LIVES BETWEEN THE LINES

Also by Michael Vatikiotis

Non-fiction
Blood and Silk: Power and Conflict in Modern Southeast Asia
Indonesian Politics under Suharto
Political Change in Southeast Asia: Trimming the Banyan Tree

Fiction
Debatable Land
The Painter of Lost Souls
Singapore Ground Zero
The Spice Garden

Praise for *Blood and Silk*

'A fascinating and many-layered portrait of Southeast Asia, brimming with colourful characters, insights and anecdotes, *Blood and Silk* is a rich palimpsest as can only be written by a longstanding student and scholar of the region like Michael Vatikiotis' – Thant Myint-U, author of *The River of Lost Footsteps*

'Vatikiotis's arguments are fluent and convincing, and his writing is suffused with a deep knowledge of and affection for Southeast Asia and its peoples' – Richard Cockett, *Literary Review*

'Books on the rise of Asia tend to concentrate on China and India. Vatikiotis fills a gap by providing a lively and learned guide to the politics, personalities and conflicts that are shaping a dynamic group of countries, including Indonesia, Malaysia, Thailand and Burma' – Gideon Rachman, *Financial Times* Summer Reads

'Vatikiotis offers a lucid portrait of this fascinating region by bringing together a student's sense of wonder and curiosity, a journalist's scepticism and diligence in making sense of reality, and a peacemaker's compassion for the vulnerable' – Salil Tripathi, *South China Morning Post*

LIVES BETWEEN THE LINES

A Journey in Search of the
Lost Levant

MICHAEL VATIKIOTIS

First published in Great Britain in 2021 by Weidenfeld & Nicolson
an imprint of The Orion Publishing Group Ltd
Carmelite House, 50 Victoria Embankment
London EC4Y 0DZ

An Hachette UK Company

1 3 5 7 9 10 8 6 4 2

All images courtesy of the author, except pp. 17, 20 and 49 © Alamy
Map design by John Gilkes

A CIP catalogue record for this book is
available from the British Library.

ISBN (Hardback) 978 1 4746 1319 4
ISBN (Export Trade Paperback) 978 1 4746 1320 0
ISBN (eBook) 978 1 4746 1322 4
ISBN (Audio) 978 1 4746 1891 5

Typeset by Input Data Services Ltd, Somerset

Printed in Great Britain by Clays Ltd, Elcograf S.p.A.

www.weidenfeldandnicolson.co.uk
www.orionbooks.co.uk

Dedicated to my parents, Patricia and Panayiotis,
and to the memory of two beloved uncles:
John Mumford and Yannis Vatikiotis

'It is very hard to live with silence. The real silence is death and this is terrible. To approach this silence, it is necessary to journey to the desert. You do not go to the desert to find identity, but to lose it, to lose your personality, to be anonymous. You make yourself void. You become silence. You become more silent than the silence around you. And then something extraordinary happens: you hear silence speak.'

Edmond Jabès, Egyptian Jewish poet (1912–91)

CONTENTS

LIST OF ILLUSTRATIONS

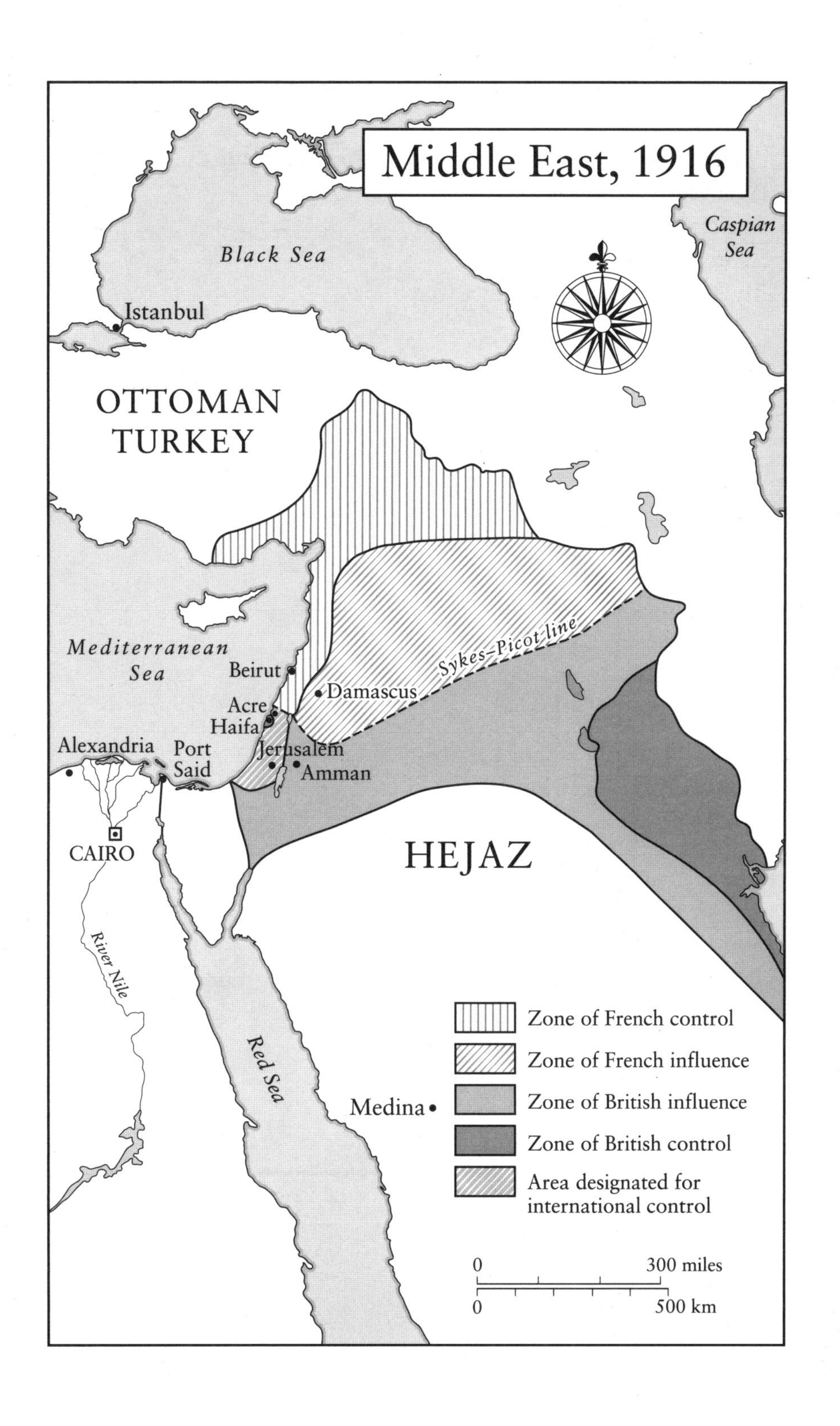
Middle East, 1916
Black Sea
Caspian Sea
Istanbul
OTTOMAN TURKEY
Mediterranean Sea
Beirut
Damascus
Sykes–Picot line
Acre
Haifa
Alexandria
Port Said
Jerusalem
Amman
CAIRO
HEJAZ
River Nile
Red Sea
Medina
Zone of French control
Zone of French influence
Zone of British influence
Zone of British control
Area designated for international control
0
300 miles
0
500 km

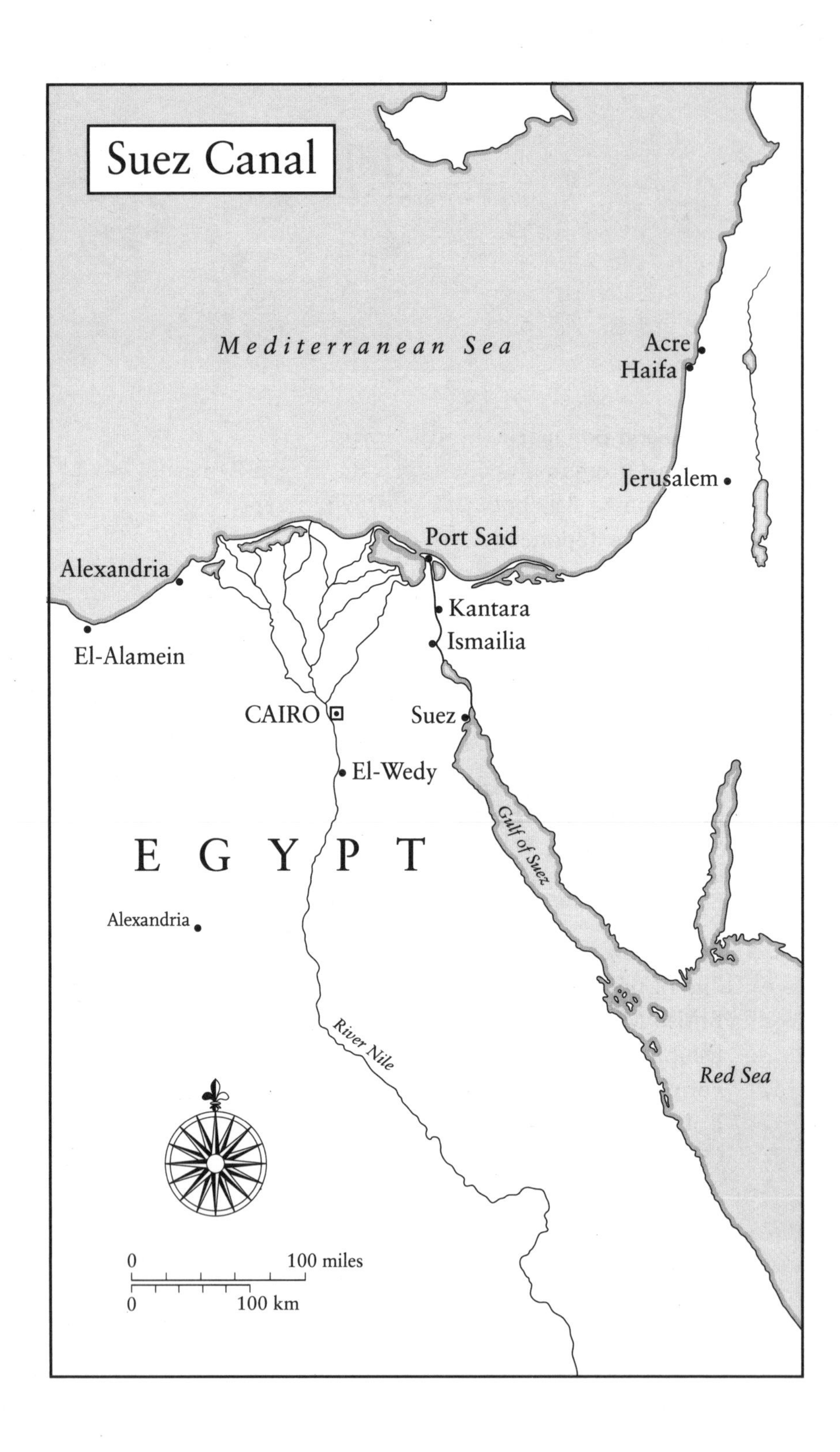
Suez Canal
Mediterranean Sea
Acre
Haifa
Jerusalem
Port Said
Alexandria
Kantara
Ismailia
El-Alamein
CAIRO
Suez
El-Wedy
EGYPT
Gulf of Suez
Alexandria
River Nile
Red Sea
0
100 miles
0
100 km

TIMELINE

1798	Napoleon Bonaparte invades Egypt
1801	Anglo-Ottoman invasion expels the French Armée d'Orient
1805	Muhammad Ali appointed Viceroy of Egypt
1854	Said Pasha appointed Viceroy of Egypt
1859	Construction starts on the Suez Canal
1863	Ismail Pasha appointed Viceroy of Egypt
1869	Grand opening of the Suez Canal
1871	Verdi's opera *Aida* opens at the Cairo Opera House
1875	Britain acquires 44 per cent of shares in the Suez Canal
1882	British bombardment of Alexandria
1914	End of Ottoman rule and establishment of the British 'veiled protectorate' over Egypt
1914	Start of the First World War
1916	Sykes-Picot Agreement
1917	Balfour Declaration
1917	Allenby enters Jerusalem
1918	End of the First World War
1921	British Mandate established in Palestine
1921	Establishment of the British protectorate of Transjordan
1922	Formal abolition of the Ottoman sultanate
1922	Britain grants independence to Egypt
1936	Outbreak of the Great Arab Revolt
1939	Start of the Second World War
1942	Battle of El-Alamein
1944	Alexandria Protocol: formation of the Arab League
1945	End of the Second World War
1947	UN Partition of Palestine
1948	Establishment of the State of Israel
1948	First Arab-Israeli War

1952 'Black Saturday' Cairo fire
1952 Gamal Abdel Nasser assumes power in Egypt
1956 Nationalisation of the Suez Canal
1956 Suez Crisis

PART I

PIONEERS

PRELUDE

'*Alla Franga*': The Ottoman Pocket Watch

The Ottomans were poor timekeepers. In their medieval empire, time-keeping was primarily a function of determining the Muslim call to prayer according to sunrise and sunset. Use of a lunar calendar made the exercise imprecise. Confusingly, there were also overlapping time frames based on dynastic anniversaries, political activities and even agricultural seasons. In addition, each confessional community was permitted to use their own calendars – the Hebrew, the Orthodox Christian Julian calendar and the Gregorian, used by Europeans. This rather arbitrary marking of time made the administration of the empire hard to synchronise, yet promoted an easy tolerance of diversity and nurtured communal harmony.

Mechanical clocks started appearing in the sixteenth century. Most of them were gifts from European ambassadors arriving in the Ottoman capital of Istanbul, referred to rather elegantly in Europe as the *Sublime Porte*. Before then, sundials and the calculations of star-gazing astronomers (using astrolabes) kept the time. Even when mechanical clocks started appearing, the Ottoman practice, *alla Turq*, was to set the hand to twelve at sunset. There was only one public clock in the entire empire by the seventeenth century, in Skopje, where, according to the British historian Jason Goodwin, 'it tolled the hours in the European manner, *alla Franga*, and its survival, or erection, was considered something of a marvel, for bells and public clocks were generally outlawed.' Islamic clerics feared that the clock, like the printing press, would dilute their authority. The clerics protested when, in the mid-nineteenth century, Sultan Abdulhamid II started erecting clock towers across the empire to mark time *alla Franga*, defined as the official Ottoman state time alongside the traditional marking of Muslim prayer times.

By then, mechanical pocket watches had become so fashionable that many European watchmakers established themselves in Istanbul, near the present-day Galata Bridge. It is one of these watches, silver, engraved and double-cased, that was the sole item left to me by my father, Panayiotis Vatikiotis.

This arrival of European mechanical timekeeping precipitated a cultural invasion of the Ottoman mind. The mechanical clocks, with their predictability and assumptions of the universality of time, breached a high wall of Ottoman particularity and marked the beginning of the end of more than half a millennium of empire. The clerics were right: scholars today argue that the empire underwent a 'crisis of the clock', referring to this transformative – and ultimately destructive – period of modernisation.

My father was born in the holy city of Jerusalem in 1928, six years after the formal end of the Ottoman Empire. He grew up with seven clock towers the Ottomans erected across Palestine at the turn of the twentieth century. Imposing and mostly built with contributions of local Christians, Jews and Muslims, the towers were symbols of progress and prominent monuments to Ottoman rule. When the British seized Jerusalem from the Ottomans in 1917, they marched into the city under an elegant Ottoman clock tower built adjacent to Jaffa Gate; a few years later they demolished the tower, just as the Ottoman Empire was ending.

Quite how my father came upon the watch is a mystery. Yet the more I delved into the history of my family in the Middle East, the more the watch, with its meniscus crystal face, marked for me the transition between the era of Ottoman rule and the start of the European period, a seismic shift in the history of the Middle East and the Levant that my family straddled and thrived in, only to fall victim to its violent legacy after the end of the Second World War.

I carried the watch with me as I traced my father's family across the Mediterranean from its ancestral home in the Greek islands to the coast of the Holy Land, a region transformed by the Ottomans before being lost to French and British colonial powers, and eventually liberated by the clashing forces of Arab and Zionist nationalism. My mother's Italian Jewish family hailed from Leghorn (now Livorno), a city that took in Jews fleeing persecution in Spain and Portugal in the late fifteenth century and which, much later, served as a jumping-off point for these same Jews trading and settling across the Ottoman Empire – my maternal relatives landing in Egypt.

My family's eastward peregrinations were a startling discovery for me, a child of modern European prosperity. I grew up in England in a time of inward migration from the former colonies. The schools I attended were filled with the children of migrants fleeing instability and insecurity across the Middle East, Africa and the Indian subcontinent.

My father's silver pocket watch was made at a time when Istanbul, the Ottoman capital, presided over an imperial realm that was a magnet for migrants; today the former empire's territory is the source of 40 per cent of the world's refugees. Not being a scholar of the region, I held on to this talisman as I ventured into a landscape of violent contention.

The hands of the silver pocket watch are fused at noon. Or midnight. For the Ottomans, noon was not only the brightest hour but also the darkest, the time of the devil. I prefer to think of the hands frozen at midnight, at the end of the Ottoman Empire's long period of neglectful but nonetheless prosperous existence, and the start of a prolonged nightmare of suffering from which the region has yet to recover.

CHAPTER ONE

Piercing the Sands

> What of this piercing of the sands?
> What of this union of the Seas
> This grasp of unfamiliar hands
> The blending of strange litanies?
> This pot pourri of East and West Pilau and potage ala bisque
> Circassian belles whom Worth has drest
> And Parisiennes a l'odalesque
>
> *Punch*, November 1869

The ferry from Port Said to Port Fuad crosses the Suez Canal in less than fifteen minutes. The ride is free. Many locals take the trip simply for a bit of breeze and a chance to be with loved ones, cramming together in the slippery gangways on either side of the rusty, flat-bottomed boat. Imperceptibly, the crossing spans two great continents, and it was here, alongside the dark, bittersweet waters of the canal where Africa and Asia meet on a flat, featureless desert isthmus, that my parents began their lives.

Over a period of almost a century my Greek-Italian family, and hundreds of thousands of other Europeans, flocked to the Middle East in search of security and stability during a time of what seemed to be relentless conflict and instability in Europe. This book tells the story of why they came, how they prospered and what eventually forced them to leave.

It begins in the mid-nineteenth century with the conception and construction of the Suez Canal, commissioned by an ambitious clan of Ottoman rulers of Albanian descent at the behest of competing European powers. The story spans a period of remarkable modern-isation and growth as well as upheaval in the Middle East from the

1850s to the 1950s and is mainly set in Egypt and Palestine (and what is today Israel). It captures an era subject to much nostalgic retrospection, characterised by a social and cultural milieu of cosmopolitanism most often described as Levantine.

These Levantine societies perfected a unique mingling of diverse peoples of different faiths and a hybridisation of European and oriental sensibilities. They thrived on the fertile rims of the region facing the Mediterranean Sea: the coasts of Turkey, Syria, Lebanon and Palestine, the mouth of the Suez Canal and the Nile Delta. They evolved under the authority of the Ottoman Empire, which, already in decline, was struggling to modernise and looked to skills and technology from Europe. The European powers, which replaced Ottoman rule after the end of the First World War in 1918, needed trustworthy and diligent non-native administrators and entrepreneurs; thus the Levantines continued to thrive.

While the Levantines mingled socially and professionally and enjoyed mostly untrammelled freedom, there was an illusory quality to their cosmopolitanism: they were not completely integrated with their host communities because they were held apart, protected and privileged by legal mechanisms based on their status as foreign citizens, which, aside from religious and ethnic considerations, militated against their assimilation. All the same, the Levantines contributed greatly to the remarkable modernisation of Egypt, and to the commercial progress of the coastal port cities of what is often called the Levant (*Al-Mashriq* in Arabic), which towards the end of the nineteenth century was comprised of significant centres of both regional and global commerce.

The Levantines, mostly people of southern and eastern European origin, but also Armenians and Sephardic Jews from the east, established for themselves a prosperous, educated existence. They maintained boundaries defined by ethnicity and religion, though mingled easily with each other and with the aristocratic and landed classes of their host communities through the medium of mostly the French language and, later, English. At the same time, they absorbed many of the customs and mannerisms of the oriental world they had inhabited for several generations. Even so, it remains hard to identify a distinctive Levantine culture; in part because so much of what they aspired to and how they lived was Eurocentric.

Like other successful minorities they cultivated close ties to the powers that be, which made them cautious and somewhat mercurial.

Later, this bound them fatally to the European, mostly British imperial project, and condemned them to eventual exile and dispersal after the Second World War. Interestingly, the term Levantine conveys a derogatory meaning, describing people who are hesitant, untrustworthy and avoid taking sides. They made ideal go-betweens, which was essentially what their Ottoman patrons wanted them to be.

The Levantine milieu, which is perhaps the best way to describe them rather than as a definable community or group, has vanished. It was upended and destroyed midway through the twentieth century in a whirlwind of violence that inaugurated what we call today, rather generically, the Middle East Conflict. Luckily, most people were permitted to leave, though not always with their wealth. The survivors are mostly, like the veterans of the last century's wars, either dead or well into their eighties and nineties. Some have told their stories, and there is a rich legacy of biography, mostly out of print. Their society served as a colourful backdrop to literary works of the last century – notably, in English, Lawrence Durrell's *Alexandria Quartet* and Olivia Manning's *Levant Trilogy*. Their descendants have gone to some lengths to trace and study what made Levantine society tick; the Italians and Greeks of Egypt are a much-chronicled diaspora. For me, a child of Levantines born in and exiled from the Middle East, this was not enough.

I was curious to explore the cosmopolitan era that nurtured and shaped the identities of my mother's family of Italian Jews from Egypt and my father's family of Greeks from Palestine. My own identity, too, for I grew up very much aware of being tethered to a mélange of cultures and places that inspired a deep sense of loss and longing. My first overseas visit was to Beirut in the late 1950s, where my father showed off his infant son to old school friends from Palestine, by then members of the Palestinian Liberation Movement and exiled in Lebanon. I have returned again and again to the region – as a wide-eyed teenager, as a student, a journalist and, latterly, as a conflict mediator. On each occasion I have experienced a strange emotional confluence of attachment and detachment. I regret being unable to see and chronicle the world my parents grew up in as one of their contemporaries, or as a participant. In today's world of sharply defined, possessively protected identities, I suppose this makes me something of an interloper. Yet I feel more like an outcast in exile.

As I embarked on a journey to explore the roots and way stations of my family, I took some comfort from the experience of some of my forebears – they were outcasts, too: Jews from Italy who distrusted the promise of a unified Italian state; Greek islanders unable to thrive in the new Kingdom of Greece they had fought the Ottomans for. The Suez Canal was in the mid-nineteenth century a kind of Statue of Liberty – a beacon, offering the possibility of refuge to those in search of a new life.

Before we get to the Suez Canal, an important historical reality check needs highlighting, one that will strike most contemporary readers as surprising: the Middle East – the home of al-Qaeda, the Islamic State, Saddam Hussein, Bashar al-Assad, rivers of blood flowing from decades of senseless wars – was once and for quite a long time a place people escaped to, rather than from. The stream of migrants from war-torn Syria and Iraq that has fed anti-migrant sentiment and boosted right-wing politics across Europe in the second decade of the twenty-first century offers a striking counterpoint to the flow of people in the other direction at the end of the nineteenth century. Today we see desperate refugees scrambling aboard flimsy rubber dinghies to cross from the coast of Turkey to nearby Greek islands such as Lesbos. Some 123,000 people, many of them from Syria, arrived in the course of 2019. Yet for long periods of history these same islands were jumping-off points for eastward and southward migrations away from Europe and towards the Middle East, which then was the central region of a relatively well-governed empire tolerant of minorities and, in fact, welcoming, in contrast to its European neighbours.

In the era before the birth of unified modern states in Europe, to be a Jew, or a Catholic in a Protestant setting, or vice versa – indeed, to belong to any religious minority – invited persecution and death. A Statute of Jewry drawn up in 1275 mandated residential segregation between Jews and Christians in England. The expulsion of Jews from England in 1290 marked the first of its kind in Europe. This was not the case in the Middle East under Ottoman rule, where tolerance of religious minorities was built into government practice – and harnessed to the progress of statecraft and commerce. There was inequality, in that Jews or Christians were considered inferior to Muslims and were taxed more; but there was no barrier to conversion to Islam, or to intermarriage. 'Such was the level of integration,' noted the British journalist Nicolas Pelham in his excellent short study of Ottoman pluralism, 'that the Ottomans had no word for minorities.'

Many Europeans from persecuted minorities and distressed areas were therefore drawn eastwards to the Ottoman Empire and to Istanbul, its bustling cosmopolitan capital. The Ottomans in fact encouraged Jews to abandon Europe, where they were hounded and persecuted in the fourteenth and fifteenth centuries, and even sent ships to collect them. Following King Ferdinand II's Alhambra Decree of July 1492, which expelled the Jews from Spain, the Ottoman Sultan Bayezid II sent a naval flotilla to pick them up for resettlement in Istanbul. 'You venture to call Ferdinand a wise ruler?' the sultan is reported to have said to his courtiers. 'He who has impoverished his own country and enriched mine?'

Indeed, those who ventured east found more opportunities to make their fortunes as merchants, officials, soldiers or even concubines. Another Ottoman Sultan, Suleiman the Magnificent (1520–66) befriended an Orthodox Albanian-Greek, later called Pargali Ibrahim Pasha, who served as his grand vizier, or chief advisor. Others followed. They were generally well-travelled, well-educated men who provided an invaluable interface for the Ottomans with the European world. They were appointed as *dragomans* to the court, effectively the diplomatic corps. But many also were wealthy traders and became administrators of Ottoman provinces, especially in the Balkans.

This is not to say that Ottoman society was uniformly tolerant or peaceful. Minorities including Jews and Christians were taxed and persecuted to varying degrees, often depending on the probity and predilections of local rulers. In medieval Egypt, for example, greedy Mamluk rulers intimidated and extorted minorities to raise revenue and enrich themselves. This pattern of casual extortion started to change, argues the Arab political scientist Sami Zubaida, only when bold and ambitious Ottoman rulers recognised the need to modernise, and realised that to do so they needed to tap into European expertise and know-how. 'It was only during the course of the nineteenth century and into the twentieth – with a combination of the processes of modernity and capitalism under the increasing hegemony of the European powers, especially Britain, and the responses of Ottoman reforms – that communal barriers become more permeable, especially in the main centres of power, commerce and culture.' The mainspring of what has been styled cosmopolitanism, therefore, was the slow collision of two empires: the Ottoman, which was desperately looking for ways to reinvigorate and preserve its existence, and the rising European imperial powers searching for trading partners and territory.

These accommodations of diversity, aimed at effectively administering a heterogenous society, evolved over time and persisted through periods when supposedly enlightened European society was busy enslaving millions of Asians and Africans and persecuting minorities at home. The fact that my family left Europe and found security in Ottoman lands turns the orientalist paradigm on its head. For by some measures, the Middle East in the mid-nineteenth century was a more advanced and stable society under Ottoman rule – a fact missed by generations of European scholars seeking to impose their own view of the region. For my family, the Orient was not an abstraction, or a career, as Benjamin Disraeli put it. It was quite simply a refuge, a place to build their lives and raise a family. There was perhaps, in hindsight, much that the emerging modern states of Europe could have learned from the carefully calibrated, if unequal, pluralism of the Orient. Then, before long, the Europeans arrived and swept everything away.

We generally consider migration as a kinetic human instinct to escape poor, backward conditions in search of something more promising and hopeful. The example most often cited is the movement of massive numbers of people from the old European world westwards to the New World in the early twentieth century; however, people had already long been on the move eastwards to a world much older, yet more promising.

By the nineteenth century, technological advances in transport in Europe – by sea and land – greatly facilitated the ease and safety of travel overseas for larger numbers of people. There were reasons to move. Wars and popular revolt affected parts of central and southern Europe, marking the birth pains of newly unified states such as Italy, Spain and Germany, as well as the arrival of new notions of social order and equality. Dislocation and economic distress generated by the Franco-Prussian War, including the Paris Commune (the radical socialist government that was in place from March to May 1871), the Carlist Wars in Spain and the Italian *Risorgimento* (resurgence) pushed many people from southern Europe west to the Americas. According to the United States Commerce Department's Bureau of the Census, more than a million Italians, mostly from the poorer *Mezzogiorno* region of southern Italy, migrated to the United States between 1880 and 1900. Another 3 million arrived in the first two decades of the twentieth century. More than 6 million Europeans – many of them Greeks and Italians – settled in Argentina in the same period.

Less well known is the fact that many of these displaced and dislocated Europeans also moved south and eastwards to the Middle East, though in smaller numbers – around 300,000 Italians to countries such as Tunisia, Morocco and Egypt by the 1920s, according to a study of Italian official data in the 1930s. By the 1930s there were around 60,000 Italians in Egypt,[1] and the 1927 census in Egypt recorded close to 100,000 Greeks. The entire foreign community in Egypt numbered more than 1.5 million by the end of the 1930s in a country of around 16 million. For a time, virtually every town in the Nile Delta had a Greek shopkeeper or innkeeper – who often exploited their Egyptian customers, lending them money at exorbitant rates, according to Alexander Kitroeff, a scholar who has made a detailed study of the Greeks in Egypt. By the end of the nineteenth century almost all modern services or professions in Egypt were heavily populated by Italians, Greeks or Jews of one European nationality or another – from the postal service to the medical profession to lowly waiters and stevedores. In Jerusalem, the Greek Colony was home to close to 8,000 Greeks until 1948, but there were also sizeable communities of Greeks along the coast of Palestine and in Lebanon. In the 1860s one-third of people inhabiting the city of Alexandria were foreigners – again, mostly Greeks and Italians.

There was as much pull as push to this migration from Europe to the Middle East. The majority of Europeans moving to the New World struggled to find work, and when they did it was often in poor, unprotected conditions. The southern Italians in America were subject to racial abuse because of their dark skin, noted the *New York Times*: 'They were sometimes shut out of schools, movie houses and labour unions, or consigned to church pews set aside for black people.' This striving new working class often fell prey to exploitation and crime.

By contrast, Europeans arriving in the Middle East found an abundance of work and, more importantly, protection under Ottoman rule. Even as arcane laws governing society were replaced by more modern forms of taxation and conscription at the heart of the empire, there remained more autonomous parts of it, such as Egypt, where exemptions could be made. These migrants generally prospered, and became the core of a Levantine bourgeoisie. In Egypt they served a new dynasty of Ottoman rulers, themselves originally from the eastern fringes of Europe, who decided at the start of the nineteenth century that the path to power and glory was modernisation in the European mould. Muhammad Ali, the Macedonian-born Albanian soldier who ruled Egypt from 1805 to 1848, and his successors needed architects, engineers and artisans to design their ersatz Europhile cities and opulent palaces; they also needed bankers to find them the money.

In Palestine, meanwhile, the Greek Orthodox Church, like other Christian churches, was undergoing a revival because of the rising tide of pilgrims availing themselves of more affordable travel to the Holy Land. Priests and merchants – often one and the same – were in demand to serve the faithful, and to profit from them. A trading and commercial boom grew on the back of servicing pilgrims. Not all of these migrants intended to settle; much of the work was seen as temporary. Some of the women from Greece and Italy sought jobs as wet nurses, maids and cooks in the growing new cities of Cairo and Alexandria. In Egypt, the best hotels advertised European chambermaids and by the end of the nineteenth century commercial premises in downtown Cairo and Alexandria were essentially staffed and run by Europeans. And, unlike the peasants from the poorer south of Italy who left for North and South America with their families, the Greeks and Italians who went to the Middle East tended to move as artisans, merchants, teachers, priests or skilled labourers, and the Italians were as much from the north as from the south of their country. By the 1940s at least two generations of Italians and Greeks had been born and raised in Egypt and Palestine, including my parents, who were second-generation members of their communities born in the Middle East. They knew no other home until they were forced to leave in the 1950s.

The Greeks were mainly island seafarers, who in the eighteenth century became the mainstay of commercial shipping in the Mediterranean after the Treaty of Kuchuk Kainarji (imposed by Russia on Turkey in 1774) opened the grain-growing areas of the East to industrial markets in the West through the Dardanelles and the Black Sea. My own Greek seafaring ancestors from the island of Hydra sailed three- and twin-mast barques and *caiques* under Russian flags plying lucrative trade routes between the ports of the Adriatic coast in Italy and the Black Sea. But the Greek War of Independence (1821–29) decimated their merchant fleet and necessitated drastic cuts in crew complements to help restart business, which explains why so many Greeks were willing to migrate, including my paternal great-grandfather.

As well as people fleeing economic adversity, there were those on the move to escape prejudice and persecution. Many migrants to the Middle East from Europe at this time were Jews, like my mother's family, and included a steady stream of mostly Sephardic Jews originally from the Iberian Peninsula but scattered across southern Europe because of earlier periods of persecution. They moved east as their communities continued to be hounded and bounded in ghettoes from the Middle Ages and '[a]ll through the early modern period,' according to Warwick University scholar Felicita Tramontana, 'the Jews moved south toward Ottoman domains in order to escape their frequent persecution in Europe.' Again, hard as it might be to imagine today, the Middle East was seen then as a safer place of opportunity. And rather than an arduous sea journey across the Atlantic, the Middle East, a pleasant two days' sail from the ports of southern France or Italy, was all the more tempting.

The Suez Canal was a primary catalyst of this movement to the ancient rather than the new world: its decade-long construction a magnet for labour and pioneering opportunity. The trade the canal spawned once it opened was an even bigger draw for migrants in search of new lives. Without the canal, and the immense transformation of commerce it heralded upon completion in 1869, much of the good fortune my family benefited from would never have materialised. Today, a third of Egypt's population live in poverty, but in the 1860s the country, 'bustling, dirty, corrupt and exciting', was also described as the 'Klondike on the Nile'.

The story of how the Suez Canal was conceived and built sheds light on a pivotal moment in the history of the Middle East, inaugurating a period of considerable hope and opportunity that lasted for almost a century. The canal cleaved Africa and Asia, and as a magnet for migration it transformed the Middle East and its peoples. The Suez Canal, one of the world's oldest hydraulic dreams, has been a focus of great-power competition for centuries. Egypt, one of the world's oldest civilisations, was from early in history a crossroads of trade, linking Europe to the Middle East and the Middle East to Africa.

The Suez Canal was first conceived in pharaonic times, and then by almost every major empire or power that traversed the area – from the

Greeks and Romans to the Persians and Venetians – all considered cutting a waterway across the 120-kilometre-long isthmus separating the Mediterranean and Red seas. Records exist of an ancient canal linking the Red Sea with the Nile closer to Cairo from the sixth century BC. Arab *dhows*, sailing boats made of hardwood and coir rope stitching originating from India, plied between the Yemeni coast of the Red Sea and the west coast of India from as early as the first century BC and helped carry Arab traders and Islam to Asia.

With the rise of competing European powers and the scramble for ever more imperial possessions, the notion of a canal linking the two seas was seen as creating a more efficient thoroughfare linking Europe through Africa to Asia. The success of the East India Company from the mid-eighteenth century made it imperative to increase the speed of communications between the company's base in Calcutta and its headquarters in London. The fastest and most certain route was by ship to the head of the Persian Gulf and then overland via Baghdad and Aleppo to the Mediterranean coast. But the 'frequent depredations of the Arab tribes' rendered this route increasingly unsafe. So in 1777 the company secured permission from the Ottoman sultan to use passage through Egypt by way of the Red Sea, then across the Isthmus of Suez.

It was at this point that the French, who had suffered badly at the hands of the British during the Seven Years' War (1756–63) started to look seriously at exploiting the Egyptian route as a way to undermine British supremacy. Napoleon Bonaparte's invasion of Egypt in 1798 aimed to establish a beachhead from which to invade India and dominate the shorter route from Europe to Asia via the Isthmus of Suez. Egypt, which straddled the fault line of empire, 'never stood a chance', said Flaubert in the mid-nineteenth century: '[she was] on the way to India and Sudan, a gateway to imperial riches.'

When Napoleon invaded Egypt (seizing the country in just three weeks), he brought along a team of surveyors who looked seriously at cutting the canal. His idea was that if he 'could pierce the isthmus, he might destroy England's commercial supremacy'. Thirty years later, having defeated the French, Britain also sent a survey team, but, given the cautious imperial tradition of the day, London worried about the cost of annexing Egypt to assure the security of the proposed canal; thus construction was opposed. Meanwhile, French diplomats had gained the ear of Egypt's new ruler, Muhammad Ali, who encouraged the idea of a canal and was an important catalyst for the country's modernisation.

Born in Kavala, today a city in northern Greece, Muhammad Ali was the son of a local militia leader and tobacco trader of Albanian origin; the year of his birth, 1769, was coincidentally the same as Napoleon's. As a young man, Muhammad Ali dabbled in trading tobacco and trained as a soldier, rising through the ranks of the Ottoman army, which held sway and recruited across large parts of Greece and the Balkans.[2] In 1801 Muhammad Ali was sent with an Ottoman force to reoccupy Egypt after Napoleon's retreat following a humiliating naval defeat by the British in Aboukir Bay close to Alexandria. In the ensuing power vacuum, Muhammad Ali emerged as a popular and effective candidate for the Ottoman governorship. The Mamluks, who ruled over Egypt before Napoleon's invasion, were a caste of Christian converts to Islam, liberated slaves mostly of Balkan origin. They were unpopular and relatively easy to push aside. Gathering all the notables of the Mamluk regime in the Cairo citadel one evening, Muhammad Ali had them massacred by his troops.

Muhammad Ali

Apart from his brutality, by far the most significant decision Muhammad Ali took was to embark on an ambitious programme of modernisation, for which he turned to Europe – as a contemporary observer, James St John, put it, 'perseveringly though quietly proceeding with the destruction of all these stupid prejudices which interrupt the free interaction of Turk and Christian'. To be absolutely clear, Muhammad Ali had no feelings for the Egyptians, nor had he any intention to do much for them. He was a foreigner, albeit a servant of the Ottoman Empire. Neither, as it turned out, was he all that loyal a servant of the Ottoman sultan in Istanbul. The country was, as the Egyptian writer Tarek Osman observes, a place for this ambitious Balkan adventurer to build an empire based on a rich country he had managed to subjugate. Or as Henry Dodwell, Muhammad Ali's British biographer, quotes the new governor of Egypt as telling a French diplomat: 'Je n'ai fait en Egypte que ce que les Anglais ont fait aux Indes.'

Compared with other Ottoman lands, which enjoyed autonomy but were treated as vassal states, by the mid-nineteenth century Egypt under Muhammad Ali possessed a stable government, a disciplined army, a free education, and modern forms of transportation, including the first postal service and railway in Africa. 'Egypt was the first oriental country in which anything like a regular system of Westernised education was established,' noted a European traveller in 1838. Initially Muhammad Ali stacked his administration with Turkish officials, but later found this bound him too closely to the Ottoman seat of power in Istanbul. So, at the suggestion of one of his Italian advisors, he started to train a local Arab cohort – only to find they were even more corrupt. The Turks, Dodwell quotes one foreign observer as noting, 'always stole more decently'.[3]

Egypt ruled by Muhammad Ali enjoyed religious freedom and offered protection to foreigners; under the preceding Mamluk regime, Christians 'were obliged to distinguish themselves by the colour of their dress. They were forbidden to ride horses.' The country was, even by European standards at the time, a relatively secure place filled with opportunities. Very soon the court of Muhammad Ali, perched at the western end of the grand bay in Alexandria in the sprawling Romanesque Ras el-Tin Palace he had built by French and Italian architects, became a cockpit of frenzied politicking among competing European advisors, and no issue was more contentious than the idea of the Suez Canal.

The French spearhead of this effort was a group of social reformers known as Saint Simonians – forerunners of the modern socialist movement – who took the idealistic view of the benefits to global trade of piercing the isthmus.[4] The British, in a bid to confound French ambitions, argued vigorously that the idea was too costly and countered with plans for a railway; they were already replacing their own canals with railways at home. Initially their bid was unsuccessful. However, when Muhammad Ali died in 1849, his grandson, Abbas, succeeded him and replaced the French advisors with British ones. Abbas moved the court back to Cairo, away from the haranguing community of foreign consuls. The railway was duly built and opened in 1851. But his reign was short-lived: in 1854, Abbas died and was succeeded as governor by Said, the French-educated fourth son of Muhammad Ali. More interested in modern reforms and despite his natural shyness, Said engaged with the foreign consuls, once again moved back to Alexandria and restored French ascendancy at court. And this was how a clever former French diplomat, Ferdinand de Lesseps, arrived on the scene.

De Lesseps, a career civil servant and a freemason with Basque ancestry, was both a dreamer and a pragmatist. The idea for building the Suez Canal came to him in the 1830s when, as a young vice-consul in Alexandria, he stumbled across an article published a decade earlier by Napoleon Bonaparte's chief engineer, Jacques-Marie Le Père. In *Mémoire sur la communication de la mer des Indes à la Méditerranée par la Mer Rouge et l'isthme de Soueys*, Le Père described the ancient pharaonic canal linking the Nile and the Gulf of Suez, prompting de Lesseps to wonder if the entire isthmus could be cleaved.

His vision was idealistic – a gift for the good of all nations. 'The Prosperity of the East', he rather pompously wrote in 1855, 'is now dependent upon the interests of civilisations at large, and the best means of contributing to its welfare, as well as that of humanity, is to break down the barriers which still divide men, races, and nations.' Little wonder, then, that his original plans for the canal included a massive statue at its mouth of a woman holding a torch symbolising 'Egypt carrying the Light to Asia'. The grand monument never materialised, but the design for the statue by the French sculptor Frédéric Bartholdi was not lost; it was built, and is now planted at the mouth of the Hudson River in New York State and known as the Statue of Liberty.

De Lesseps was no engineer, but he had the persuasive skills of a good diplomat and played on idealistic notions of trade as a civilising influence that were popular with emerging liberal thinkers. He drew together some of Europe's finest engineers and tramped across the continent to generate support and financial backers. This wasn't easy. In addition to concerted opposition from the British, there were those who feared the environmental impact of the project. 'Many people believed that the level of the Red Sea was so far below the level of the Mediterranean', wrote P.H. Morgan, a contemporary American observer, 'that, the canal once dug, all the water of the latter would pour through it leaving its bed dry.'

Yet de Lesseps didn't win the day because of his powerful idealism and networking skills. Fortuitously, he had spent some time as a youth in Egypt, where his father Mathieu de Lesseps had been Napoleon Bonaparte's political agent and later French consul. When de Lesseps arrived back in Alexandria in 1832 as vice-consul, he developed a bond with Muhammad Ali's son, Said. The two grew close, so the story goes, because Said's father had bullied him as a boy for being too fat and denied him food. De Lesseps fed him in secret – they both loved pasta, apparently. Recalled from a disastrous posting in Rome, de Lesseps hastened to Egypt as soon as his friend Said was appointed viceroy in 1854. It is said that when de Lesseps presented his school friend with the plan to develop the canal, Said Pasha signed his approval without reading it. This, after years of argument between great powers and despite opposition by the Ottoman court in Istanbul.

Ferdinand de Lesseps

The proposed channel would allow shipping to avoid the long sea passage down the African coast and around the Cape of Good Hope, a costly journey of six months or more depending on the winds. This new, alternate route would shave more than 6,500 kilometres off the passage between London and Bombay alone. As an added bonus, the canal was to be built for steamships, not sailing ships, which helped further reduce the costs of using steam-powered ships on longer routes.

The decade-long construction began in 1859, attracting labourers and engineers from far and wide and, notably, stimulating the first great wave of immigration from Europe to Egypt. As the British desert traveller Charles Doughty observed: 'There was a Babel of nations, a concourse of men of every hard and doubtful fortune . . . Moslems and Christians . . . mingled together.'

With hindsight it is hard to appreciate the ambitious scale – and steep cost – of the canal. The project initially relied heavily on forced labour, an ancient practice that had been in place since pharaonic times. At one point more than a million men toiled in the desert heat digging and carrying sand, often by hand or in baskets. P.H. Morgan, a liberal American judge, wrote a savage critique of the canal's construction in 1880:

> those who carried the earth away from where it was dug were not furnished anything in which to carry it. They were required to stoop. To place their arms behind their backs, the left wrist clasped in the right hand, and then as much earth was placed in the hod thus made as it would hold. They were forced to walk away with it up a steep acclivity and, when they reached the dumping spot, they let go their hold, straightened up, and, shaking themselves like a spaniel who has just come out of the water, relieved themselves of their burden.[5]

Thousands of labourers died from disease and of dehydration – the numbers are not precise; shelter was sparse and water supplies, carried on the backs of camels, were sometimes interrupted. There was an outcry in Europe which brought a halt to the use of forced labour, and increased costs, adding to Egypt's mounting debts. This in turn created opportunities for many Greeks and Italians to take the place of Egyptians working on the canal: as many as 5,000 Greeks, most of them from Kasos, a small island south of Rhodes and one of the closest points in Greece to the coast of Egypt. Many stayed on and settled in the towns that sprang up along the canal, and then also worked as shipping pilots until the Egyptian takeover of the canal in 1956.

A few years after construction began, Said Pasha died – in 1863 – and his nephew, Ismail Pasha, became the new viceroy. (As fate would have it, Ismail's elder brother and Said's presumptive heir, Ahmed Ri'fat, drowned when his railway carriage fell off a bridge into the Nile.) Like Said, Ismail was French-educated and greatly taken with the idea of Egypt as a modern country in the European mould. He famously declared that Egypt 'is no longer in Africa: we are now part of Europe'. But, more like his grandfather, Muhammad Ali, Ismail promoted ambitious reforms and spent liberally on infrastructure and the lavish remodelling of Cairo, pushing Egypt further into debt. Not that this prospect ruined the party.

Once completed, the grand opening of the Suez Canal on 17 November 1869 was one of the most extravagant events of the era. Ismail Pasha presided over the event, at which the guest of honour was the French Empress Eugénie de Montijo, then one of the most admired aristocratic figures in Europe. It was then that he also encountered some of my mother's Italian forebears, the Catholic Piattolis and the Jewish Sornagas. As emerging members of the new European bourgeois elite in Egypt, they were invited to the festivities attending the opening of the canal. Luigi Piattoli, an Alexandria-based architect whose sons married into the Sornaga family, represented the Chamber of Commerce in Florence, which was where the family hailed from.

Crowned heads of Europe and all manner of socialites flocked to Egypt for months of festivities that cost millions of dollars and almost bankrupted the country. Here was another manifestation of the Middle East's shiny allure at a time when many of Europe's older cities were still recovering from decades of war. Cairo's new downtown area gleamed, its sycamore-shaded avenues swelling with well-heeled visitors who enjoyed extravagant soirées and nightly firework displays by the Nile. One eyewitness of the opening ceremony of the canal described it as 'a gorgeous and glittering scene at the doorway of the desert, there were fifty men-of-war flying the flags of all nations of Europe, firing salutes, playing their bands, whilst the sandy littoral was covered with tented Arabs and Bedouin from far and near who had come with their families on horseback and camel to join the greatest festival that Egypt had seen since the Ptolemies'.

The extravagance endured. Port Said, the eponymous city established to command the canal's Mediterranean entrance, became, albeit briefly, one of the world's most cosmopolitan centres and sought-after destinations. The newly established city was one of the first in the world to be gas-lit. As Rudyard Kipling, who frequently passed through the canal on his way to and from India, put it: 'If you truly wish to find someone you have known and who travels, there are two points on the globe you have but to sit and wait, sooner or later your man will come there: the docks of London and Port Said.'

The story of the Suez Canal and how it was built, the impact it had on the evolution of modern Egypt and the role of outside powers runs in parallel to the story of my family, whose history in the Levant is intricately linked to it. My mother Patricia's parents first met in Port Said at the mouth of the canal on the African side; she was born there in 1930. My father Panayiotis's parents lived on the Asian side in the first years of their marriage in the mid-1920s; his earliest years were spent in a flyblown place called Kantara East, where the Hejaz railway from Damascus joined the railway line to Cairo, linked by a ferry. I grew up hearing about the canal from an early age, and visited the area once as a student traveller in the mid-1970s. But it was only when I started to research its development, not to mention the significant role it played in Middle East history until the end of the colonial era, that I realised how it had changed everything and defined the Middle East for the century during which my family lived and prospered in Egypt and in neighbouring Palestine.

For, once built, the canal stimulated tremendous growth and development alongside European economic migration. Just a year after its opening in 1869, and as far away as Singapore, the value of trade doubled. Suez henceforth became a byword for international trade and travel. And while the canal was built and largely funded by the French, it was British shipping that dominated the early years of its use, making the security of Egypt and its African hinterland a priority of British colonial policy.

The huge debt created by the canal drew in bankers – mostly European Jews – to help the struggling viceroy reorganise his finances. The canal required skilled pilots, engineers and administrators – they were all European, mainly experienced Mediterranean seamen. As already described, Europe in the 1860s was poor, often destitute, and in many places unstable. Italy was consumed by the *Risorgimento*, uprisings and wars in the struggle for a unified kingdom. Greece, newly established as a kingdom in 1832, was afflicted by poverty and unrest. Opening the doors to immigration was a deliberate move by the rulers of Egypt; foreigners brought in technology, professional skills and commerce, reinforcing their autonomy from the Ottoman sultan in Istanbul. Meanwhile, the principal imperial powers of the era, France and Britain, vied for primacy in Egypt, intent on using the country to gain access to Asia and the rest of Africa.

But this is not solely a story about imported European skills, technology and politicking. It speaks, too, about the very different nature of society under Ottoman rule, which generally allowed people of different origins to mix and prosper unhindered, even if equality as such was not granted.

The Ottomans found a way to foster and harness diversity across their empire without the complications of ethnic or religious hegemony that has plagued the modern Middle East. It amounted to a pragmatic mobilisation of social capital. Egypt's ambitious dynasty of Albanian descent, perhaps because of their European origins, strived for more than the normally granted degree of autonomy from their Ottoman masters. They understood that their survival depended upon the need to embrace the wider world – and this meant primarily the European powers to the north. They did so with remarkable effect; however, this was only really possible because they utilised practices and institutions fashioned by the Ottomans that tolerated diversity, and could use them more liberally because they came to power at the start of the long decline of the Ottoman Empire.

The Ottomans, a people of Turkic descent who migrated across the steppes to Anatolia from Central Asia, ruled over much of the Middle East, and eventually the greater part of what we know today as Greece and the Balkans, for a period spanning more than 600 years (1299–1922). One of the secrets of their success was that they established effective practices to preside over such a vast and heterogeneous domain that harnessed non-Turkic manpower to administer and fight for their empire, and allow inhabitants of whatever race or creed to lead relatively untroubled lives.

In addition to Anatolia, the Ottomans ruled over the entire Fertile Crescent, Egypt, the Arabian Peninsula, and as far as the Maghreb in North Africa. To the west, Ottoman rule extended through the

Balkans to the western shores of the Greek Peloponnese. At the height of the empire's power in the sixteenth and seventeenth centuries, the pragmatic Ottoman Turks hit upon a way of circumventing its outward Islamic identity; they simply continued the receding Byzantine Empire's practice of granting rights and privileges to heathen citizens trading within the boundaries of the empire. These enduring and remarkable mechanisms of exception became known as Capitulations. France was the first country to benefit in 1535. The English followed in 1583 – apparently arguing that, like the Muslim Ottomans, newly Protestant England had banned the worship of idols and should be given special treatment. These Capitulations – so-called because they were charters drawn up in the name of the Ottoman ruler and divided into articles and chapters – permitted the free flow of trade and provided the protection of extraterritoriality: they allowed foreigners to travel all over the empire and to trade according to their own individual laws and customs; it gave them liberty of worship and freedom from taxation except for customs on imported goods.

The practice of granting such freedoms was an ancient tradition in the Mediterranean; early Arab caliphs granted such leeway to traders from Venice and Amalfi; Frankish crusaders did the same when they reached the Holy Land. It was a nice way to disentangle the reality of the region's commercial interdependence from the ideal of conquered conformity.

It was perhaps Alexander the Great (356–323 BC) who first devised cosmopolitanism as a tool of empire. Ruling over a vast expanse of South and Central Asia as well as Europe, he recognised that effective control could only be achieved by allowing his subjects to retain their own identity. To cement his rule, he encouraged his generals to marry into local elites, thus diluting the classical Greek distinction between citizens and barbarians. This more fluid idea of identity passed into classical Greek philosophy as the notion that all people, regardless of which city state they lived in, share the same basis of common reason and divine origin. The Greek philosopher Diogenes, who lived in the fourth century BC, considered himself a 'citizen of the world'. At the time, Diogenes was considered by his contemporaries as a ribald eccentric – he allegedly masturbated in public, ate raw meat and lived in a large jar. Yet his ideal of people identifying with the wider world as opposed to just one place influenced later Roman thinking about citizenship within the empire and was passed on to the Ottomans, probably via the descendants of Byzantine courtiers who served as their viziers.

The Ottomans absorbed elements of these ideas of universal citizenship, which translated into a high degree of tolerance for the many different confessional communities under their expansive rule, alongside a system that preserved Muslim primacy. According to the Ottoman historian Jason Goodwin: 'The most impressive feature of Ottoman rule was its opposition to the thin inadequacies of national identification.' For the Ottomans, past practice was combined with a general indolence and disinclination to travel and learn new customs and practices; far better to let others do the work. As Goodwin points out in his history of the Ottoman Empire, the Capitulations were also essentially an extension of the system of collective responsibility, which the Ottomans applied to all subject communities: 'Police yourselves, the Ottomans said, or suffer the consequences together.'

The same degree of lassitude was applied to the manner in which the Ottomans dealt with non-Muslim communities. They were entitled to be governed by their own laws under the '*millet*' system. So long as these were religions of the book – Abrahamic faiths – they had limited powers to regulate their own affairs and were not forced to convert to Islam. One by-product of the system of Capitulations was that it encouraged a degree of competition among foreign powers. As trade with the empire expanded, the French and later the English were granted the right to offer protection to other powers not covered by Capitulations. This meant that all kinds of foreigners could claim to be 'protégés' or even citizens of other places, and enjoy extraterritorial rights in the empire. The newly independent Greeks were one such tribe: by the end of the third decade of the nineteenth century as many as 120,000 were protected by the Russian Consulate in Istanbul. These rights, shamefully abused, encouraged the growth of consular power, including legal clout and a certain amount of muscle in the form of *dragomans* – people who could serve as translators and go-betweens with the Ottoman authorities. Many emigrated Greeks and Italians served as *dragomans* to larger foreign powers.

As the balance of power started to tilt towards Europe in the late eighteenth and early nineteenth centuries, the Capitulations became a licence for foreign consuls to exercise sovereignty over sizeable communities in Ottoman lands. 'What began as a contemptuous concession became a gross abuse,' wrote Sir Andrew Ryan, a British diplomat who in the late nineteenth century served in the *Sublime Porte*, as the

Ottoman capital in Istanbul was known. 'Corrupt and power-hungry European Consuls drew increasing numbers of local inhabitants under their protection.' Imagine a country full of turbulent foreigners, wrote Viscount Milner, a British aristocrat-chronicler of imperial Britain, 'whom its police cannot arrest except *flagrante delicto*, and whom its courts cannot try except for the most insignificant offences. Imagine the Government of this country unable to legislate for these foreigners without the consent of a dozen distant Powers.'

Imagine, indeed; Ottoman practice was an early manifestation of Britain's allergy to a conglomeration of nations with fuzzy, undefined borders. Thus a concession that Ottomans themselves initially thought they were bestowing upon a 'weak and poor Europe as a favour' ended up violating Ottoman sovereignty and paving the way for colonial predation.

Yet as much as these crude instruments of extraterritoriality invited the violation of sovereignty, the Ottoman Capitulations – along with the *millets* – laid the foundations of diversity and cosmopolitanism in the Middle East. Making the best of the reality of the special privileges enjoyed by Europeans, the Egyptians launched a unique system of Mixed Courts in 1875 which allowed a panel of judges conversant in different legal codes, though preponderantly that based on French law, to adjudicate in cases involving foreigners.

These mechanisms enabled Christians, Jews and Muslims to live among one another, and to regulate and govern each other without creating communities separated by walls or boundaries; this allowed for hybrid, fluid identities that militated against friction and generated understanding between East and West, between Orient and Occident. By the 1860s foreigners in Egypt enjoyed a privileged position, such that 'no house of a foreigner could be forcibly entered without the knowledge and concurrence of the consul representing his nationality.' Foreigners were also exempt from local and state taxation and could not be tried in Egyptian courts. By 1860, around 30,000 foreigners were streaming into Egypt a year: 'the European concession hunter and loan monger, the Greek publican and pawnbroker, the Jewish and Syrian money-lender and land-grabber, who could always with ease obtain "the protection" of some European Power'. In 1864 Alexandria's population of more than 100,000, was almost a third European, with around 15,000 Greeks and 15,000 Italians in equal measure. It was at this time, in the early 1860s, that the first members of the Sornaga family arrived in Egypt.

CHAPTER TWO

Grand Hotel de la Poste

'All things are for sale in Port Said.'

Rudyard Kipling, *The Light that Failed*, 1890

The Suez Canal, one of the world's most strategic waterways, a lightning conductor of imperial design and exploitation, as well as a vital channel of communication between East and West, was the start of my family's Levantine sojourn. It was also the starting point of my journey in search of my family's almost-forgotten history. For reasons mostly of my own making, the journey was long overdue.

I grew up in the mind-numbing normality of an outer London suburb. England in the 1970s, where my parents settled after a brief spell in the United States, was reaching the end of a long period of difficult post-war and post-imperial recovery and embarking on a half-hearted embrace of Europe. I attended private schools in the best elitist British tradition, where I was taught subjects rather than shown the world. My unusual heritage was obscured and suppressed in the interest of blending in; my foreign name and relatively recent provenance were halters on advancement up the pillar of the English establishment. Yet there were telltale signs of a Levantine past, scraps of evidence littered across my childhood. Pewter and copper artefacts from the souks of Cairo that my mother lovingly polished; old prints and engravings that depicted idyllic scenes by the Nile, and some remarkably delicate porcelain decorated with ornate flower patterns in rich burnt ochre, indigo and vermillion. When I was growing up, my parents told me stories about their childhood on the fringes of the desert, of their large and quarrelsome families, and of the dark times that engulfed them all in the 1940s, leading to their eventual exodus as refugees.

Foreign languages were regarded as peculiar in the England of the 1970s, yet Greek, Italian and Arabic wafted through our suburban north London home with visiting friends and relatives, down muffled, long-distance phone lines and through the gramophone speaker on which my father would play scratchy records of Lebanese and Egyptian songs. Much later, and regrettably towards the end of the lives of my parents and relatives of their generation, I grew more interested in finding out about their life in the Middle East. I had two children of my own growing up in a multicultural millennial world; they had no idea of their provenance. I started conversations with relatives, pored over musty photo albums, scanning feverishly with my handphone, and eventually delved into stacks of yellowing family papers in my mother's Oxford home.

There were hints of colourful characters lurking in the faded sepia wash of old photographs: a successful mustachioed and be-flannelled entrepreneur on the Italian side; a wandering Greek Orthodox monk with a long flowing beard and piercing dark eyes on the Greek side; incongruously wedged between these Italians and Greeks there was my maternal grandfather, a wounded British veteran of the trenches in France who went on to serve the British Empire in the deserts of Jordan. My mother, Patricia, toggled between her kindly but distant British Catholic father, with his modest achievements and loose flannel trousers hitched up high, and her mother's more sociable and successful Jewish Italian clan. Towering over all of these fleeting glimpses of my Levantine family was the charismatic personality of my father, Panayiotis, who made a successful career of the Middle East as a scholar and university professor. He loved the land in which he was born and grew up – he loved the music, he loved the food, and most of all he loved the whole madness of its tortured history, about which he wrote just as lovingly. He delighted, a former student recalled, in 'revealing the artfully concealed deceptions behind grandiose political projects, deflating the claims of nationalists'.[1] His teaching and writing inspired two generations of students to do the same at universities across the United States and then at the universities of London and Oxford.

I have to confess I don't recall too many conversations with my father about the Middle East in his time. I was either away at school or he was away at some conference. My early interest in the family and its background was awakened at the dining table, where my father regaled us with stories about the old world he and my mother came from. Before dying far too young at the age of sixty-nine, he left a brief and curiously meagre memoir of his life among Arabs and Jews in Palestine.[2] Published in 1991, the book left many gaps, some of which I have pieced together by talking to those who knew him and reading his unpublished personal diary that mostly covers his academic career from the late 1960s to the mid-1970s. My father confided his most candid thoughts to fiction. I discovered a collection of short stories that were never published in a pile of his papers.[3] Eager to learn more, my memories filled with fragments of history and evanescent patches of colour of a world all but lost in the sands of time, I embarked on a journey of several stages.

Every journey has its beginning: I arrived in Cairo on a flight from my home in Singapore on an overcast, blustery day in March 2019. Trudging through the featureless and unremarkable airport, I was struck by the absence of any of the opulent European flourishes the Viceroy Ismail Pasha was so fond of; the gateway to Egypt today is decorated with grimy ceramic tiles and pallid plastic, lit by flickering fluorescent tubes. It was early evening and very chilly when I emerged from the terminal and found a taxi. Weaving through heavy, honking traffic on uneven, elevated roads, we passed the grey stone piles of medieval Mamluk mosques and the mud-brick hovels of old Cairo crouching in the shadows below. On either side of the road I was assaulted by brightly illuminated billboards, luminously incongruous, like scenes from a Ridley Scott movie, offering intangible escape from drudgery to luxury resorts on the Red Sea coast.

It's always disconcerting to arrive in an unfamiliar place at dusk, as I did – difficult to get a feel for your surroundings, which reveal themselves the next day, for better or worse. Then there is the perpetual anger of the Cairo taxi driver. Years ago, I learned to swear in Arabic from Cairo taxi drivers. I could recite all the different ways to violate somebody else's mother, or describe people and their relationship with dogs. Today, Cairo taxi drivers have toned things down; they are more likely to invoke God and mutter Koranic verses under their breath. Piety instilled by the Muslim Brotherhood, a semi-secret Islamic populist movement that has led a long struggle against military rule in Egypt, is evident everywhere. A dark patch of hard skin on a taxi driver's forehead denotes devotion to God, rather than the absence of seat belts. The taxi I took from the airport had a small lighted Koran placed on the dashboard; the driver had a knob of darkened skin on his forehead and wore a white cap. He waved his hands a lot and honked his horn, muttering Koranic verses under his breath all the way to Zamalek, the upscale district of Cairo that sits on the north end of an elongated island in the Nile in the city centre.

The following morning, I stepped on to a dusty balcony overlooking the gleaming expanse of the longest river in the world. The Nile flows from Lake Victoria in Uganda almost 7,000 kilometres to the south and, running up through the desert before fanning out into a rich alluvial delta, gives life to Egypt. A weak winter sun reflected off myriad ripples, cast like a net of fine gold threads on the remarkably blue waters below. The dust underneath my bare feet reminded me, as Lawrence Durrell nicely put it, that 'the desert is always there at your elbow.' The throaty roar of Cairo at full throttle filled my ears with the commanding insistence of a cathedral pipe organ: a discordant symphony of car horns and worn, old, screeching tyres, the sounds punctuated by distant, mournful mid-morning calls to prayer. I was reminded of the Cairo I had known as a student in the mid-1970s; the same throbbing roar and the aroma of old rubber, cheap gasoline and human toil. Awestruck by one of the world's oldest – and, with almost 20 million people, one of its largest – cities at my feet, I was also seized with a mild sense of panic: alone in search of a lost era. Poor and beset by the frustrations of a failed popular revolution, Egypt today is a world apart from Ferdinand de Lesseps and his idealistic vision of Egypt as a prosperous crossroads of global trade and the splendour of the ambitious viceroys who modernised the country. Where to begin?

After a light breakfast involving warm bread, bitter black olives and creamy yoghurt laced with thick green olive oil which had the consistency of engine oil, I headed downstairs in the ageing lift that descended with creaks and groans in semi-darkness to find the *boab*, or door guard, slowly lifting his head and casting a watery eye over the dimly lit lobby. The building dated from the 1940s and hadn't seen a lick of paint since.

'*Sabah a-keer*'; I extended a polite morning greeting on my way out to meet the driver I had engaged through a friend. He arrived punctually, at nine o'clock as arranged, wearing a broad smile that offset his cheap blue suit and unnecessary formality. His name was Omar, and he had a faint whiff of oranges about him. As we set off, Omar launched into his life story. Before working as a driver, Omar told me, he was an optician. He had worked for a while in Saudi Arabia, which he lost no time saying he hated.

'They told me I would be paid a certain salary and have a free ticket there and back; they lied,' he said, swinging the car on to the 26th July Bridge and heading into the city passing Tahrir Square, the epicentre of the 2011 popular revolution that brought down then President Hosni Mubarak and for a brief moment liberated the country from army rule.

The easy familiarity, the immediate sense of trust – something that accompanied me throughout my journey in the Middle East – was a striking contrast to the unspoken suspicion that pervades initial encounters in Asia. The endless litany of grievance aired so readily was another constant on my journey. Egypt's troubled situation has prompted an exodus of labour, mostly to neighbouring Arab states. Yet Egyptians reserve a special dislike for the Saudis, whom they consider thieves and brigands, much as they look down on their own desert Arabs, known as sage people, after the wild bushes that grow so abundantly there.

'Why leave a respectable profession for life as a driver?' I asked Omar. 'The pay was terrible – and I was fed up staying in one place, sometimes as long as twelve hours a day in the optician's shop, peering into people's eyes.' Omar tapped his hand nervously on the steering wheel as we waited at a traffic light. His leg pumped up and down. The cool air outside was infused with exhaust fumes and the organic scent of decaying meat and vegetables. Omar was a nervous man clearly in need of an outlet, and it wasn't very long before he started talking politics. Ahead of us a gigantic battle tank painted in pale desert camouflage was being transported on a slow-going lorry and holding everyone up. The tank's long gun barrel stared menacingly down at us. Omar turned to me and said with remarkable clarity: 'Our military is like a closed watermelon.' I later learned that he meant it is a question of luck: either the watermelon turns out red and sweet, or it is only fit for the garbage.

We turned off the main road near Ataba Square in downtown Cairo and headed towards the city's older Mamluk quarter. A press of people carrying fresh vegetables brushed past the car as we nudged carefully through the Al-Ghayara produce market. Pyramids of dusty oranges and gigantic cabbages lined either side of the narrow street. Omar explained that, after the 2011 revolution, President Muhammad Morsi's government, elected in 2012, tried to open the army's books and expose its vast wealth and command of the economy. Morsi was a leader of the Muslim Brotherhood, which has championed the poor in Egypt since the 1930s and is loathed by the elite, who fear its levelling aims more than its dogmatic religious beliefs. The army's response was to unseat the government and engineer General Abdel Fattah el-Sisi's elevation to president in 2013. Omar professed no support for the Brotherhood – which could land you in jail – but he was bitterly critical of the military-led government. He did admit to being an avid consumer of dissident talk shows beamed in via satellite from Turkey. One of the most popular is presented by exiled Egyptian journalist Moataz Matar, based in Istanbul, on the Arabic-language El Sharq network. 'The authorities try to stop it,' said Omar, 'but the Arab satellite range is close to our own Nilesat.'

Much as my eagerness to uncover family history urged me to relegate modern Egypt to the sidelines, it had already begun to intrude. I have been visiting Egypt for forty years. Each visit was coloured by impending crisis or the aftermath of upheaval: bread riots as I left Cairo in 1976, unrest following the rigged elections in 2005 ahead of my second visit, and then the sour taste of disappointment I encountered on the streets of Cairo amid the disillusionment of the failed Arab Spring on another visit in 2012. The immense sadness and anger of my Egyptian friends today offsets the bourgeois Arcady as recalled by my family before 1952. Contemporary Egypt is ruled by a strict military regime, which is taking no chances, fearing a repeat of the 2011 popular uprising. The army rules by fiat, and there is nothing even approximating the kind of demi-democracy I was used to in Southeast Asia, which offers political and economic safety valves that mostly keep violent protest at bay: much smarter authoritarianism. In Egypt, dissenters pay a high price. Omar talked about people disappearing, about thousands held without charge in jail: 'I have friends I haven't seen in three years. I don't know if they're alive or dead.'

Omar paused to concentrate on merging into a broad avenue in heavy traffic. The sun was rising higher and chasing away the long shadows cast by the city's magnificent stone buildings, their grey-brown hue a blend of the natural surrounding desert and centuries of human detritus. Conversation that heats up in tandem with midday temperatures in Cairo makes for an angry, combustible brew. I remember in the 1970s how terrified I was of the beggars who scrambled like beetles out of dark corners in the heat of the day and turned their pleas for a few coins into foaming fury as the sweat poured off their faces. Poverty in Egypt isn't endured stoically the way it is in parts of Asia; it is a perpetual source of anger.

'You know,' Omar resumed, his watery eyes on me and then again the traffic, one hand raised from the wheel to gesticulate, 'the fake-news TV here likes to describe Sisi as a prophet sent by God to save us from the Muslim Brotherhood. But we don't think Sisi is a good Muslim. He looks happiest when he goes to non-Muslim functions.'

After a long silence during which I gazed at a line of people patiently queuing for bread, their faces lined by daily struggles and stamped with resignation, Omar shook his head before continuing the litany, each point stressed with a frantic wave of hands.

'You know, just last week, they killed twenty-one young people. Killed them!'

'Who were they?' I asked, alarmed but also a little sceptical. 'And who killed them?'

'The *Mukhabarat*, the secret police. They accused them of blowing up a senior official.'

Like so many things in modern Egypt, it is hard to distinguish hard fact from angry, hysterical rumour. There have been some pretty serious acts of violence, like the car bomb in August 2019 that killed twenty people outside a hospital in central Cairo.[4] The government was quick to blame Islamic militants. Then the news was buried. All the same, Egyptians drink deep from the rumour mill – it slakes their thirst for something to be angry about, partly because the media is so crushed and cowed, but also because so much is hidden behind high walls, tinted glass and veils of paranoia. For many years the smiling face of President Mubarak, who assumed power in 1981 after the avuncular Anwar el-Sadat was assassinated by the Muslim Brotherhood, presented a more benign image of military rule. After 2011, when thousands of young Egyptians faced down the military and toppled Mubarak's sclerotic and corrupt government, the army was taking no chances.

'We knew where Nasser lived [Egypt's first president of the Republic]; we all knew where Sadat and later Mubarak lived,' Omar told me.

I noticed the veins on his throat throbbing. He turned and offered a vague, nervous smile to mask his anger: 'Sisi is the first president of Egypt we have no idea where he sleeps at night.'

I asked Omar to simply drive me around the first day in order to get my bearings. The next day we ventured further, to Port Said, and before setting off Omar greeted me with a recounting of the previous evening's anti-government dissension. 'Last night Moataz Matar asked the people to gather in groups at sunset and say to one another #besafeyouarenotalone.' With that he flashed me one of his soon-to-be-familiar toothy grins and we commenced our journey.

The drive took about three hours along the recently built 30th June Highway, named after the day the Egyptian army seized power from the Morsi government elected on the back of the 2011 popular revolution. The military government claims that almost 40 million Egyptians came out on the streets on that day to overthrow the president, who was subsequently arrested, along with many of his Cabinet colleagues. Morsi was put on trial for treason and later collapsed and died in court in June 2019.

I observed that the desert road – much like the events of that fateful day – was unfinished and in parts hard to discern. Omar found this 'too funny', his bulbous head bobbing in angry accord as we jolted up and down on gravel-strewn, unfinished stretches of tarmac.

We sped past what seemed a never-ending series of walled compounds behind which sits the Egyptian army. I counted dozens of watchtowers and guard posts – all manned by an armed soldier at the end of the slender black barrel of an automatic rifle. From a distance they seemed so harmless, like toy soldiers. In between, new housing developments with names like Future City sprouted in the otherwise open desert and arrayed so higgledy-piggledy that they looked like Lego assembled by a five-year-old.

Once in Port Said, I immediately sensed the city's prosperous past. Omar nosed the car down dusty streets fronted on each side by crumbling stucco façades embellished with rich rococo flourishes and shaded, iron-lattice balconies hanging like loose camisoles. Early accounts of the city describe its hasty construction, and the challenge of erecting buildings without a ready source of local stone – so perhaps they have always looked makeshift. Ferdinand de Lesseps chose the site because it was the shortest distance on the isthmus from the coast inland – and French surveyors found it was the spot opposite the deepest channel from the sea. It was on Easter Monday in April 1859 that de Lesseps swung a pick to 'break ground that will open the way to the Orient for the trade and civilisation of the West'. A traveller at the start of the twentieth century, barely forty years after Port Said was built, wrote scathingly about the poverty of its attractions, dismissing Port Said as nothing but a coaling station. 'An imaginative writer once called Port Said the "Venice of Africa,"' wrote the irritated American Eustace Reynolds-Ball; 'the comparison might for its inappropriateness rank with the proverbial one between Macedon and Monmouth. Both Venice and Port Said are land-locked and that is the only feature they have in common.' Yet for a city built from scratch, Port Said grew quickly. Barely twenty years after it was established there were more than 16,000 inhabitants – almost half of them foreigners. The city was laid out in binary form; there was a cramped and squalid Arab quarter, and a foreign quarter with wide streets lined with elegant buildings named after crowned heads of Europe – and, of course, Ferdinand de Lesseps.

Omar drove us through what would have been grand squares, their iron-fenced gardens now invaded by plastic garden furniture in garish colours. Main street buildings had shaded arched porticos on either side, reminding me of the covered five-foot-ways of the Straits Settlement town of Penang in Malaysia, though they were much wider here in Port Said. Eventually, turning into the main commercial thoroughfare of El-Ghomirya Street, which used to be called Rue du Port and later King Fuad Street, we reached my destination: the Grand Hotel de la Poste, established in 1892, as a sign outside proudly declared. It was here that my mother's parents first met in the mid-1920s. And it was here that I decided to truly begin my journey in search of the lost era in which they, and my father's parents to the east across the Sinai Desert in Palestine, grew up and thrived more than a century ago.

The Grand Hotel de la Poste has seen better days. The grubby signboard outside what is today a five-storey building could barely be read and, appropriately, the word 'Grand' had been removed. Tattered awnings in what was once a cheerful tangerine sagged with a thick coating of desert dust and black grime from probably decades' worth of traffic. Port Said, as Egypt's principal port, was something of a freewheeling entrepôt for much of the second half of the nineteenth century and until the outbreak of the Second World War. After the opening of the canal it was known for its bustling brothels, smoky gambling dens and music-filled night clubs, much as you would expect of a desert Klondike. In his early novel *The Light that Failed*, published in 1890, Rudyard Kipling wrote: 'there is iniquity in many parts of the world, and vice in all, but the concentrated essence of all the iniquities and all the vices in all the continents finds itself in Port Said.' The Egyptian Jewish writer Sylvia Modelski, who grew up in Port Said in the 1930s, laments the reputation Port Said acquired for being a city of 'women to buy and boys for sale'. The Grand Hotel de la Poste, which sits around 200 metres from the dockside, must have seen some wild times.

Today the hotel looks weary and long past caring. The lobby smelled of the boiled lima beans which constitute the staple diet in Egypt. It was littered with tattered chairs and tables scattered in no particular order. The front desk sat hiding in the back. Two young girls wearing hijab completed the check-in formalities with no conversation. One of them slid a key attached to a chipped and cracked plastic fob towards me with the merest hint of a smile, but nothing more. The lift, one of those without an inner door, gave me a perfect view of stain-smeared, cobwebby walls as it groaned its way to the third floor, although when the doors opened I saw there had been some attempted recent renovation. Room 308 faced the street and was graced with a precarious balcony, its rickety railing coated with dust thick as hazelnut icing and not for leaning on. There was no longer a bar in the hotel; the chandeliers and gilt furniture I saw depicted in a grainy 1904 postcard have vanished, but alcohol could be procured from a dingy counter off to the side of the hotel under a faded sign saying: 'Drinks'. I purchased a cold Stella beer and retired to my room to gaze out and upon the city's crumbling past. Late in the afternoon, with an early spring sun casting filigree shadows on the buildings along El-Ghomirya Street, I headed out for a stroll along the edge of the canal.

Many of the buildings here were once owned by shipping companies. Many still are. Some had the city's characteristic ornate iron balconies and terraces – veritable crows' nests from which employees could be on the lookout for arriving ships. These balustrades were also important to provide shade and a place to snatch passing breezes during the suffocatingly hot summer months. I came across the Bauhaus-style Simon Arzt Building, intact but empty. The Jewish-owned business was once the city's biggest emporium, famous for a brand of cigarettes popular across the region. And all that remains of the ten-metre bronze statue of Ferdinand de Lesseps is a marble pedestal at the end of the long *ilot*, or concrete jetty, that frames the mouth of the canal and was one of the first structures built in Port Said. The statue was dynamited in 1956 by Egyptians protesting Britain's vain attempt, in a last gasp of imperial arrogance, to seize the canal in what came to be known as the Suez Crisis. Nearby, a stately nineteenth-century lighthouse, one of the first buildings erected in Port Said, watched resolutely over the entrance to the canal. It is said that Gustave Eiffel, who built the famous tower in Paris, vied to build the lighthouse. When completed it had the most powerful electric light in the world and could be seen from a distance of forty kilometres on a clear night.

It was here in 1925 that my grandfather, Richard Mumford, arrived, having left the British Colonial Service in Transjordan a few months earlier to take up an offer of a clerk's job with Savon and Co., a shipping company with offices in Alexandria and Port Said. There is no record of where their office in Port Said was, but I found an old shipping announcement from the last decade of the nineteenth century that mentions a company based in Alexandria called Savon-Bazin and Co., which later closed and became simply Messrs L. Savon and Co., specialising in the supply of coal to steamships traversing the Suez Canal. This was no small business: in the early decades of the twentieth century, Port Said was the leading coal-bunkering station in the world, importing 2 million tons a year before the outbreak of the First World War in 1914. There were dozens of other companies providing shipping services of all manner. Archives from the major French merchant bank and shipping conglomerate Worms & Cie testify to frequent disputes over coal-pricing and supplies with Savon and other canal-based companies.[5] Being the head of the Suez Canal made Port Said a bustling place, '[f]our days' sailing from Marseilles,' wrote a former director of the Alliance Française, Valérie Nicolas, 'four days to meet up with this Tower of Babel where Egyptians, Arabs, Greeks, Maltese, Cypriots, Levantines, Syrians, and Tripolitanians mixed and where they took ocean liners by storm'.

The Grand Hotel de la Poste as it is today

Arriving after a spell in Alexandria at head office, Richard lodged at the Grand, and it was at one of the hotel's tea dances that he met my grandmother, Lidia Sornaga, the youngest daughter of a family of Italian Jews who were prosperous and well connected in Egypt. The Sornagas, like other Levantines, fled to Port Said during holidays to escape from the stifling heat of Cairo. The Grand was one of several of Port Said's upscale hotels. Others were the Continental, the Royal and the Eastern Exchange, all situated along the elegantly laid out Rue du Port, now El-Ghomirya Street, which ran alongside the canal, back from the jetty. The Eastern Exchange, damaged then demolished after the Suez Crisis in 1956, was one of the first iron-structured buildings in Egypt – believed to have been inspired if not executed by Gustave Eiffel, and which boasted the country's first passenger lift. Beyond the jetty there were beaches with bathing huts and fresh fish to be had at fine restaurants. Despite Kipling's less savoury view of Port Said's seedy dockside life, it was a summer riviera for the Cairo elite. Sylvia Modelski recalls the beach scene in her delightful memoir *Port Said Revisited*:

> It is hard to think of a better summer resort than Port Said in the thirties . . .Those with cabins arrived late, around lunchtime. They

> brought their food with them as no snacks were available on the beach itself except for *granita* and iced tea dispensed by an ambulant seller in an Annamite hat. For lunching in style there was the *Pavillion Balneare*, which stood over the surf on algae-coated pilings. A branch of the Casino Hotel, its restaurant served delicious spaghetti with seafood sauce. A live dance band brightened the atmosphere further.

Port Said and other towns up and down the canal became veritable playgrounds for people living in Cairo, and it was the same in the early 1940s, my father recalls in his diary.

He and his university friends fished for crabs in Port Tawfiq at the Red Sea end of the canal and played soccer against the Greek Club:

> Driving from Cairo to Ismailia and up or down the Canal was like rushing near a ditch which was about level with the desert and on either side of it. The mad hotel in Port Tawfiq in a narrow alley by the harbour populated by Greeks and Italians; Coucouris and Belelis and his insane Jazz Band. Then there was the Hotel Aore in Port Said with its terrace restaurant on the roof looking down to the harbour. Some fifteen of us one evening bought every giant shrimp found in the baskets of the itinerant vendors moving from table to table, and had the restaurant cook them for us.

Over a long, hot summer of beachside fun and evening entertainment, Richard and Lidia courted, and married soon afterwards. Lidia gave birth to twins, John and Josie, in 1928 and to my mother, Patricia, in 1930. I have no idea, but imagine that perhaps the couple spent their first night together at the Grand – and I wondered, if so, in which room.

As night fell and the city darkened, a cacophony of stray cats invaded the gutters, hunting for scraps. I closed the rickety shutters of Room 308 and fell asleep dreaming of starched white flannel, panama hats, dance bands and well-lubricated tea dances.

The first years of my mother's childhood, until 1936, were also the final years of the canal's effective occupation by British forces. Remember, in 1875 the British government bought the shares owned by the heavily indebted viceroy, Ismail Pasha. After the British occupation of Egypt in 1882 the country, and especially the canal zone, became a virtual British colony, despite the almost completely French-staffed and -run Canal Company, based in the more sedate town of Ismailia halfway down the canal towards the Red Sea.

As in other British colonies, the number of British personnel and their impact on society was minimal; they confined themselves to the imposing British Navy House, the Customs House and the Port Police HQ, built along the jetty near the mouth of the canal.

Sylvia Modelski recalls that the British 'were among the least visible communities.' There was an English Hospital, where my mother was born, but no English school. The British and Foreign Bible Society opened a depot for the global distribution of its Bibles in Port Said, both because of its efficiency as a distribution centre and, conveniently, because of its proximity to holy sites mentioned in the Old Testament – this was, after all, the location of the Wilderness of Sin, through which the Israelites passed on their passage out of Egypt! The British community leaders, including the British Consul, were mostly Maltese Catholics – although the British did build a cricket pitch on land set aside for a municipal park. Certainly, in Port Said my grandfather Richard would have felt closer to England than when he lived in the deserts of Jordan. My grandmother Lidia, however, probably missed her large Italian family, which helps explain why the family moved to Cairo shortly before the outbreak of the Second World War.

Old building in Port Said today

Port Said today is a free port and duty-free zone, but with so little traffic that the customs checkpoint simply waved us through on our return to Cairo. Omar began the morning drive with the latest from Moataz Matar in Istanbul, who had revised his advice: instead of coming out in mass numbers on the weekend, he recommended they wait until Mother's Day on Thursday. Changing the subject, Omar asked if I was satisfied with my visit to Port Said. 'Yes, but . . .' I replied.

The city was infused with a sadness I found hard to understand, given its spectacular setting and storied past. People's faces were pinched and scarred; on the ferry to Port Fuad, on the other side of the canal, there were few smiles and little conversation. And as the sun set gloriously on the African side, at the Port Fuad Greek Club I was shooed away by an irritable guard and told that everything was closed. It was as if I were being told: forget it, the era you are looking for is long dead, don't even try to conjure it up. It was advice that others offered regularly along my journey, which I sensed stemmed from a mixture of emotions and evident realities. Some Egyptians don't like to be reminded of the khedival era or the colonial past – and of the manner in which the revolution that expelled the British and deposed the king heralded a bright new future, how this promise of freedom was squandered, and for many Egyptians has become a totalitarian nightmare. Others reminded me that there was nothing about the Levantine era that ever did very much for the average Egyptian, even if the privileged Levantine elite were eventually just replaced by a more grasping parochial elite. This sense of parallel but disconnected histories haunted me throughout my journey. I found no easy way to connect them.

Turning back from the old Greek Club, which seemed to have an inviting terrace that glowed as the sun dipped behind Port Said, I watched young couples stroll through a clothing market situated along the quayside in Port Fuad, in the shadow of two soaring minarets casting long shadows.

I returned to the other side of the canal disappointed to find the streets of Port Said deserted by early evening, with few cafés occupying the generous shade offered by the stately porticos on El-Ghomirya Street. Gone were the elegant tea houses of my mother's era. I found refuge in a small, brightly lit coffee shop serving limp chicken sandwiches and run by two young men glued to smartphones.

This was rather different from my memory of the Port Said I visited in 1976. Then, just three years after a war with Israel that saw parts of the town destroyed by the Israeli air force, Port Said was quiet but still had an edge to it, together with some of the iniquities Kipling wrote about. I found speakeasy bars serving beer and whisky filled with rowdy young Egyptians psyched about fighting Israel and stashing notes under the bra straps of corpulent belly dancers, their sweating, pouted flesh shimmering with sweat under dim-red lighting. The Egyptian army was everywhere, and the security situation tense. Port Said was dotted with air-raid shelters and life-size decoys of Egyptian soldiers manning fake missile batteries. I was travelling with a group of foreign students; we played football with local kids in the street and joked with horse-drawn carriage-drivers rolling joints and waving them at local policemen. We had fun, but, even then, there was a sense of lamentable loss about the place.

'You know why people are so sad?' asked Omar, jolting me back to the present. 'It's because of what happened in twenty-twelve.' I confessed I didn't follow. 'It was after a football match between my team – Al-Ahly – and the Port Said team, Al-Masry. I was right there, in the stadium, with a group of supporters; we'd won, and were cheering wildly. All of a sudden, Al-Masry supporters charged on to the pitch and attacked us. They beat us up and stabbed us with knives. Many people died in the crush to escape. I saw a pregnant woman killed in front of my eyes. Seventy-nine people died that day. We were all terrified. We couldn't drive our cars here for fear of being attacked. At the time the army was blamed. Too much killing; too much sadness.'

Omar, who had a knack for bringing alive his country's tragic present, once again frustrated all my efforts to lose myself in the past. After a long pause we changed the subject, and I asked for the best place to find fresh fish – something I remembered from my first visit: the taste of freshly caught sea bream, grilled simply, drenched in lemon juice and served with salad, washed down with local white wine. The fish market, of course! Omar had eaten there the night we arrived, while I had had to make do with a less-than-appetising chicken sandwich, washed down by a not-so-cold beer in Room 308 of the formerly grand Hotel de la Poste.

On the morning I left Port Said, gazing towards sleepy Port Fuad, dominated today by the twin minarets of a modern mosque, I found it hard to transpose the images from the early-twentieth-century photos

I had seen: a bustle of barges and labourers servicing the liners and cargo ships passing through the canal, the coal hauled up in sacks on their bare backs into the bowels of the ships; all manner of goods and services on offer to passengers and crew from tenders and stretching across the jetties. This slender body of water served as a vital artery feeding, fuelling and filling ships that funnelled through the canal outward-bound to Asia or inwards to the ports of Britain and Europe. There was nothing very Egyptian about Port Said's community of customs officers, pilots, brokers, merchants and chandlers, other than the manual labour they hired. Nor was much of any profit returned to the Egyptian people, who did not even exercise sovereignty over the canal zone for more than half a century of its operation. When the end of this halcyon era of freewheeling opportunity for anyone but the Egyptians arrived, it was sudden and violent.

Endless flat, featureless desert flashed by as we picked up speed to join the new highway. In ancient times, the Egyptians built the great trading city of Pi-Ramses just to the south of Port Said. It was known as the Thebes of the North and, much like de Lesseps and the Canal Company in the nineteenth century, the Egyptians drew in large numbers of seafarers and merchants from the Mediterranean, manning shipyards and warehouses – again, a cosmopolitan trading community, which thrived here almost 3,000 years earlier. For a long time afterwards it must have seemed improbable that anyone could have made anything of this place, with its salty marshes rimmed by waterless desert. Yet three millennia later, Ferdinand de Lesseps, the resourceful and cunning Frenchman whose imposing bronze likeness no longer surveys the canal, pierced the sands Moses-like, his project drawing people of all kinds to its banks to build a new life. Here, as in other parts of the Middle East for a time, people prospered as who they were.

After visiting Port Said I made a beeline for Kantara from the western side of the canal, aiming to cross by ferry. Kantara lies on the other side of the canal from Port Said in what today is the Sinai province of Egypt. In the early decades of the twentieth century it was a busy crossing: where the railway from Palestine met the canal and before a modern bridge was built, passengers transferred by ferry to a railway line that went on to Cairo. Here, in 1923, my paternal grandfather, Jerasimous Vatikiotis, was posted as a junior clerk for the Palestine Railways. He was newly married to Paraskevi, a Greek woman of good standing from the island of Rhodes whom he had met when they both lived in Jerusalem.

In the early 1920s '[t]here were Greeks, even in Kantara East, a god-forsaken spot in the desert in 1923,' wrote my father; 'they founded a lively community with its own church [Saint Spyridon] and school, organised their own celebrations commemorating various national-religious occasions and holidays, and generally continued to be as Greek as ever.'

I was eager to look over the remnants, and was told the Greek church was still standing.

We drove south from Port Said for about an hour to reach the sizeable, modern Mubarak Peace Bridge, which crosses the canal at Kantara, but it was closed to traffic 'for security reasons'. For the past decade or more, the north-eastern quadrant of the Sinai has been designated a war zone by the Egyptian government. The army is said to be engaged in a desperate battle it never quite wins against Islamic extremists, in particular a branch of the Islamic State that has been active in the area since the collapse of the 2011 revolution. The war in northern Sinai is very much a hidden war. Independent human rights organisations have tried but failed to verify reports of draconian security operations on the Asian side of the canal, which are said to have included forced evictions, widespread arrests, torture and aerial bombardment resulting in thousands of deaths. For its part, the Egyptian government blames Islamic State and its affiliates for savage acts of terrorism – including the August 2019 hospital car bomb in Cairo.

No surprise, then, that I was met at the ferry crossing in Kantara West by a wall of security. First there were police wearing white, ill-fitting uniforms and sloppy black berets who raised their hands and waved them like windmills and said '*mish mumkin*' – 'impossible'. I queried this decision, and after a brief discussion among themselves they referred me to army security, kitted out in slim-fit striped tennis shirts, sleek black jeans and Nike trainers. After scrutinising my passport their injunction was firm: go back, no foreigners allowed.

Ahead of me I spied a pick-up truck being forensically dismantled by security personnel, while its occupants squatted in the meagre shade of a date palm. On the way back past the checkpoint a policeman suggested we seek a permit from the *Mukhabarat* – the feared security police. So we drove into Ismailia, the elegantly laid-out and rather bucolic town that hosts the Canal Company headquarters.

Ismailia is famous for three things: the Suez Canal Company; the foundation of the Muslim Brotherhood in 1928; and in 1973 a desperate battle between Israel and Egypt, in which Egyptian troops narrowly averted the city's capture by the Israeli Defense Forces. Today the city is popular with weekend visitors from Cairo, who come to eat fresh fish by the side of Lake Timsah. Much of what you see physically is the legacy of the Canal Company's long presence, complete with elegant homes surrounded by manicured gardens and neatly laid-out streets, influenced by French taste and style. It was at one such mansion that we found the headquarters of the *Mukhabarat*. The large house was situated along a busy main road, and the entire property was ringed by a high wall of thick iron sheets with a guard turret at each corner. The place looked more like an armoured tank than a Canal Company villa. There was no obvious entrance. One of the soldiers manning a turret languidly pointed to a door cut into the iron wall. It was firmly shut, but I rang a doorbell that I found hanging casually by the side. I rang it again, and waited for about ten minutes. Then, with a clang, the door opened and what looked like a nervous, T-shirt wearing teenager appeared clutching a walkie-talkie.

'I was told I could come here to secure a permit to visit Kantara East.'

'No permit,' the boy said, clanging the door firmly shut. There was a fearful look in his eyes. Again, I rang the bell. Again, I waited – this time for about five minutes. Then the door was opened, this time by an older man in a white sleeveless vest. No walkie-talkie, less nervous and almost relaxed. 'There is no possibility of getting this permit unless you apply in Cairo at the HQ,' he said.

He was neither rude nor polite. He was probably just stating the truth. I withdrew, imagining a month of visits to the headquarters of the *Mukhabarat*, waiting in tobacco-reeking, dingy offices for yet another round of questioning with forms to fill in and ultimately no outcome other than drawing attention to myself in a high-security state. After a cup of bitter coffee at a roadside café we drove back to Cairo, where I took up the search for the greater part of my mother's large Italian family and tried to ignore Egypt's sad contemporary predicament.

CHAPTER THREE

The Khedive's Gold

> 'In times gone by, when stones threatened us, we wandered from place to place. But by the mercy of God we have now been enabled to find a resting place in this city.'
>
> Maimonides (1138–1204)

Christmas Eve in Cairo in the year 1871. A well-dressed crowd including dignitaries from all parts of Europe are settling into the plush seats of the brand-new opera house. Men wearing starched dress shirts and black tails peer in the dim gaslight at their programmes; women in richly coloured silk dresses glitter with a kaleidoscope of jewellery. Four tiers of ornately decorated boxes look down on the stage and the rather constrained orchestra pit, where the players tune their instruments with a discordant hum. Behind the curtain a cast that includes powdered Italian divas and scantily dressed Ethiopian slaves waits in the wings and in the cool, dry air outside. The performance that is about to begin will be remembered not just in Egypt, but across the operatic world. For it seems, on this particular night, that all roads lead to Egypt, and a great modern future lies ahead. Giuseppe Verdi, grand maestro of the opera in the modern age, has written a new work about Egypt, commissioned especially by Egypt's ruler, the Viceroy or Khedive Ismail Pasha, to mark the opening of the Suez Canal. At least, that is what the well-heeled and expensively coiffed audience has been led to believe.

The reality is more complicated. The opera house is spanking-new, but a bit of a compromise, hurriedly designed and built in just six months, 'like so much else of Ismail's Cairo, by gangs of forced labour'; the Tuscan architect Pietro Avoscani endeavoured against the odds to imitate Milan's famous La Scala. As a result of the rushed timetable, the building wasn't as grand or sturdy; to save money and time it was built partly of wood and could hold only 850 spectators. Extra audience space was taken up by Egyptian women of the viceregal court, who needed to sit in boxes behind gilded screens.

Verdi initially refused the viceroy's generous commission, saying it was not his custom to write 'occasional pieces'. But the story is that he changed his mind after hearing that Ismail Pasha had been considering appointing his German competitor, Richard Wagner. Perhaps Verdi wasn't happy with the idea that one of his operas would be used to mark an occasion he wasn't at the centre of – not the opening of the canal, but of the opera house itself. But the generous fee, 150,000 lire, was enough to buy a sizeable house in Italy. 'We must at least keep the fee secret,' Verdi wrote in June 1870. 'Someone would be sure to point out the 400 *scudi* for the *Barbiere di Siviglia*, Beethoven's poverty, Schubert's misery, Mozart's roaming about just to make a living, etc, etc.'

The idea for *Aida* – a tale of love and treachery set in the Old Kingdom of the pharaohs – was proposed by the French Egyptologist Auguste Mariette. Although written and scored according to the demands of the commissioned schedule, the premiere had to be postponed because the elaborately designed sets were stuck in Paris, which was under siege from the Prussian army at the tail end of the Franco-Prussian War. Irritated, Verdi reportedly exclaimed: 'Bloody Goths, source of all my troubles!'

With a ruffling of taffeta and silk followed by a wave of hushes, the lights of the opera house begin to dim, leaving only the twinkling of jewels as the house goes dark. The audience are barely able to contain their excitement: for not only are they about to watch Verdi's greatly anticipated new opera, but there are European nobles and notables among them, including the French Empress Eugénie, with whom Ismail Pasha is secretly (or perhaps not so secretly) besotted.

Most of the audience are Europeans of one sort or another – from the high-born and noble to the new bourgeois elite: Greeks, Italians, Jews and Armenians, perhaps a few down-and-out Russian counts and countesses here and there – 'foreigners of high extraction who are numerous in Cairo', wrote one observer. Their conversations slide bewilderingly between Italian, Greek and mostly end up in French. Also among the audience are the new rich of Egypt: 'It is a perfect miracle to see a fez in the theatre of Cairo,' wrote the Italian critic Filippo Filippi. 'Copts and Jews, with strange headgear, impossible costumes, colours which clashed so violently that nothing worse could be imagined.'

Many in the audience are hangers-on at the viceroy's court, indebted in Europe, and living off the pasha's largesse. The Empress Eugénie, wife of the exiled Napoleon III and the last French empress, wears her favourite emerald tiara, and is seated in the royal box on a gilded armchair upholstered in red velvet. Verdi himself is absent, unhappy, it was said, with the fact that no members of the general public had been invited to attend the gala opening. Filippi wrote that the frenzy to attend the premiere was such that 'at the last moment spectators sold boxes and stalls for their weight in gold.'

The Cairo Opera House as it was in 1871

As much as the glittering premiere was a significant moment for Egypt, and one that has been dissected and debated ever since, the distinctive diversity of the audience that night reflected a period of turmoil in Europe. For a continent of old princely states and monarchies was in the violent throes of transformation as wars and revolts heralded the formation of larger states, which in turn set the stage for even bigger upheavals to come at the start of the new century. In 1871, after France's defeat in the Franco-Prussian War, Germany's northern and southern states combined to establish the German Empire, Kaiser Wilhelm was installed as emperor and Otto von Bismarck became its first chancellor. Also, in 1871, after more than half a century of armed uprising and revolt, Rome became the capital of the new unified Kingdom of Italy.

Meanwhile, at lower levels of society, there were signs of impending revolution: in June 1871 the Paris Commune was brutally suppressed after a disorganised mob of republicans tried to hold parts of the city after the end of the Franco-Prussian War. After loyalist troops eventually suppressed the resistance, more than 20,000 of them were killed. (The Emperor Napoleon and Empress Eugénie sought refuge in England, after France's defeat at the hands of the Prussians in the same year.) There were also the first signs of the foundations being laid for the Nazis' persecution of the Jews: in 1873 Wilhelm Marr published his book *Der Sieg des Judentums über das Germanentum vom nichtkonfessionellen Standpunkt aus betrachtet*, or *Jewry's Victory over Germandom*, considered by some to be the intellectual wellspring of anti-Semitism.

These and other ructions in central Europe and on the margins of the Ottoman Empire, which was embarking on its own stately decline, set in motion a major movement of people away from the ravages of war, insurrection and rising racial and religious prejudice. Many of these people found refuge and made new lives for themselves in Egypt, which was at peace and modernising, and where foreign labour and expertise were much in demand. Some of these newly arrived foreigners even made it to the opening night of *Aida*. Among them were members of my mother's Italian Jewish family, the Sornagas.

My maternal great-great-grandfather Samuele Sornaga and his wife, Stella, had arrived in Egypt from northern Italy about a decade earlier, shortly after the start of the Suez Canal's construction. They came in search of opportunity and quickly found their feet working in the cotton-ginning business based out on the Nile Delta south of Alexandria. As such, by 1871 they were already well-off and respectable members of society with connections to the viceregal court when the Opera House opened for its gala performance.

The story of why and how these Sornagas went to Egypt, the fortune they made and then lost, captures an important strand of a forgotten cosmopolitan era in the Middle East. Consider the manner in which refugees are treated today, especially those fleeing the Middle East for Europe: evading coastguard patrols; surviving the risk of drowning in small, often flimsy and overcrowded boats on the high seas; herded into grim transit camps and condemned to uncertain overland journeys across Europe, only to face racial taunts and prejudice once they find a safe haven. From today's perspective, it is almost unimaginable that people seeking refuge from turmoil would be so warmly received and protected, even privileged, in their place of refuge. Yet enterprising Europeans who made their way to Egypt two centuries earlier found not only shelter but also protection and a path to prosperity, and those in the audience at the opening night of *Aida* participated in a singularly productive moment of Egypt's history.

Unlike the bedraggled, shell-shocked families from the ruined cities of Syria and Iraq who today stumble over the obstacles to uncertainty in Europe's recession-hit economies, the Italians and other Europeans who went to Egypt in the mid-nineteenth century were more fortunate. Commerce and trade, stimulated by the opening of the Suez Canal, helped a young and equally foreign ruling dynasty determined to detach itself from the overstretched Ottoman Empire drag Egypt into the modern world. This development largely occurred on the back of trade in a single commodity – cotton – which by the 1870s accounted for more than 90 per cent of Egyptian exports. And, much like many ruling houses of Europe, the rulers of this new Egypt relied on bankers, principally Jewish bankers, to arrange their financing. Many of these Jews would have arrived from other parts of the Ottoman Empire, where anti-Semitism was more common than in Egypt. Pre-modern Egypt was already a diverse society with a community of Jews that settled in the Nile Delta as far back as pharaonic times. The Egyptian viceroys needed engineers to build their infrastructure and professionals to run services, teach in schools and train soldiers and officials. In the process, the Sornagas and countless other families like them – Italians and Greeks, but also Jews and Armenians from elsewhere in the Levant – prospered, and achieved a measure of security they would have found hard to match in their countries of origin. It was, very briefly, a golden era of progress enjoyed by many, but certainly not by all.

Yet these Europeans, my mother's family among them, were also profoundly complicit in proud Egypt's eventual hobbling at the hands of the European powers. While my mother and her siblings enjoyed the fruits of Sornaga wealth in the 1930s, cavorting at the family villa by the banks of the Nile, or enjoying sultry weekends in another sumptuous villa by the pyramids of Giza, around them Egypt was already a broken country subject to the whim of indirect but suffocating British rule. Muhammad Ali and his successors initially enslaved the Egyptian population, preferring to enlist foreigners to run their new modern country. The majority of senior civil servants and military officers were Turks – trained and advised by Europeans. Arabs weren't trusted by these imported rulers, who hailed after all from the Balkans. The marginalisation of Egypt's native population was unsustainable. Indeed, for all of its glamour and glitter, that opening night at the Cairo Opera House marked the beginning of a long arc of decline that ended in a bloody revolution and the expulsion of foreigners, including the Sornagas.

The Sornagas traced their ancestry to the Jews of Tuscany, and before that to the Iberian Peninsula. They were Sephardic and settled in the seaport of Leghorn (Livorno) along with other Jews fleeing persecution in Spain and Portugal towards the end of the sixteenth century.[1] The muddy wetland on the west coast of Tuscany developed as a port for Florence and nearby Pisa, falling under the rule of the enlightened Medici family, which controlled most of Tuscany. Livorno was connected to the Tuscan interior by a canal dug in the sixteenth century, propelling its development as a free port and major trading centre. To encourage Jews escaping Spain to settle there, the Medici allowed them to engage in commerce and moneylending. Grand Duke Ferdinando I de' Medici drew up a set of charters in 1593, known as the *Livornina*, which guaranteed full religious liberty, amnesty for crimes previously committed, and provided exemption from taxation, and commercial freedom. 'Jews could own houses, inherit property, carry arms at any hour, open shops in all parts of the city, have Christian servants and nursemaids, study at the university, work as doctors and did not have to wear the Jewish badge.'

Given this high degree of liberty, the Jews of Livorno thrived and preserved their Sephardic culture. At one time in the seventeenth century Livorno housed Europe's second-largest Jewish community after Amsterdam. They spoke Spanish and they were referred to by the Italians as *Ebrei*. Records from the city show that one Samuele Sornaga, son of Binyamin Sornaga, was circumcised on 9 January 1704; quite possibly he was a forebear of my great-great-grandfather of the same name who settled in Egypt. By the late seventeenth century Livorno had become a major port in the Mediterranean, attracting Greeks fleeing Turkish rule as well as European Protestants escaping

Catholic persecution. The British Levant Company established a trading house there. This exposure to trade in the Levant meant the *Livornese* Jews were familiar with the region, and indeed their music and Jewish ritual styles extended as far as modern-day Iraq. So why did the Sornagas leave Livorno? A quick recap of Italian history offers some clues.

The Roman Empire fell to invading Goths at the end of the third century AD, and over the course of the next 1,700 years what we know today as Italy morphed into a collection of separate states, all with their own identities, cultures and languages. A sense of Italian national identity only started to bloom in the late eighteenth century. Gian Rinaldo Carli's *Della patria degli Italiani*, written in 1764, related the story of a stranger who entered a café in Milan and puzzled its occupants by saying that he was neither a foreigner nor a Milanese. 'Then what are you?' they asked. 'I am an Italian.'

By the mid-nineteenth century the Italian peninsula was in turmoil. This was the period known as the *Risorgimento* – the aim being unification of the country. 'Few people in 1830 believed that an Italian nation might exist,' wrote the British historian Denis Mack Smith. 'There were eight states in the peninsula, each with distinct laws and traditions.'

Italian states in their disparate forms were ruled by foreign princes imposed by the main imperial powers of France and Austria. The weight of oppressive outside rule meant that many of the key nationalist intellectuals and political leaders were in exile. The patriotic poet Ugo Foscolo, for example, lived in near-obscurity in London teaching Italian in Chiswick. Nationalist leaders like Giuseppe Garibaldi fled into exile after each of the failed uprisings. Italians fighting for nationhood, it seems, came and went, establishing a tradition of exile as a political statement.

As French and Austrian armies tramped up and down Italy stamping out the successive revolts and wars of independence that rocked the peninsula from about 1830, something else began to happen. To appease their uppity subjects some local rulers started to grant citizen's rights under constitutions. These had a liberating impact, especially for Jews who had lived in Italy since Roman times. The Savoyard King Charles Albert made Piedmont the first Italian state to grant its Jewish citizens equal rights and allow them to enter the military. In Tuscany Grand Duke Leopold II issued a series of edicts that culminated in Jewish emancipation in 1848. As a growing number of Italians experimented with republican notions and struggled to throw off the archaic rule of aristocratic outsiders, they embraced liberal ideas of freedom and equality that attracted many Jews to the patriotic cause. Jews were particularly active in Giuseppe Mazzini's *Giovine Italia* (Young Italy) movement. Campaigns for Italian unification and Jewish emancipation therefore went hand in hand. 'The *Risorgimento* was good for the Jews,' wrote a reviewer of a biography of the Italian Jewish writer Primo Levi in the *New York Times* in 2006. 'It was a liberal, secular, enlightened movement, all three of whose great leaders, Mazzini, Garibaldi and Cavour, were philosemites; and it had already freed them. Not surprisingly, therefore, Jews were among the most passionate supporters of a united Italy.'

Accordingly, my Sornaga antecedents were drawn to the struggle. Some joined the *Garibaldini*, the red-uniformed followers of the great Italian republican General Giuseppe Garibaldi, one of the key military leaders of the *Risorgimento*. It is thought some of the Sornagas were in Rome with Garibaldi himself in February 1848 when he declared the Republic, which, among other things, advocated freedom of religion. Pope Pius IX, who presided over the Jewish ghetto established in 1555 by Pope Paul IV, feared he would be deposed – or worse – and fled. The ghetto, which celebrated its liberation in 1849, was located in an area comprised of several blocks of stately old buildings stretching from Venice Square to the tree-lined banks of the Tiber and encompassed the ruins of an old fish market crowned by a triumphal gate erected by the Emperor Octavian. Today the area is a popular tourist attraction, offering supposedly kosher food and gefilte fish in open-air restaurants employing Middle Eastern immigrants as waiters. When I visited, the man who served me a dish of fresh octopus and pasta and a glass of refreshing Frascati was, as fate would have it, Egyptian. As I walked around the stately old synagogue facing the river one early summer's afternoon, I was reminded that Jews, although freed from the ghetto in 1849, were not assimilated as citizens until after the unified Kingdom of Italy was established in 1871.

The early emancipation of the Jews under Garibaldi's new Roman Republic was short-lived: it soon fell under French attack. Garibaldi fled to New York in 1850; a great many of his Jewish supporters followed him out of the country. Just as the new nation had begun to evolve, there was reason to leave. They were exiles, wrote the Alexandria-based Italian writer Fausta Cialente, and, fleeing from the Pope or the Bourbons, they 'embarked at night in fishing boats from Barletta, or Taranto, or from the coast of Sicily, and after weeks at sea disembarked in Egypt. I imagined them, the legendary fugitives of the last century, wrapped in their cloaks, with wide-brimmed hats and long beards: they were mostly professional men or intellectuals who, after a while, sent for their wives from Italy or else married local girls.'

There were other reasons to leave Italy, including the burgeoning opportunities abroad and the means to reach them. As much as violence and prejudice were a mark of the times, the arrival in the mid-nineteenth century of regular steamship services across the Mediterranean made such journeys safer and ultimately cheaper. By 1850 several commercial companies, including Cunard, started running steamships out of British ports to the west coast of Italy and then on to the eastern Mediterranean, calling at Alexandria and Istanbul. The Crimean War of 1853–56 saw a boom in the construction of troop ships, which were subsequently retrofitted to take on passengers and named to reflect the identity of those on board: *Grecian*, *Italian*, *Egyptian*, *Dalmatian*, etc. Once the Suez Canal opened in 1869, these steamship services through the Mediterranean multiplied.

Italians went to Egypt in the mid-nineteenth century, around the time the canal was being dug. One of these Italians, Samuele Sornaga from Livorno, was my great-great-grandfather. Samuele arrived in Egypt around 1860 after the Rubattino Italian Shipping Company established a steamer route calling at Livorno. He and his family landed at the port of Alexandria. Italians who went to Egypt in this period joined thriving and colourful communities; Alexandria's neighbourhoods included the old Jewish *Harat al-Yahud* quarter, which, with its Italians congregating from the early nineteenth century onwards, had the look and feel of an Italian town, complete with barber shops, wine-sellers and *tavola calda* restaurants, out of which wafted the smells of fresh baking and rich tomato sauces. Along the Rue Fuad, or in and around the Place des Consuls, then known as the Place des Armes, more established Italians mingled with Greek and Armenian shopkeepers and other Levantines; they lived in modern apartment buildings embellished with classical columns and arches that survive to this day, even though many are crumbling with neglect. They attended balls and tea dances at cafés and hotels situated just off the city's generous, sweeping seafront.

Many of these Italians enjoyed a privileged position, serving the khedive as architects, engineers and running all kinds of professional services. They congregated at Italian clubs and associations and had their own newspaper in Alexandria, *Il Messaggero Egiziano*. An observer in 1863 noted that: 'The Italian language is, after Arabic, the most generalised. All Levantines and Greeks speak it well enough and the Arabs that deal frequently or trade with Europeans speak broken Italian by necessity.'

Nestled in the library at the Italian cultural centre in Cairo is a three-volume history of the Italian community in Egypt published in 1906. The compiler, Professor Balboni, noted that at the start of the nineteenth century most of the viceroy's foreign advisors were French, but that this started to change in the 1820s, when Italians were invited to help establish the postal service. By the 1850s Balboni presents potted biographies of hundreds of architects, engineers and other professionals: men like Ciro Pantanelli from Siena in Tuscany, who worked on designing some of the viceroy's early palaces, such as that at Kasr el-Nil in Cairo. Many of these architects came from different parts of Italy to build in khedival Egypt, each with their distinctive style. Defying the stereotypical orientalist narrative, writes Cristina Pallini, who has made a study of architecture in Egypt from this period, these refugee artisans were attuned to local cultural needs, coining the term *okelle* to describe the grand buildings they constructed with neoclassical façades that were essentially Turkish caravanserais – places of trade and commercial exchange where people also slept, ate and transacted business. One of them, the Okelle Monferrato, which still stands in the heart of old Alexandria, was designed by my mother's great-uncle Luigi Piattoli, a Florentine who went to Egypt as a young man in the 1840s and who was eventually appointed by the viceroy, Said Pasha, as one of his engineers and architects. Piattoli worked on various major palace projects and public buildings in Cairo and Alexandria.

Okelle Monferrato as it is in Alexandria today

An accomplished artist as well as an architect, Piattoli painted large religious canvases for the Roman Catholic Saint Catherine's Cathedral, which can still be seen. His sons, Giorgio and Alfredo, married into the Sornaga family. Another Tuscan, Carlo Biagini, owned a bank and, together with Luigi Piattoli, built Alexandria's Italian Theatre in 1858. The courtyard of the theatre originally housed a statue of the Tuscan Grand Duke Leopold II, who had helped emancipate the Jews.

By the time Samuele Sornaga arrived in Alexandria sometime around 1860, the Italian community, many of its richer members Jews, was well established and numbered close to 10,000. Samuele, his wife Stella and five children would have been well looked after by one of the many resettlement associations and might have first been housed in the densely inhabited old Turkish quarter, where many newly arrived immigrants stayed.

Samuele soon moved away from Alexandria and settled a little to the south in the Nile Delta region, which was home to fast-growing agricultural enterprises. A note based on a dictated account by one of my mother's cousins, Iole Arrigotti, before she died in 1987 speaks of Samuele owning a cotton-ginning factory in Kafr el-Zayat, a modern industrial town where before the Second World War the name Sornaga could be seen from the train, painted on a factory wall. Samuele was considered in family circles a roguish adventurer. It's possible, though not entirely clear, that his wife, Stella, was an Italian Jew from Tunisia, whom he met along the way to Egypt. 'The Khedive Ismail, who lived nearby, often [spent] his evenings at the Sornaga house playing cards,' Iole recalled. I picture the ebullient viceroy wearing a velvet waistcoat and a red-felt fez sitting at Samuele's table, the soft sound of shuffling cards the backdrop for discussion after an evening meal, cigar smoke the background fragrance. In the morning, said Iole, the servants would find gold coins littering the floor.

Ismail Pasha was a passionate Europhile who had been schooled in France. He brought back many ideas and spearheaded efforts at education reform and established the country's first national assembly. He once said that Egypt 'is no longer in Africa; we are now part of Europe. It is therefore natural for us to abandon our former ways and to adopt a new system adapted to our social conditions.' He clearly did and, grateful for the Sornaga family's friendship, and who knows what else, the khedive provided the dowry for Samuele and Stella's three daughters: Rosa, Teresa and Maria – almost certainly in gold sovereigns.[2]

The Sornagas had arrived in Egypt just as the country was experiencing an economic boom built on cotton. The Egyptian scholar Mona Abaza, whose family owned a cotton plantation, relates a story that one day during Muhammad Ali's reign a French botanist discovered a plant growing in a Cairo garden that he recognised as a shrub from the Americas known as *Gossypium barbadense*, popularly known as Sea Island cotton, prized for being disease-resistant and especially for its light, silky texture; it was thus valuable.

Seeing an economic opportunity, the foresighted and enterprising first viceroy, Muhammad Ali, ordered this high-quality variety to be planted and cultivated over wide swathes of the country. Within half a century cotton was Egypt's dominant agricultural product and the main source of its revenue. Egyptian cotton experienced a boom after the sudden loss of production in the cotton-producing American South on account of the Civil War, which erupted in 1861. As a result of an effective blockade of the Confederate troops by the Union forces in the North, the mills of Lancashire in England, which had been starved of supplies, were soon filled by Egypt.

Cotton was profitable for those who grew and exported it, but generated twin evils: crushing inequality as a result of forced or slave labour, and colonial dependency, which the economy's inevitable reliance on European markets engendered. It's more than a little ironic that the Egyptian cotton industry generated so much hardship for the native peasant on the back of a war fought in a far-off continent over the abolition of slavery.

The Sornagas' cotton-ginning business prospered. Samuele's two sons, Giacomo and Clemente, and three daughters, Teresa, Rosa and Maria, were well educated. One of the hallmarks of the cosmopolitan era in the Middle East was the multiplicity of languages people were fluent in – mainly French, Italian and Greek, in addition to Arabic and English. It was common for rich immigrant families to have an Arab wet nurse, perhaps an English nanny, and Italian domestic staff. The best Italian schools taught Arabic as a second language, and all the Sornaga children born in the nineteenth century could speak French, some English and could read and write Arabic and found professional jobs in Egypt's burgeoning institutions. By the time the next generation came of age in the first two decades of the twentieth century, the use of Arabic had been relegated to the kitchen and the marketplace, as French and English became the means of effective social and economic mobility. My mother and her siblings knew only basic 'kitchen Arabic', which was my first exposure to the language as a child.

Cultural nuance and ambiguity of identity was standard in the Italian community, writes the Levantine scholar Anouchka Lazarev: 'the sense of national belonging [to Italy] was just as strong as the opposing sense of rootedness within the country.' The ambiguity was compounded by a liminal quality to their existence, living a privileged life, as the Egyptian Jewish writer Jacqueline Shohet Kahanoff notes: 'What were we supposed to be when we grew up if we could be neither Europeans nor natives, nor even pious Jews, Moslems or Christians, as our grandparents had been?'

Giacomo, the eldest of the Sornagas' five children, who had been born in Italy, finished school and started work in the Post Office, where he rose to become general manager; his brother, Clemente, worked in the law courts. 'The two brothers were rather different in their outlooks and tastes: Clemente (known in family circles as Uncle Gogo) was rather democratic and mixed with ordinary people and workmen,' according to my mother's cousin Iole: 'Giacomo was happier in high society and social gatherings.' The two brothers were young men with bright futures, particularly because they lived and worked in Cairo, which in the 1870s was at the dawn of what is often called Egypt's belle époque.

Sornaga family outing c.1905 (Lidia Sornaga on the far right)

The Cairo Post Office is a dusty *grande dame* of a building, well past her prime, yet still proud and keen to keep up appearances. She squats on one corner of Ataba Square, hemmed in on one side by an elevated expressway, and with a seedy market underneath selling cheap Chinese mobile phones and other gadgets cobbled together at its elegant marble skirting. As part of his modernising thrust, Muhammad Ali dreamed of a nation connected by an efficient postal service. Early on, he asked Italians – later including my great-grandfather, Giacomo Sornaga – to establish a new postal service. This explains why the first Egyptian postage stamps were printed in Italian.

The Cairo Post Office today

The Post Office was high on my itinerary of places to see during my stay in Egypt, and I set out to see it on a chilly but bright and clear March morning, taking a taxi to the square. As I got out of the cab and approached the building on foot, I started taking pictures. A portly policeman carrying an ageing automatic weapon came shuffling over.

'Who are you?' he asked in broken English.

'A tourist,' I replied, wielding my camera aloft in a gesture of surrender.

'Let me see,' he demanded, gesturing towards the camera.

I scrolled through the digital file of images on the small screen behind my trusty Fujifilm SLR. Squinting at views of the Nile and Ataba Square, preceded by shots of my infant grandchildren, the mustachioed constable in his threadbare uniform seemed satisfied I was not plotting an attack and waved me on.

The Cairo Post Office boasts a museum, as befits one of the earliest of the modern institutions created by Muhammad Ali. The museum is reached through the main door and up a grand central staircase made of marble. A guard at the door snapped a string of beads and waved a finger and thumb at me in a classically Egyptian form of interrogation: 'Ticket?' No ticket.

I was directed to one of the main booths in the main hall, a small open-air atrium decorated with murals depicting ancient Egyptian motifs, hinting at a fact I later learned – that my great-grandfather Giacomo was no pioneer: according to an Egyptian government website, 'Postal services flourished in Egypt since the Pharaonic Old and Middle Kingdoms and have been a paradigm of precision.'

Trudging up the worn marble staircase, museum ticket in hand, I was directed by a stout woman wearing a hijab to a musty, high-ceilinged room lined by dusty glass cabinets. Here I found myself completely alone with the ghosts of postal workers past, a thought made spookier by the manikins dressed in faded old uniforms arrayed within the glass cases. I peered in the dim light at documents pertaining to Giacomo Muzzi, who, along with other Italian partners, had set up a private 'Posta Europea'. Viceroy Ismail Pasha, continuing with his uncle Muhammad Ali's plans, bought over the private postal service and then contracted Muzzi and his partners to establish the government postal service on 2 January 1865 – which also marks one of the stranger commemorative dates I have encountered: National Postal Day. Muzzi, who was granted the title 'Bey', made a considerable profit on the deal and stayed on to manage the service, which utilised rail and river transport and needed qualified staff, many of whom were Italian.

I imagined Giacomo stepping out from his office, greeting his colleagues with a tip of his straw boater or Panama hat and striding into Ataba Square, which marked the frontier of Ismail's modern Cairo with the medieval Mamluk Cairo. He and the family lived close to the current fire station just off the square. Perhaps he would have gone to the nearby Cairo Opera House to buy tickets for a weekend performance. Or have his watch repaired at 'Montres Francis Papazian', the Armenian shop beside the fire station. He may have strolled over to Soliman Pasha Street, now Talaat Harb, to have a sherbet and a coffee at Groppi's, an Italian coffee house that is a Cairo institution. Its cream cakes and ice creams were famous, especially for the European berries they imported to grow on farms in the Nile Delta. Today's *farawla* (strawberry-juice) vendors on Cairo street corners owe a debt to Groppi's, for whom the fruit was first cultivated.

Today the streets are clogged with traffic and it is hard to imagine the international bustle of Ataba Square in the last decade of the nineteenth century. In the dusty little park outside the Post Office, as honking cars and dilapidated buses spewing fumes speed past, peasant families spread cloths on the ground and try to have a dignified meal of flat bread and hard cheese under the shade of the noisy flyover.

Giacomo was the equivalent of a hi-tech worker for the modernising Egyptian state. The contemporary Egyptian writer Alaa Al Aswany captures how the Italians helped fashion 'paradigms of precision' and drag Egypt into the modern age. He tells a story of the first motion picture shown in Egypt, *The Arrival of a Train at La Ciotat Station*, made by the Lumière Brothers. The event was held in Alexandria in 1896, in a hall owned by an Italian, Dello Strologo. The audience panicked when they saw images of a train speeding towards them and, imagining it was real, they fled – as they had done in Paris when the film was first shown. After that, Strologo began each screening with a 'behind the scenes' tour, thus assuring his audiences that what they were seeing was merely a projection, caught on camera and replayed for their amusement.

By the end of the nineteenth century the Sornagas had multiplied, marrying into other wealthy Italian families, among them the Balls and the Piattolis. Not all these unions were with other Jews, reflecting the Sornagas' rather liberal perspective on their Jewish faith. This was possibly driven by Samuele's Italian nationalist credentials – making him notionally a Jew, but more identifiably Italian – or the need to adapt and blend into a context not all that friendly to Orthodox Jewry. Giacomo married a native of Rome, Celeste Campagnano. Together they had six children, including my maternal grandmother, Lidia, who was born in 1887. Life was 'cheerful and gay' in the household of Giacomo Sornaga. My mother's cousin Iole again:

> Conversation at the . . . table was always about cheerful things: marriages, baptism and so on. Nothing sad was allowed. Celeste always had a starched bag made from a pillowcase full of Tuscan home-made biscuits with almonds and also some *rosolio* [a kind of liqueur], also home-made . . .There would be receptions and entertainment and the young girls would make fun of some of the young men who came to visit. There was much fun and humour.

Even as more Italians emigrated to Egypt, a great many of them were also born there and felt just as attached to Egypt as they were to their nearby homeland. When they died they were buried in one of the city's many foreign cemeteries.

'I know the Latin cemetery,' declared Omar triumphantly. 'It's close to where I grew up, and now live.' We headed south towards the citadel, perched on a rocky outcrop on the Mokattam Hills overlooking the (relatively) new section of the city. 'Egyptians like to call it Muhammad Ali's citadel, but it was built by Salah al-Din,' Omar said as we approached the imposing thirteenth-century walls behind which soar the rocket-shaped Ottoman-style minarets of the Muhammad Ali Mosque. We drove through the expansive Muslim cemetery known as the 'City of the Dead' before reaching an Anglican Protestant cemetery, next to a Commonwealth War Graves site. But still no Latins.

'Where's *Makubur Lateen*?' Omar asked another driver when we pulled up at a set of traffic lights. After some toing and froing we set off again, this time finally, after venturing carefully down a few narrow side streets and past a church, finding a narrow gate and another caretaker, who seemed more harassed than perhaps he should have, considering he was looking after a cemetery full of souls who had been dead for almost a century. A few graves were more recent; otherwise, the names are almost exclusively those of people my mother's family would have known in the heyday before 1952: the Piattolis, the Scottos, the Paladinos, the Castellanis. I could not find any Sornagas. I was told they might be buried in a Jewish cemetery; no one knew if it still existed. In any case, Giacomo Sornaga, my great-grandfather, died in Rome in 1903 and is buried in the city's main Verano Cemetery in an imposing tomb not far from that of the Garibaldi family. For those buried in Cairo, over the years bodies once individually laid to rest in marble niches have been grouped together under family names. The bones are there, the caretaker assured me, gesturing to rows of square marble panels along a rectangular wall with the names of architects, bankers, engineers. The Cairo these Italians helped build has now all but engulfed their last resting place. Across the street the grey stone aqueduct built by the Mamluks in the fourteenth century to carry water from the Nile to the citadel casts a severe shadow: a reminder of the city's enduring relics. I wandered around the cemetery, its expanses of white marble reflecting the light of the bright, mid-morning sun.

Omar took the ring road back into town, passing through what seemed to be an endless corridor of apartment buildings, rough and unfinished.

'Before the twenty-eleven revolution this was all green fields,' said Omar, gesturing expansively. Many of these brick-and-concrete structures were so pockmarked, often with whole floors and walls collapsed or caved in, that it looked as if bombs had hit them. *Is this Cairo, or Aleppo?* I wondered.

'They're mostly illegal, so the government comes and demolishes them,' said Omar, going on to explain that the law required external walls to be faced and painted; but the owners erected the buildings hurriedly for sale, to make a quick buck.

I heard a slight catch in his throat that hinted at suppressed emotion. He gripped the wheel with one hand and scratched his belly with the other.

'Agh, what a waste,' he muttered and then, after a while, he turned to me: 'You know, the next revolution isn't far off.'

I was not sure what to say. I had seen none of the gathering of Egyptians Moataz Matar has been calling for from his television studio in Istanbul. But I didn't want to ruin Omar's moment of hope.

'You make me feel very comfortable,' Omar said. 'I can't talk about these things to Egyptians. They'd report me to the *Mukhabarat* and I'd be arrested.'

Later that evening, on my balcony in Zamalek overlooking the Nile, I allowed myself to be mesmerised by the great river. Garish purple and yellow lights on the side of passing restaurant boats danced on the rippling, dark water, which drifted along like some giant electronic water beetle. In the distance, the call to evening prayer competed with the honking cacophony of evening traffic across the 26 July Bridge. The press of humanity below gave off a musty smell of dust, sweat and onions. Omar's anger and frustration with his people, stuck in a rut of perpetual underachievement, living in shabby, half-built, illegal structures that could be destroyed without warning, brought into sharp relief the contrast with my Italian family's transition from Jews of the ghetto to pillars of the professional class. For the Sornagas, Egypt was at first a life raft and then a bountiful cornucopia. They enjoyed the privileges of education, wealth and connections, as well as protection under the Capitulations. The contrast troubled me. With a few taps on my phone, I started playing the famous 'Grand March' from *Aida*.

CHAPTER FOUR

Blue Bricks by the Nile

> 'It was an odd world where people both belonged and didn't belong, mixed and didn't mix.'
>
> Jacqueline Shohet Kahanoff, 1959

The elegant grandeur of downtown Cairo's late-nineteenth-century layout and architecture survives, but barely. The darkened entrances to once-stately apartment buildings along Kasr el-Nil Street gape like aged, toothless maws. Idle *boabs* wearing dull-coloured *galabiyas* lounge outside on plastic chairs, languidly flipping beads, to escape the foul, musty breath of these neglected interiors. Above them, balustraded balconies sag under the weight of rattling air conditioners dripping water on to pedestrians below. Rotting louvered wooden shutters hang at odd angles off broken hinges and shabby clothing dries on balconies once decorated with potted palms and aspidistras.

At ground level, shopfronts are hard to discern. Lighting is scarce and signage sparse. A century-old pharmacy preserves the carved wooden design of its dispensary counter. The finely decorated art-deco façade of the Cosmopolitan Hotel, once a famed nightspot, is obscured behind geological layers of dust. I peer inside and see that the lobby, brightly lit by finely wrought stained glass, is intact but deserted. A pair of sleepy guards jerk into life and indicate with furiously wagging fingers that entry is forbidden. Forbidden! Nearby, the grand equestrian statue of Ibrahim Pasha, Muhammad Ali's eldest son, who led military campaigns across the Middle East, no longer overlooks the fine opera house he built to celebrate Egypt's debut in the modern world, but stares grimly instead at a mouldy concrete edifice insultingly called the Opera Office Building and Garage. Khedival Cairo survives as a shabby, fossilised remnant.

Groppi's, the famous coffee house established by a Swiss-Italian family from Lugano in 1891, is one such remnant. The original corner shop on the sharply angled edge of Soliman Pasha (now Talaat Harb) Square has been shuttered for renovation. A larger premises nearby continues the transplanted European fashion of creamy cakes ringed with glazed fruits. Its outdoor garden, hung with fairy lights, was once a favourite spot for afternoon tea and early evening drinks. The coffee is insipid and weak – though the mint lemon crush is delicious. A little further down the avenue leading to Soliman Pasha sits the 'Café Riche', established by a Greek in 1909. Its dowdy, dark-wood interior has long been a meeting place for intellectuals and activists, its walls lined with portraits of fiery, chain-smoking Egyptian thinkers with wide lapels and wild eyes. Umm Kulthum, Egypt's legendary singer, once performed here. More recently, the 'Café Riche' was home to Cairo's foreign press association. My father and his friends frequented the place in the mid-1940s, as did I in the mid-1970s, enjoying cold beer and greasy pasta flecked with mouldy pecorino cheese. The 'Café Riche' limps on, its ageing waiters and their careworn expressions a living memory of the past, the faint scent of lemons emanating from the kitchen.

Downtown Cairo today is a pale shadow of its former self. From the mid-1860s Egypt's Europeanising viceroy, Ismail Pasha, built a gleaming new downtown as a facsimile, its streets laid out and appointed to resemble those found in any European capital, with grand neoclassical expressions involving stout marble columns and undulating stuccoed carvings. The city centre was built on land formerly flooded by the Nile, around a triangle of tree-lined streets: Kasr el-Nil, Soliman Pasha and Fuad. Their layout was a paean to the geometric harmony used by Baron Haussmann's plan for the renovation of Paris, with its grand avenues radiating out from monument-laden circles, which had so impressed Ismail Pasha on his many visits there. Thus, with Ismail's approval, modern Cairo was dubbed the Paris of the East, here recalled by the Egyptian professor of letters Magdi Wahba:

> Here were the department stores (guarded by mustachioed Albanian doormen, in their fustanella and high boots). And here the French and English bookshops, the tea rooms and Parisian cafés, mingled with fashion boutiques, milliners, art galleries, clubs for the well to do, banks, court photographers, automobile showrooms, antique shops and jewellers . . . The Europeans, rich Egyptians and

Levantines of any class did their shopping here, conducted business in offices, sipped coffee in cafés.

The modern downtown area had gas-lit streets shaded by sycamore trees, leading into geometric squares of manicured, palm-fringed gardens. As in Alexandria, the architecture was grand and reflected the liberal European and largely secular vision of the Muhammad Ali dynasty. As with the Okelle Monferrato, which my grandmother's uncle Luigi Piattoli designed and built in Alexandria, Italian architects working on downtown Cairo, many of whom were from Tuscany, imported the secular idea of the city state pioneered in Florence during the Renaissance. In the stone-carved features and decorations they celebrated the Greco-Roman heritage of Egypt's past. In this sense, the city wasn't regarded as part of the divine order dominated by mosques or churches, but rather as a self-sufficient secular society dedicated to the advancement of its citizens and recalling classical forms of the pre-monotheistic era. A walk around downtown Cairo is an architectural masterclass. It also presents an uncomfortable paradox with the contemporary orthodox Muslim and Arab face of Cairo – not to mention its more austere Mamluk past. The residents of these buildings were predominantly foreigners. Contemporary accounts of the city by the turn of the century mention that there were few native Egyptians to be seen; even the waiters and shop assistants tended to be European.

Well-heeled Europeans and the few rich Egyptians in situ sipped chilled Hock or Chablis and held salons in rooms lined with gilt mirrors, flock wallpaper and Louis XVI crockery. The upstairs dining hall of Groppi's was *the* place to be seen, where society weddings were held and formal balls convened. Here the champagne flowed freely as a mountain spring and layers of icing and cream glistened white under gleaming crystal chandeliers. Cigar-chomping men in starched bibs and tails steered their heavily scented partners around the dance floor to the accompaniment of music from a band kitted out in brass-buttoned uniforms. The table chatter was mostly in French – the language of refinement for everyone who aspired to be somebody in Egypt. Around this area of the city, lavish villas, apartment and office buildings were owned by big Jewish and Armenian families – the Cattaui, Mosseri and the Yacoubians, as described in Alaa Al Aswany's novel *The Yacoubian Building*:

> It was considered quite inappropriate for natives to wander around in downtown in their *galabiyas* and impossible for them to be allowed in this same traditional dress into restaurants including Groppi's, but also A L'Americaine, and the Odeon, or even the Metro, Saint James, and Radio cinemas, and other places that required their patrons to wear suits, for men, and evening gowns, for ladies. The stores all shut their doors on Sundays, and on the Catholic Christian holidays, such as Christmas and New Year, downtown was decorated accordingly, as though it were a foreign capital.

This separation of poor Egyptian native from the Levantine elite was marked and became more pronounced in the early years of the twentieth century. Greeks and Italians mixed with Jews and Armenians – they met in the classrooms of English or French schools and in the clubs and bistros of Cairo and Alexandria. There were some formal unions across ethnic and religious lines, but mostly illicit ones. Intermarriage with Egyptians was rare. This partition of communities was of course innate to the prevailing British colonial context, and not all that different from the civil and military 'lines' separating the British from their Indian subjects. Except that Egypt wasn't formally a colony. Its parvenu Albanian rulers had initially invited enterprising foreigners to modernise the country. Britain and France, the two largest imperial powers with interests in Egypt, were initially content to invest and take profits, rather than intervene and exercise control. Yet as Egypt grew the country became indebted to mainly European creditors. By the 1870s Egypt's national debt, which stood at merely £3 million when Ismail became khedive in 1863, was around £100 million in a country that generated annual revenues of less than £10 million. The khedive was unable to repay these debts, despite the bounty of the Suez Canal, the boom in cotton and, later, after American cotton production resumed and the price of Egyptian cotton fell, a swerve into sugar.

Profligacy and financial mismanagement brought about the effective collapse of khedival rule and instigated a form of indirect British rule after 1882 that was colonial in all but name. This neocolonial context enhanced the protection of the Levantine community and saw the fortunes of my mother's family, the Sornagas, soar, but also drove a bigger wedge between them and the Egyptian people.

Set against the disastrous management of national finances and the growing impoverishment of ordinary Egyptians, the Levantines were doing rather well. Protected by the Capitulations and later the Mixed Courts, the Sornagas and other immigrant families wallowed in wealth, parading in fine linen suits and straw boaters around Ataba Square and the nearby Azzbakkiya Gardens. As anxious creditors besieged the khedive for repayment, they sipped lemonade at Groppi's and played tennis at the Gezira Club in Zamalek. Established in 1882, the Gezira Club was carved out of the Khedival Botanical Gardens and was used at first exclusively by the British army. The Royal Fencing and later Shooting clubs were favourite haunts of the incipient Egyptian elite, who benefited from and served the neocolonial elite. And at the Tipperary Club on Fuad al-Awi Street, the following amenities were available:

> air-conditioned tea rooms and balcony overlooking Ezbikieh Gardens, reading rooms with easy chairs, ping pong and darts, barber's shop and showers and a Musky shop from which purchases may be despatched home. Films are developed and printed, watches repaired and there is a small lending library. There are facilities for telephoning. The menu consists of tea, coffee, Horlicks, Ovaltine, hot and cold, milk shakes, ice cream sodas, ices, fruit salad, minerals, home-made lemonade, cold ham and tongue, sandwiches, salads, hot buttered toast, eggs, cakes, etc.

This was the domain of my great-uncle, Samuele Sornaga, son of Giacomo the Post Office manager and grandson of the pioneering Sornaga of the same name. Samuele Sornaga's story captures the heyday of Levantine society in Egypt in the first three decades of the twentieth century. Samuele made his start in the cotton business established by his grandfather, later branching out on his own to found a ceramics business in 1905, which became a model of the country's modern industrial potential – in terms both of the quality of its wares, some still manufactured, and the contributions he made to the welfare of his employees, a legacy remembered fondly even today. As a testament to his labour, the two lavish villas Samuele built still stand, as does the now-idle ceramics factory that bears his name.

Giacomo Sornaga and his wife Celeste's only son Samuele was born in 1870. Samuele embarked on his career as a young man in the final years of the nineteenth century, after the British invasion and establishment of the so-called 'veiled protectorate', the quaint labelling of so-called indirect British rule after 1882. After a spell with his grandfather's cotton-ginning business, Samuele worked as a trader for a rich Jewish merchant called Rostowitz Bey, an Austrian citizen from Trieste who imported cement and grain and was granted the honorific 'Bey' by the Ottomans. Samuele was talented, energetic and determined to succeed in business. Although he never married, Samuele eventually became the head of the family because he was rich and successful. By the 1930s he had transcended the hard-working, professional, middle-class background representing the majority of his Italian contemporaries and become a member of the wealthy and well-connected capitalist upper class, rubbing shoulders with other prominent Italian Jewish families. He eventually became head of the Federation of Egyptian Industries and was a member of the Economic Council of Egypt.

Other rich Jewish families included the Mosseris, who were also from Livorno, the Suarezes, prominent bankers who built railways, sugar refineries and owned a bus company, and the Menasces, who established a chain of free schools. The Rollos owned railways and Robert Rollo was director of the National Bank of Egypt. These Jewish families mingled with Egyptian royalty, and several of their women were rumoured to have been mistresses to kings and princes of the Egyptian line. King Fuad and his son, King Farouk, who reigned in the first half of the twentieth century, were particularly close to the Italians, surrounding themselves with pampered courtiers and courtesans.

Cairo in the last two decades of the nineteenth century was built to cater for this new capitalist elite, its downtown rivalling the sumptuous bourgeois quarters of Paris and Vienna. Whether they were Jews, Catholics or Greek Orthodox, Italian, Greek or Albanian, they subjugated as far as possible their religious and ethnic differences using the convenient cloak of cosmopolitanism facilitated by the khedival regime. This gave Levantine society a rather louche and liberal reputation. While the Sornagas and their Italian cousins munched on cream cakes, Ismail Pasha languidly played with Abyssinian dancing-girl slaves and down-at-heel European courtesans in his new palace, the Abdin, designed by French and Italian architects and designers at the south-east corner of the modern downtown triangle.

The situation generated two contrasting reactions in Egyptian society. There were those who benefited from a foreign education and mingled well in the mostly French-speaking milieu of the belle époque.

Taha Hussein, one of Egypt's most prominent nationalist thinkers of the early twentieth century, and who became minister of education in the 1950s, embraced the idea. In his 1938 book *The Future of Culture of Egypt* he argued that Egypt's culture and civilisation had more in common with the Mediterranean and in particular Greek culture than with the Arab world. For many middle-class Egyptians, however, even as they started to attend foreign schools and aspire to careers as professionals or in industry, it was frustrating to see so many plum jobs going to foreigners, which planted the seeds of resentment.

The Sornagas were aware of these glaring inequalities, and according to my mother's cousin, Giorgio Eberle, whose grandmother was Samuele's elder sister Enrichetta, were generally careful not to flaunt their wealth. Behind the veil of languid luxury, however, the Sornaga family harboured fissures typical of the day; the resulting unhappiness was passed down.

My mother, Patricia, was the youngest of three children; her elder brother and sister, the twins John and Josie, proved to be a handful for their mother, Lidia. When they were three months old it was decided that they would be separated and that Josie would live with Lidia's unmarried elder sisters Margherita and Beppina. These well-educated Sornaga women led comfortable but unfulfilled lives, all notions of love and ambition trampled by family interests and intrigues.

At sixteen, beautiful Beppina fell in love with her cousin, Aldo Ball. They decided to marry. But Aldo's family insisted that, for the marriage to proceed, Beppina's brother Samuele, who clearly had prospects, would also have to marry a cousin: one of Aldo's sisters. Samuele readily agreed, to help his sister, even though he was in love with another woman. This is how Levantine families plotted their rise to wealth and fortune – feelings had little to do with it. Nevertheless, Beppina and Samuele's mother, Celeste, felt this was going too far and intervened. The engagement was broken off and Beppina remained a spinster. Aldo, after an unhappy arranged marriage, died by suicide – not the only one to mark the family. Meanwhile, Margherita was courted by a young Italian naval officer, and according to convention she was expected to provide a handsome dowry. The Sornagas refused to do so; their modern, liberal way of thinking looked down on the convention. Added to this, Samuele did not like or trust his sister's suitor. The engagement was terminated and another unhappy life was assured.

Known in the family simply as 'the aunts', Margherita and Beppina migrated to England to join Lidia and Richard after their brother Samuele's death in 1951. Like my grandmother Lidia they had long, handsome faces with strong Sephardic features but, unlike hers, their eyes were cold and grey, betraying bitterness and regret. I remember meeting them when I was a child, and recall their distinct lack of warmth; they did not even embrace me, quite the opposite of Lidia, who smothered me in hugs and kisses, leaving traces of Max Factor powder on my cheeks.

My great aunts' stories mirror the suffocating conventions of the period, yet in Egypt they lived well; their brother Samuele provided them with a spacious, well-appointed apartment in downtown Cairo on Kasr el-Nil Street. It was a pronounced contrast to my grandparents' more modest home in Heliopolis – a contrast so marked it caused enough jealousy to impair my mother's relationship with her sister. 'The aunts had two manservants, Ibrahim and Abdou, and a Sicilian cook, Grazia, who lived in,' my mother recalled with a trace of bitterness. 'What to my mother must have been a welcome respite', she wrote, 'turned into a nightmare of regret . . . when we became full-blown teenagers; this situation led to a dysfunctional relationship between my sister and I.'

Josie, witty and flamboyant, went on to have a successful career in journalism, later working for a popular women's magazine in England. This family rift survived the Mumfords' exodus from Egypt, and though I became a journalist myself, I knew Josie only superficially. I was, though, close to my uncle John, a Catholic schoolteacher and later headmaster, who taught me much about the Sornagas and the Mumfords when I was growing up. In fact, it was at his urging that I first conceived of telling their story.

Fortuitously, Samuele Sornaga extracted himself from the cotton business before it collapsed by the turn of the century. Even so, he generously supported his old Egyptian trading partner, who had been reduced to virtual poverty by the downturn. As freethinkers who were generally liberal in outlook, drawing on their Italian cultural and nationalist roots, the senior Sornagas strived to be modest, especially given how they were surrounded by poverty, and neglect. 'We felt ill at ease because we knew that the bonanza and the privileges for some of us were very high, compared to those of the poorest Egyptian classes,' my mother's cousin Giorgio

Eberle told me; remedial action, though considered, 'came too little and too late'.

My mother described a seasoned style of interdependence: 'One felt at ease and comfortable with the many languages spoken, the many faiths practised and tolerated.' Yet the sophisticated lifestyle of these wealthy families presented 'too sharp a contrast with the visible poverty and misery of many Egyptians'. There wasn't strict social segregation – my mother's neighbours in Heliopolis were Egyptians. Her parents could afford to send their children to the expensive British school because the fees were graded according to income; they could afford a *sofragi*, or manservant, because wages were so little by comparison. During the summers spent in Port Said, she helped her mother's cousin, Giselda, who lived there, sew garments for the poor, which they donated to charity. The cook, Grazia, was a professed socialist. None of this charity or social 'awareness' made up for the actual social and economic divide between foreigners and Egyptians. Yet for all their wealth and privilege it would be hard to overestimate the contribution these foreign families made to Egypt's growth and development at the turn of the century. And given Egypt's significant external problems and internal turmoil, this contribution was even more remarkable.

Ismail Pasha's lavishly appointed belle époque was short-lived. No sooner had he presided over Cairo's remaking in a modern European image than he began to lose control to the very Europeans he longed to emulate. Within a decade of the opening of the Suez Canal, Egypt's coffers were empty and Ismail Pasha was buried in debt – no doubt the gambling he was fond of contributed to this. And here at last was an opportunity for Britain, for so long an ardent opponent of the canal but now a key beneficiary. The Suez Canal made Egypt vital to British interests, which at the time were focused primarily on the security of India, the lynchpin of its empire. The British moved into Africa, noted two veteran scholars of the imperial age, Ronald Robinson and John Gallagher, not aiming to create a new empire on the continent but to protect India. Sudan and neighbouring East Africa were keys to the Upper Nile, which in turn held the key to Egypt and the Suez Canal. At the same time, British prime minister, Benjamin Disraeli, was looking for a way to benefit from the decaying power of the Ottoman Empire – and prevent other European powers, especially France, from capitalising on it. Khedive Ismail was desperate to stave off bankruptcy.

Securing a loan of almost 4 million pounds from Rothschild's Bank, Disraeli outbid the French in 1875 to buy up Ismail Pasha's shares in the Suez Canal, which amounted to almost 50 per cent. With the stroke of a banker's pen, Britain gained virtual mastery of Egypt's economy and a huge say in how the country would be run.

Nevertheless, despite the bailout, the khedive and his court continued to spend extravagantly, showing no inclination to reform. By 1876 a Commission of the Public Debt established dual British and French control over state finances. In 1878 Ismail Pasha owed the equivalent of ten years' worth of revenues from the country's cotton crop. His mostly European creditors applied the screws. Then, in 1879, the British and French governments forced the Ottoman sultan in Istanbul, who still nominally claimed the loyalty of Egypt's viceroys, formally to depose Ismail. Never very happy with the brashly independent Albanian dynasty, the sultan promptly did, replacing him with his twenty-seven-year-old son, the rather weak Prince Tewfik, who was apparently so unhappy at being named successor that he beat up the servant who had brought the news. Ismail's abrupt departure and Tewfik's lack of interest left control over Egypt effectively in the hands of British advisors and a coterie of self-interested European *flâneurs*. The British agent overseeing disposition of the debt was Sir Evelyn Baring, who as Lord Cromer later became London's proconsul in Cairo until 1907. As a member of a prominent banking family, his appointment demonstrated the extent to which British intervention was initially aimed at financial stabilisation as well as extending imperial rule – though the ultimate impact was the same.

The effective loss of Egypt's independence did not go unchallenged. Reaction to the sudden imposition of European control, as well as the manner by which Egypt's rulers passed on the burden of debt to ordinary Egyptians, prompted the rise of a nationalist movement. Imbibing this proto-nationalist spirit, one of the viceroy's generals, Ahmad Urabi Pasha, stoked the flames of anti-European sentiment.

In early June 1882, an argument between an Egyptian donkey-owner and a Maltese merchant in Alexandria sparked a riot that left several hundred people, including around fifty Europeans, dead. Although alarmed, the new British government led by William Gladstone was inclined to avoid intervention, distracted at the time by a restive Ireland, where, like Egypt, a nationalist movement challenged British control. Urabi used the rioting to reinforce Alexandria's defences with modern artillery. Commanders of British warships anchored off the city considered this a threatening move and, ignoring the cautionary views of their superiors in London, bombarded Alexandria, silencing the Egyptian guns and moving to occupy the city in the first weeks of July. Alexandria turned, in the words of A. Hulme Beaman, a British consular assistant posted to the city at the time, into 'a Dantesque inferno, alight almost from end to end, the flames running riot from street to street without any attempt being made to check them, with wild figures here and there pillaging and looting and ghastly corpses swollen to gigantic proportions lying charred and naked in the roadways'.

Almost a century after Muhammad Ali had seen off Napoleon and established an Egyptian dynasty independent in all but name from Ottoman rule, proud, modern Egypt was subjugated by another invading foreign army. After 1882, the British restored Tewfik as a puppet, therefore gaining control of most aspects of administration and the army. Some scholars argue that Britain, in this period of rising liberal influence aimed at avoiding intervention, placed faith in the 'power of trade and Anglicisation to turn nationalists into friends and partners'. But as Robinson and Gallagher point out, just as in India, 'this assimilationist approach wasn't working out, so they turned more often from the technique of informal control to the administrative orthodoxies of the Indian raj.'

Egypt, ruled by Lord Cromer's 'veiled protectorate' of puppet Egyptian ministers whose strings were pulled by British officials in white flannels from their club quarters, became the fulcrum of Britain's imperial domains in Africa, as well as the key to the East via the Suez Canal. As for claims that Britain never wanted to occupy Egypt, the celebrated Arabist who helped incite the 1916 revolt against the Ottomans on behalf of the British, T.E. Lawrence, better known as Lawrence of Arabia, cited Feisal, a prince from Arabia: 'They hunger for desolate lands to build them up.' Cromer's view was simply that imperial aims could only be achieved if the 'subject race', by which he meant the Egyptians, were told what to do.

Poor Ismail. He mostly gets a bad rap for being as profligate with money as he was a womaniser: 'Luxurious, voluptuous, fond of display, devoid of principle,' wrote Lord Milner. Nationalists blamed Ismail for allowing foreigners to dominate and control Egypt's wealth: 'a bacchanalia of follies, making Egypt a hot-bed for parasites of civilisation.' My father, in his *Modern History of Egypt*, first published in 1969, took a more charitable view. He argued that Ismail was a great moderniser who left a lasting legacy: he built schools and established institutions that pulled the country into the modern age, and laid the foundations of an intellectual elite that was of political and cultural importance to the rise of post-war nationalism and the reassertion of Egyptian sovereignty. The irony is that in promoting reforms and building his country's industrial capacity Ismail, like his grandfather Muhammad Ali, was hoping to secure for Egypt a future dependent on neither Ottoman nor European control. But Ismail had inherited many disabilities: he was unable to tax the rich foreign community under the Capitulations, nor bring an estimated 100,000 foreigners under local administration of justice because of the Mixed Courts, which 'constituted an *imperium in imperio*'.

After being deposed, Ismail was exiled initially to Italy. I wonder perhaps if the Sornagas helped him financially in return for his earlier generosity and friendship. Later, old and corpulent, Ismail settled near the Ottoman capital, where he lived as a 'despised supplicant . . . a virtual captive, at the Court of Constantinople'. He died in 1895, reportedly guzzling champagne from the bottle.

As the new century dawned, Egypt's economy stabilised under thinly veiled British rule. Facing domestic pressure to recoup the money the government had borrowed to acquire the Suez Canal, the British empowered the private sector, which mostly benefited immigrant-owned enterprises. Jewish family firms such as the Suarezes and Cattaui in Cairo were among the first to prosper.[1] Samuele Sornaga wasn't far behind. They were all helped by the fact that after almost a century of European immigration, the Levantine community was the lynchpin of economic activity in Egypt; they had capital, expertise and connections.

In Alexandria to the north the Greeks dominated, among them the Benakis, who in modern times have endowed the largest private museums in Greece. The Greek community had done well in Alexandria, mainly by establishing a close-knit trading community which extended beyond the city into rural areas, where at one time in the late nineteenth century virtually no village was without its Greek moneylender. The Greeks did not have a merely superficial, colonial-type presence in the country, wrote the Greek-American scholar Alex Kitroeff, 'but instead penetrated deep into its fabric, its economy and its cities and provincial towns'. Indeed, as early as 1856 *The Times* of London reported from Alexandria that 'the Greeks threaten at no distant period to absorb the entire trade of Egypt.' Perhaps the closest parallel elsewhere in the world are the overseas Chinese communities in Southeast Asia.[2]

Some of these foreign families had long settled in Egypt, some as early as the seventeenth century on the back of trading opportunities, mostly in textiles, for which Egypt was famous. But because of the benefits under the Capitulations and later the Mixed Courts, they were mostly registered as foreign citizens: Greek or Italian. In community terms, following the Ottoman *millet* system, they regarded themselves as either Jewish or Greek Orthodox – forging community ties that helped consolidate wealth and status. Equally, they were not beyond sacrificing religious identity for social standing. Religious ties tended to weaken with success, argues David Landes in the artfully titled 1958 book *Bankers and Pashas*:

> Connections of this kind were of greatest importance for the beginner, the man without the strength and contacts that wealth and time confer. The established banker may have had preferences, but he did not need his countrymen or co-religionists; even more, he sometimes preferred to do without them. Many Jewish financiers in particular sacrificed their faith to their social ambitions and did their best to cut themselves off from their fellows.

Later immigrant families, including the Jewish Sornagas, married into rich and not necessarily Jewish families, like the Piattolis. The connections these unions created provided the capital to go into business. At the same time, the agricultural-based economy, overburdened with debt and facing greater global competition, was giving way to industrialisation, which then formed the basis of wealth for the next generation of Sornagas and others like them.

The burden of foreign overlordship, not just a loss of independence but also denial of access to capital, weighed heavily on Egyptians and before long there were stirrings of revolt. To the south, the British almost lost control of Sudan to an Islamic rebellion in 1881 that was only defeated in 1899. Elsewhere in the Muslim world Islamic sentiment was stirring in response to advancing imperial predation. In Egypt the al-Watani group fanned the fires of nationalism, and violence erupted in Cairo and elsewhere protesting British control. Early outbreaks of violent revolt after 1906 gave way to more moderate, staunchly political opposition after the First World War, which culminated in a popular revolt in 1919. It was within this context – of flourishing capitalism and brewing nationalist discontent, in the shadow of the outbreak of the First World War – that Samuele Sornaga embarked on an entrepreneurial gamble to establish a ceramics factory by the banks of the Nile.

In 1905 Samuele decided to strike out on his own. He had been told by an Egyptian, familiar with a place called Helwan, just south of Cairo, of rich clay deposits there. Curious, Samuele accompanied him on a tour of the site. Their guide was the paternal grandfather of the prominent modern Egyptian architect Abdelhalim Ibrahim Abdelhalim.[3] In an article published in the English edition of *Al-Ahram*, Abdelhalim recounts that his grandfather, a Jesuit graduate, was recommended to 'Mr Sornaga – an Italian who had arrived from Alexandria with the intention of establishing his business in Egypt – to act as translator during a boat expedition along the Nile, in search of the perfect clay to manufacture refractory bricks and decorative ceramics'. Many samples were tested, and eventually the shores of Al-Saff in Giza district, near Helwan, were selected. Arrangements were made with the village head, Sheikh Mohieddin – who would later become Abdelhalim's maternal grandfather – to build a factory at a village called El-Wedy according to Samuele's specifications. Samuele told the story in a company catalogue produced in 1912:

> Following technical difficulties which had seemed unsurmountable more than once, I was on the point of abandoning hope of ever seeing any result. Furthermore, the specialists that I had brought from Europe at great costs, albeit hasty experts, had left confirming that we would never be able to use Egyptian clay. And thus, I personally put myself to task, transforming myself as an industrialist and thanks to much perseverance and constancy, the small Factory became an important Establishment, with a surface area of 38,000 square meters, with a value of 2.000,000 francs, with 500 workers and producing 40.000 pieces per day.

The clay was transported in boats from the banks of the Nile. The factory and accommodation for engineers, artisans and workers were designed by Alfredo Piattoli, son of Luigi, the Alexandria-based architect from Tuscany. Alfredo had married Samuele's younger sister Teresa; their son, Guido, also later worked for the factory. Soon recruitment of traditional craftsmen was under way in the adjoining villages and an array of qualified artists, draftsmen, calligraphers and technicians flocked to Al-Saff from all over Egypt. Several decades later, Abdelhalim was born, and grew up on the grounds of the prosperous factory and its close-knit community.

The Sornaga enterprise benefited initially from the outbreak of the First World War, with two immediate consequences. The first was that the war made it virtually impossible to import foreign manufactured goods, mainly because of the demand for shipping elsewhere. This enabled local companies to supply the Egyptian market without competition. Secondly, because the government and consumers were unable to spend money on imports, there was more capital available for investment in local enterprises. In due course, the tiles, bricks and porcelain fittings produced by the Sornaga factory were in high demand as Egypt experienced an industrial boom in the inter-war years. The factory's famous blue bricks were mixed with a material that resisted corrosion, and were ideal for use in other factories and for lining sewers. Its deep-red bricks with a smooth finish and its ceramic tiles are still used, and I have been to people's homes in Egypt where I am told: 'Look! Sornaga tiles!'

The success of the factory enabled Samuele Sornaga to live very well. In addition to a villa next to the factory in El-Wedy, he built another out by the pyramids near Giza. The Pyramids villa, with its exquisitely designed Islamic tiled interior set in an extensive four-acre estate, is currently owned by the Kuwaiti royal family. According to Giorgio Eberle, the villa, located four kilometres along the Cairo–Alexandria desert road, 'included a beautiful residential building, housing for the servants, a large swimming pool, a farm, a henhouse and several orchards. A small paradise on the edge of cultivated land, glued to the desert, irrigated by a small canal with Nile water.' Samuele loved to entertain here, regularly hosting evening soirées for the Italian opera troupe that visited, with famous singers performing at the Cairo Opera House.

Samuele comes across as the archetypal successful capitalist grandee, almost a '*Godfather*'-type figure. He took mistresses and holidayed in Rimini on the Italian Adriatic coast, where family rumour has it that he had a torrid affair with a woman and threatened suicide after she left him. He was respected and loved by his sisters, nephews and nieces, even if he was hard on them sometimes. He denied financial support to his nephew, Mario, who was bent on a course of academic studies in literature. Samuele, who needed an accountant, insisted that his nephew study accountancy instead. Samuele offered my grandfather Richard Mumford, whose salary as a civil servant wasn't all that much, a position at the firm, which he politely turned down.

My mother remembers her uncle Samuele as quiet and unassuming: 'he had the aura of a man who had worked hard with and for the people. He took great pride in his achievements but particularly knew he had always cared for his family and employees, helped and supported them. There was not a trace of vanity or selfishness in him . . . He was much loved and respected by all. When he died,' she notes, the Sornaga family 'began to show its weakness and lost its unity.'

For my mother, the strength and happiness of the Sornaga family was embodied by her uncle's domain at the factory, where she spent many happy weekends as a child. She describes '[t]he factory, the villas, the gardens [as] staffed by natives from the neighbouring village of El-Wedy . . . These gentle, handsome *fellaheen* were trained to become gardeners, domestics and learned the skills required to work in the Islamic art section of the factory. Many learned to speak Italian. In return, they had good working conditions. There was even a purpose-built medical dispensary and a mosque for their use.' On family weekends there were picnics along the Nile, 'family dinners followed by coffee, jokes and gossip on the verandah'.

In Cairo, Samuele kept an apartment on fashionable Soliman Pasha and lived there with two successive mistresses – both Italian. He had a passion for decorative ceramic vases made in a post-art-nouveau style by skilled Egyptian artisans. He decorated his villas and the apartment with vases and other ceramic artefacts using old Arab figurative designs. These vases can sometimes be found – even today – in the dark and dusty antique stores dotting the streets of Zamalek in central Cairo, the shops filled with the artefacts of a lost age of prosperity. The porcelain has a mother-of-pearl glaze, with a liberal use of aquamarine, burnt ochre and deep sienna. Many of the designs were taken from the Islamic art of Anatolia from the fifteenth century, examples of which I saw at the magnificent Islamic Art Museum in Doha, the capital of Qatar. An account of the factory in the mid-1930s evokes its output in romantic and rather flowery terms:

> I find myself in the middle of an immense lit workshop where young fellows, under their attentive masters, decorate with love and with a surprising talent, art objects of all shapes which their colleagues have patiently manufactured. A door is opened and I am introduced to the exhibition halls . . . where [there are] fine specimens of 'Sornaga' pottery with harmonious shapes and iridescent colors which we have so admired in London, Turin, Liege and Cairo exhibitions. I am dreaming in front of this creation, looking at this loyal reproduction of masterpieces of Pharaonic and Arab art . . . I think of this formidable work which is being realized silently by this pioneer and his devoted collaborators supported by their sole will, and perhaps by an unknown force nevertheless irresistible, for the renaissance of the industry and of the Egyptian art.

I had to visit the factory. Following my trip to Port Said, I asked Omar to help locate the place and take me there. He surfed the web and found an obscure article in an Egyptian newspaper that reported the closure of the factory in 2002, so he had some idea of where it might be.

We set off from Zamalek early in the morning, and drove to the regional ring road to begin a long drive about eighty kilometres south. The road was broad and well paved; articulated trucks carrying concrete rumbled along the slow lane, shared taxis packed with passengers sped past belching dark fumes – the Peugeot 504 built in the 1970s remains the long-haul passenger vehicle of choice in Egypt, commanding a value three or four times that of modern Japanese imports.

Along the way we passed Al-Masa, Egypt's new administrative capital, which lies almost thirty-seven kilometres from Cairo and near the desert road to Suez. It is a massive complex planned for more than 6 million people at a projected initial cost of US$ 45 billion in a country that can't afford to feed all of its people. When finished, Al-Masa will include what is said to be the largest mosque and the largest cathedral in the Middle East, as well as a theme park many times larger than Disneyland.[4] Their juxtaposition speaks to the military government's effort to preserve the semblance of religious tolerance in a country that has more recently seen attacks on Christian churches. (Churches in Egypt are guarded by sleepy, AK-47-toting guards who make perfunctory checks on all who enter.) I have visited two other such new capitals: in Malaysia and Myanmar. They are soulless visions of authoritarian grandeur and air-conditioned bureaucratic tedium. You know leaders have lost touch with their people when they dream of living in gilded grand palaces far away from them. The massive structures of Al-Masa I spied in the distance suggested a similarly escapist approach to governing.

Billboards along the ring road boasted of Al-Masa's five-star hotels and luxury apartment buildings. Omar told me that it was all being built for officials and diplomats only, and would be a walled city. 'It's only for super-rich people, not normal rich,' he said with a grimace of disgust and dismissive wave of his hand. 'The rest of us will continue to live in Cairo. We're happy to do so. *Khallas*, please, leave us alone with our city and all of its troubles!'

With that, we turned off the ring road and entered the real world of Egypt. We drove through villages populated by rough-hewn peasants riding on donkeys; by men in long *galabiyas* smoking shisha, glass-bottomed water pipes bubbling with fruit-flavoured tobacco, and squatting against bright-green bails of freshly cut alfalfa; by women in great flowing gowns that flailed in the dusty slipstream of passing traffic as they haggled in roadside markets. We stopped outside a mosque that loomed large in this bucolic setting, its twin minarets soaring like rockets, skywards. Omar rolled down a window to ask a bearded old man for directions. The man wore thick spectacles and a kindly smile; a dark, round patch in the middle of his forehead, rough as an old scar, denoted his devotion. After giving directions, he invited us to tea and a meal, an offer we politely declined.

Driving on, we encountered a few bends in the road passing close to the Nile, which at this point flows languidly by lush fields planted with leafy legumes and dotted with date palms, their fronds hanging limply in the breezeless midday sun. The scenery was so idyllic it could have been lifted from illustrated childhood Bible storybooks – the kind that depict how baby Moses was found in a basket floating in reeds along the banks of the Nile. The majestic, stately river washes deep-emerald when it passes through Cairo; here, only sixty kilometres upstream, it appeared more youthful and fresher, more blue than green. This is the land of the *fellaheen*, the Egyptian peasant.

Omar hummed and wore a smile, his focus both on the winding road, and inwards. He was dreaming, he said, of sitting by canals and green fields with his shisha and a fishing rod – something he does in his wife's region of Fayum, an oasis a little further south.

After a few more kilometres we rounded another bend and came across a sprawling construction site covered with a complex of linked, whitewashed domes and cupolas. They looked out of place, unlike the austere vertical mosques built in the Mamluk style more commonly found in rural Egypt. Then, almost missing it, I spied a red-brick structure with an angular roof, a European style that also looked out of place, almost engulfed by all the domes and ogee arches. 'Perhaps that's the villa,' I said excitedly.

Something intuitive, a subliminal imprint of old photographs on my mind, told me it was. As we pulled off the road I felt a jolt of emotion, a physical connection to a family history I have mostly pieced together from black-and-white photographs and the sepia-tinted memories of my last living relatives, which suddenly came to life in full colour. The three-storey, red-brick structure was surrounded by scaffolding. Parts of the roof were being rebuilt; the crenellated brickwork on the twin towers crowning the building had been refaced. The villa was being renovated! Not torn down!

Restored Sornaga villa at El-Wedy

We turned into the compound and carefully followed the directions given by workmen to the adjacent factory. I immediately recognised the place – the soaring chimney and two larger, ochre-coloured buildings with a touch of Bauhaus about them. My parents had visited in the 1980s and taken many photographs. Omar parked the car and I got out with my camera poised. Almost immediately a man dressed in a dark suit came running out waving his hands for me to stop. Picture-taking is not for the faint-hearted in Egypt.

We made brief introductions: I decided to declare myself as a Sornaga descendant – why else would I be there? He was Mr Hany, the foreman, who was pleased to meet me, he said, though his face showed more fear than pleasure. Mr Hany reluctantly invited me inside the factory, where it took a few moments for my eyes to adjust to the gloom. There were clouds of dust and a loud din. Workmen were using hydraulic drills to jackhammer the floor.

They had already exposed the tracks of a narrow-gauge railway. Other workmen using sledgehammers were trying to dismantle a long row of stout brick kilns. An account of the factory from the mid-1930s describes its layout: 'The ovens are aligned in the middle of the dryers for the continuous baking of the red bricks, roof tiles and tiles. With its gigantic proportions, it gives the impression of Roman fortresses. All around there are wagons constantly transporting raw material on one side and baking material to discharge.'

Now it seemed I had arrived as the factory was being demolished. But why? Barely able to hear, and with my hands covering my ears, I was introduced to a Mr Wafez, who wore a natty tweed jacket and had the authoritative bearing of someone in charge. 'I'm a Sornaga,' I said almost shouting to overcome the jackhammers. Mr Wafez broke into a broad smile and immediately asked, 'Have you come to buy the factory?'

I laughed and wasn't sure what to say. When my mother was here with my father in the 1980s a caretaker at the factory told her that everything had turned to garbage after the government took over. As we walked around, stepping over loose bricks and twisted iron rods, Mr Wafez told me the story. The factory had been idle since 2000, when production was halted after nearly 100 years. After nationalisation in 1960, Sornaga Ceramics was renamed the El-Nasr Company for Refractories and Ceramics, and was held under the state-owned Holding Company for Metallurgical Industries, which established a new factory to the east of Cairo. The company was sold off in 2002. In news reports from the time Sornaga Ceramics was described as 'one of the oldest private-sector manufacturers in Egypt'. A separate company listing from 2005 declared a turnover of 20 million Egyptian pounds and 200 employees in 2005.

Judging from contemporary accounts, in its heyday the factory resembled a modern tech-company campus. The mosque Samuele built for his workers was the largest in the area. He also constructed a small power station, and El-Wedy became the first village in the entire region to benefit from electrification. The enterprise was so well known that King Farouk visited the factory in 1937. Today the mosque and diesel-generated power station, itself tastefully faced with azure-blue ceramic tiles, are being renovated to be integrated into what Mr Hany – who looked harassed and exasperated, as if he has been given an impossible task – told me would become a holiday resort. 'It's a pity,' he said, looking somewhat gloomily at the white domes surrounding the villa that will form the main structure of the resort. 'As a factory it employed so many.' Around 15,000 people at the peak of operations, I was told – with all degrees of work from craftsman downwards, stoking the kilns, mixing the clay, decorating and glazing the tiles, firing the porcelain and feeding the workers.

We wandered over to the site office, where I was introduced to two men dressed in tattered *galabiyas*. Hegazy Abu Kasr and Hussein Yusof, both in their sixties, had worked at the factory until it closed. Their fathers had also been employed there, and knew the Sornagas. They reeled off some family names: Mr Samuele, Mr Guido, Mr Mario, the Piattolis. They were testing me. 'Would you like to see the chairs?' Hegazy asked. 'We can show you a sign – an original,' added Mr Hany.

Satisfied by my responses, they seemed eager to please me – a Sornaga – with the meagre remnants of my great-uncle's empire. Overcome with nostalgia, I wandered out and over to the banks of the Nile, where my mother and her relatives once sipped lemonade and relaxed on a wooden pontoon moored to the bank. The garden full of herbs and the swimming pool that my mother remembered is gone. The old banyan tree by the villa under which she sat with her cousins and played has been replaced by recently planted young palm trees.

Back in the cramped site office we were offered tea and I was taken into a room where they kept an old sign recovered from the rubble. It was an enamelled plan of the factory, as viewed from above and over the river.

I raised my camera, but a hand went up to stop me.

'You cannot take a photograph,' warned Mr Hany.

'Why not?' I protested.

'It is forbidden.'

Photography was forbidden everywhere, it seemed.

'But this is for my family,' I pleaded.

'You won't post on El-Face?'

I look puzzled.

'Facebook,' chimed in Omar, who was helping with translation. Facebook, as in many other countries, Indonesia and Myanmar, for example, is the principal source of news for Egyptians. More than 40 million of them have Facebook accounts – that's almost half the population. Egyptians worry that the government is spying on their accounts, so are terrified that a posted photograph will bring the dreaded security police, the *Mukhabarat*, to their door. I stood my ground, camera in hand, and promised not to post anything on El-Face. Mr Hany relented with a great show of generosity and the plan was captured for my mother and other family members to see.

Samuele Sornaga (standing left)

Sornaga Ceramics factory advertisement

Outside, Hegazy and Hussein were eager to show me a pair of ceramic chairs of stylised pharaonic design that had been rescued from the villa. They could have been discarded props from the Hollywood set of *Antony and Cleopatra*. Although broken, they illustrated the elaborate and imaginative designs the Sornagas worked with. Nearby, two large jars made of a material hard as granite lay on the ground covered in dust. They appeared to be made of the same treated blue clay suitable for the bricks used in sewers. Around me, much of Samuele's industrial enterprise seemed to have survived the ravages of time because it was built of strong materials.

As I inspected the pharaonic chairs, a little knot of curious people gathered; they had all once worked for Sornaga. 'For the people of El-Wedy, Sornaga was our lifeblood,' explained the older man, Hegazy. 'Next time you come, I can show you some of the ceramic pieces I've saved over the years.' *Next time I come*, I reflected as I surveyed the stylised Nubian domes now encircling the Sornaga villa with its proud Tuscan heritage, *I will be using the spa and sipping mint lemonade in the shade of my family's legacy to Egypt.* Except that no one in the little group sipping tea in the foreman's office believed the people of El-Wedy would ever again benefit as much.

'I wonder who owns the resort,' I asked Omar as we got in the car to leave.

Omar looked at me and grinned: 'The army of course. The army takes everything of value.'

Not long afterwards, I did go back to the factory. I was keen to take up the invitation to visit the homes of former workers, and looked forward to seeing some pieces of ceramic art, as promised. Omar and I found our way quickly this time. South down the main Upper Egypt Highway, turning off to El-Wedy. Then heading west to the Nile and taking a sharp turn south. Along the way I saw rows and rows of tall chimneys in the desert beside the ring road, the brick kilns still using the clay from the area my great-uncle Samuele recognised as so valuable.

On reaching the factory the first thing I noticed was that a new wall had been erected around the property. The fully restored Sornaga villa was now the centrepiece of a maze of domed buildings built around courtyards that harshly bolted modern desert 'chic' on to my great-uncle's dreamy Tuscan reverie.

At the factory entrance gate a group of people emerged from the same makeshift office where six months earlier I had argued over taking photographs. As before, we sat on old café chairs under the shade of a tattered awning. A few timbers lay on the ground, their ends on fire under a roughly made grating for boiling tea. The oldest introduced himself as Ibrahim. He wore a *galabiya* and a white cloth wrapped casually around his handsome head. He had worked at the factory since 1983, as had his father and grandfather before him. He knew the Sornaga family history a little and recalled Guido and Mario managing the factory in his father's time.

'Mr Guido, he made good things for the people around here. He gave cows and other livestock to the village so we had meat to eat. The wages were very good.'

Our conversation was quickly stifled by the arrival of a well-dressed man wiping his bald head nervously.

'You should not be here unless you obtain a licence to visit,' he declared gruffly.

'Same story as before,' Omar said under his breath; only this time it wasn't.

Ibrahim handed me a glass of sweet tea and made a sign I understood to mean he couldn't talk. Almost in a whisper he told Omar that two security men had been called and were on their way. Suddenly, my tea barely touched, gone were the friendly smiles and handshakes as well any willingness to continue reminiscing. Ibrahim indicated that he must go. I pointed to the unfinished domes. He would not say anything except that here, by the factory, there was still some freedom to come and go. Over there, he said, pointing to the new buildings, the army ruled.

'We can't go there.'

What kind of resort was this? I asked.

The kind the army builds for itself, came back the muffled reply.

Coincidentally, earlier that week President Sisi had made a speech to fend off criticism that he was building luxury palaces with public money. Yes, he was building palaces, he responded, but for the Egyptian people. Around the brazier the mood turned dark and silent. Eyes darted sideways, which I took as a signal to go, but as I walked towards the car I glanced back at the factory and noticed that huge chunks of stonework had been demolished. I left with a heavy heart.

Samuele Sornaga died in his mid-eighties in 1951. My mother recalls that he had a massive stroke after fearing that the rising tide of nationalism would destroy his life's work. His obituary describes him as a man who 'appeared invincible, always the same with a pioneering spirit exactly half a century ago – his bold enterprise following his father and grand-father's tradition. It was a blessed time where the Nile encroached the fields and formed those great lakes with glinting palm trees and flame trees.'

So far in the course of my journey I had stumbled across the ruins of another era, rather like visiting the Parthenon in Athens or the Forum in Rome: I could see where a civilised, prosperous society once thrived, but all that was left were old bricks and neglected graves. A few of Muhammad Ali's descendants took refuge in nicer parts of Europe after the last of them, King Farouk, was deposed in 1952. Yet for average Egyptians today, memories of the khedives and their Europeanising zeal are relegated to the crumbling grand façades of downtown Cairo. As they toil to earn enough to buy their staple of unleavened bread sold from carts on almost every street corner, they barely look up. It was time for me to continue my journey to Palestine, where my father was born and where his Greek family grew up in a more modest but equally cosmopolitan setting.

CHAPTER FIVE

Baba Yannis Settles in Acre

'Do not spurn any infidel, for it may be hoped that he will die a Moslem.'

Jalal ad-Din Muhammad Rumi (1207–73)

The Greek Orthodox Cemetery in Acre lies due east from the main gate through medieval stone walls into the town. It nestles beneath a low hill, from which it is said that Napoleon Bonaparte stuffed his famous tricorne hat into a cannon and shot it into Acre, angry that after two months of siege in the spring of 1799, and the loss of 2,000 men, his army was denied victory. The great Marshal of France had thought he could easily take Ottoman-held Acre in a couple of weeks, march to Jerusalem, then through Syria and on to Istanbul to crown himself, as he put it, 'Emperor of the East'. At Acre he was defeated by stout walls that still stand, by motivated defenders who feared they would be massacred if they lost, and not least by British warships providing artillery support from offshore. The governor of Acre who fended off the French, Ahmed Jazzar 'the Butcher' Pasha, was a former Bosnian slave known for his brutality and military prowess. Today, a modest statue of Napoleon sits at the top of the hill to mark the presumed spot where the little emperor threw his tantrum. The cemetery and the hill are overshadowed by a new shopping mall, the sculpture of Napoleon on his horse almost eclipsed by a pair of revolving McDonald's Golden Arches.

Just below Napoleon's statue I picked my way through long, yellowed grass growing between the graves, mostly weathered stones set flat in the ground rather than standing erect; very few of them bear the names of their occupants. The still, late-winter air was pungent with the aroma of rosemary and sage, both of which grew profusely in this unwitting garden. Somewhere here, in this 300-year-old graveyard, my great-grandfather Yannis Vatikiotis – whom everyone called Baba Yannis – is buried. He was the first member of my father's family to settle in Palestine.

Greek Orthodox Cemetery in Acre

I had arrived in Acre earlier by train from Jerusalem. A friend there had given me the name of a local poet, Nazeer Shamali, who greeted me with: 'You're welcome,' near his apartment on Herzl Street, which lies outside Acre's ancient city walls. 'Now we go meet somebody.' 'But I've barely met you,' I protested.

Nazeer, a portly man with wheezing lungs and a ready smile, was one of many others on this journey who accepted the task of helping me with a sense of urgency and commitment that took me by surprise, as if my quest was also theirs: looking for something valuable that was lost. 'It's important,' said Nazeer, who has an active presence on Facebook. 'The person we will meet is Greek.'

We crossed the street and entered another apartment building. Nazeer had called ahead on a mobile phone way too small for his pudgy fingers. He called again to make sure. A woman with bright eyes and wispy grey hair opened the door and introduced herself as Rita. 'I am the last Greek in Acre,' she declared, inviting us in with a warm smile. Her husband's name was Alex. Rita's mother came from Santorini; her father was a Greek from Smyrna, today's Izmir in Turkey.

The family name was Sarandos. Her father had migrated in the 1920s after the expulsion of Greeks from Asia Minor. An old portrait hangs in their lounge of a European-looking gentleman wearing a *tarbush* (fez) and dressed as an Ottoman pasha. His name was Spiritus and he was from Sicily, says Alex of his great-grandfather: 'He took the name Hamar.'

What a profusion of origins and names! I was becoming used to the misdirection this prompted in the Levantine context: Greeks and Italians who assumed new names and different garbs. Such chameleon-like behaviour helped them blend in with the Ottoman mainstream. This became easier with the modern thrust of Ottomanism, or *Osmanilik*, which gained momentum at the end of the nineteenth century with the launch of political and economic reforms. It was a mixture of economic liberalism and constitutional centralisation which the old empire vainly used to save itself from archaic decay and the predations of European power. This modernising thrust allowed foreigners who had sought protection under the Capitulations to become Ottoman citizens, or *rayya*. As it turned out, this was not the path chosen by my great-grandfather Baba Yannis.

Over sweet coffee and cinnamon-infused, honey-glazed pastries there ensued a discussion about graves. Rita said a lot of Greek Orthodox graves have been destroyed – and that she and her family have fought to preserve their own ancestral tomb. Eventually, a telephone number was found for the cemetery-keeper. *Who keeps such a number?* I wondered.

Nazeer rang the man and I heard him say: 'Please help, there is someone here from Indonesia whose grandfather was born in Acre. We must find the family grave.'

Somehow, in the chain of contacts that started in Jerusalem, I had become identified as Indonesian. I must have said I had once lived there. It didn't bother me, as my identity has been a long process of accretion: Greece, Italy, the Middle East, then the United States and Britain. Why not Indonesia, where I made my home for five years in the late 1980s, where my children were born, and where I learned so much about the complex blending of cultures?

At the cemetery gate I met Salim, the caretaker. Those who oversee the dead have a lonely, unending job; Salim had watery grey eyes set in a careworn face, grey stubble more pronounced than a five-o'clock shadow. He greeted me with a tired look, threw on a tattered anorak and took me on a tour. Vatikiotis? He didn't recall the name. Most of the more recent gravestones are inscribed in Arabic because they hold the bodies of Greek Orthodox Arabs who dominate the modern congregation. There were a few Greeks in Acre, and they would be buried here, Salim noted as we trudged along. Alas, we didn't find anything that marked Baba Yannis's resting place.

Later, we sipped hot black tea out of small glasses in the shed that served as his office. It was lined with ecclesiastical calendars and icons projecting the baleful two-dimensional stares of sainted personalities. Salim looked apologetic and explained that many graves have been robbed over the years. 'Did Baba Yannis come from a rich family?' Salim asked me gently. No, I replied. He left nothing to his widow Evmorphia but debts. 'Ah, that's it, then,' Salim said with a gentle slap of his palm on the table. He sounded relieved: 'Your great-grandfather is buried in an unmarked grave because he could not afford a stone.'

Disappointed, I walked out among the graves one last time. Baba Yannis is here. I know he is because my father hiked out to the cemetery below Napoleon Hill as a kid when visiting his grandmother, who lived outside the town with her sisters. On the way out, I cut a short stem of flowering rosemary and slipped it between the pages of my notebook.

After my fruitless visit to the graveyard, I joined Nazeer for a frugal lunch of mashed eggplant and meatballs served with hummus that he cooked himself on a stove in his tiny apartment. I was touched, and already felt very much at home.

Acre (known in modern Israel as Akko and in Arabic as Akka) sits at the northern end of what used to be called the Gulf of Acre, a broad bay facing the Mediterranean that today is dominated at the southern end by the Israeli city of Haifa, so it is now called Haifa Bay. But before Haifa grew in the 1920s as an oil refinery and principal port for Palestine, later Israel, Acre was the more important place, for it was the gateway to Palestine from the west and, indeed, to Asia beyond. Acre's access to the overland Asiatic spice trade in the Middle Ages made it a critical connection by sea to the ports of Europe. Marco Polo sailed to Acre from Venice in 1271 with his brothers on one of their first journeys to Asia. First established around

4,000 years ago, Acre was one of the ancient world's most important port cities and is said to be among the oldest continuously inhabited places on earth. Conquerors lusted after Acre. 'Of all the towns along Syria's shore, from Antioch to Gaza, there is no other town whose history is so full of events such as Acre, and there is no other town whose influence on the whole country's fate was so grand,' wrote a nineteenth-century American visitor, Laurence Oliphant. The first sieges were in the first century BC; subsequently Greeks, Romans, Persians, Arabs and later Crusaders, Egyptians and Turks all stormed the city, which juts out into the bay overlooking a long, sandy beach littered with speckled brown cockle shells, used in medieval times as tokens by Christian pilgrims, who landed here on their way to Jerusalem.

Acre's Crusader history neatly captures the method and the madness of medieval European intervention in the Middle East. Starved of wars in devoutly Christian Europe, and faced with the burden of too many male inheritors squabbling over parcels of land at home, the Crusades were a convenient marriage between the need for war and fanatical religious belief. Acre fell to the European Crusaders in 1104 and became the site of an impressive fortress, still standing, that provided shelter for arriving pilgrims and also a strategic port to supply the European-led Crusader Kingdom of Jerusalem.

This long history of conquest meant that Acre was a place whose fortunes cyclically rose and fell. Much blood was spilled taking and retaking the city. Saladin and his Kurdish-Arab Ayyubid army seized Acre in 1187, only to lose it to the Crusaders – a four-year campaign led to victory by the kings of England and France – two years later.

Walking along the beach outside the city walls that is today a popular picnic area, I tried to visualise the 'plague-ridden shanty encampment of royal marquees, filthy huts, soup kitchens, markets, bathhouses and brothels' that Simon Sebag Montefiore conjures up as a picture of the area during the Third Crusade in 1190. The Israeli authorities have built an open-air recreation ground right outside the walls by the sea front, now a favourite hangout for young couples, but where much of the fighting would have taken place. The Crusader camp also housed brothels full of prostitutes, who in the words of Imad, a secretary to Saladin who visited the camp, 'invited swords to sheath, made javelins rise towards shields, gave birds a place to peck with their beaks, caught lizard after lizard in their holes [and] guided pens to inkwells'.

In 1291 a Mamluk-led army from Egypt expelled the Crusaders from the Holy Land once and for all. Thereafter Acre languished until the eighteenth century, when the city prospered under the Ottomans and their powerful local rulers such as Ahmed Jazzar Pasha, 'the Butcher', who fended off Napoleon. The city grew rapidly on the back of trade in raw cotton exported to Europe and boasted a population of more than 30,000, the majority of them Christians – mostly Catholic and Greek Orthodox. The Ottomans encouraged immigration, much as Muhammad Ali and his successors did in Egypt. Many Greeks arrived from the Aegean islands in search of commercial opportunities and were quickly Arabised, intermarrying and blending in with Arab Christians.

After Napoleon's attempt to seize the city in 1799, Acre was again fought over by Muhammad Ali, who aimed to extend Egyptian power at the expense of Ottoman rule in the region. Sacked, rebuilt and sacked again, by the time Baba Yannis settled in Acre in the mid-1870s the place was experiencing a period of relative prosperity under restored Ottoman rule.

The way in which Baba Yannis went to Acre, lived as a proud Greek in a mainly Arab society, survived and raised a family during hard times of economic flux and periodic war offers a contrasting picture to the fortunes of my mother's family, the Sornagas, in Egypt. For unlike the Italians – or for that matter, the Greeks – of Egypt, Greek immigrants to Palestine migrated for two main reasons: to trade, or to serve the Church. My father's family straddled both these métiers, and their story helps shed light on the peopling of Palestine – its brief but less spectacular development in the nineteenth century as a thriving agricultural economy and place of pilgrimage, followed by a longer period of descent into conflict over land and identity into which the Greeks were drawn, and which ultimately left them stranded as refugees.

Baba Yannis was an island Greek. Hydra, the island where he was born in 1840, lies around eighty kilometres south-west of Greece's main port of Piraeus in the Saronic Gulf. About twenty-three kilometres long and less than six kilometres at its widest point, Hydra's steep, rock-strewn hills were once covered in lush pines and gushing streams.

The majority of its inhabitants were refugees from mainland areas such as Albania and Asia Minor who had fled Ottoman expansion in the fifteenth and sixteenth centuries. Around the time that Baba Yannis was born, the island was a thriving centre of maritime commerce, with its own shipping companies, busy shipyards, and a population of around 30,000. Today, Hydra is a barren, water-starved speck, over-populated by tourists during the summer, but in winter its effective population falls to around 3,000. Hydra was first made famous after *Boy on a Dolphin*, starring Sophia Loren, was filmed there in 1957. The songwriter and poet Leonard Cohen and his Norwegian muse Marianne Ihlen were at the core of a group of bohemian artists and writers who flourished on the island in the 1960s. Today's pulsating beach clubs and seasonally crowded, noisy tavernas give little hint of Hydra's storied past.

High up on one of the walls of the little Hydra Museum sits a portrait of a man with a narrow face and large, dark eyes. Meet George Vatikiotis. One of a handful of Hydriots whose portraits hang alongside his, George helped win the Greek War of Independence as a fire-ship captain by navigating swift and manoeuvrable wooden barques up against lumbering Ottoman men-of-war and setting them on fire.

Hydriot fireship attacks an Ottoman man-of-war c.1827

They are known as the firebrands, and are celebrated heroes of the Greek Revolution. This is somewhat ironic, given that Hydriot sailors, renowned for their seafaring skills, were sent every year to man the Turkish fleet. The Turks commissioned many of their vessels from Greek shipbuilders, who built the boats in Hydra's picturesque Mandraki Bay (which explains why the once-lush pine forests have disappeared). George Vatikiotis sank Turkish ships at the battles of Gerontas, Eresos and Chios, according to Panayiotis Tzitzizas, who works in the untidy, book-strewn archive that occupies one floor of the museum. George rose to become a vice-admiral of the new Greek navy and a representative of Hydra in the National Assembly. So what made his close relative, almost certainly a nephew, Baba Yannis, leave Hydra?

Yannis is thought to have worked on a Greek merchant vessel carrying goods between Greek and Italian ports and the Levant ports of Izmir, Mersin, Beirut, Jaffa and Acre. 'I suppose Yannis first saw Acre,' my father wrote, 'because his ship called into port at what is known today as the old harbour . . . either to discharge a cargo or receive one – possibly grain, olive oil, currants and the like . . . having befriended a few Greeks in the town, Yannis, like other men before and after him, must have been brainwashed about quitting seafaring and urged to marry and settle down.'

According to my father's account, the keeper of one of Acre's Greek taverns and his wife introduced him to Evmorphia, an Arab girl much younger than him from a poor Greek Orthodox family of Nazarene origin. She was staying at the tavern, presumably working the tables or in the kitchen. 'The engagement was proverbially and melodramatically a long one – seven years,' according to my father. 'Yannis must have continued to sail.' Acre was a mostly Arab town, with many of the merchants from Genoa, Pisa and other trading cities only visiting the city and rarely settling down. The story my father relates is that Evmorphia finally issued an ultimatum: if they were to be married, Yannis had to give up the sea and settle down in Acre, which he did sometime after 1874, taking a job as a ship's chandler.

Evmorphia (seated in the middle), wife of Baba Yannis, pictured in the 1920s

Baba Yannis almost certainly worked near the harbour, where the ships docked and unloaded their cargoes. Facing the harbour is the only Greek tavern left in Acre, where I enjoyed a plate of fried red mullet and some very palatable white wine. 'Abu Christo' is run by an Arab Orthodox family, Hellenised like my great-grandmother Evmorphia; the tavern was established in 1948. I found no trace of the original tavern where Yannis was introduced to Evmorphia, but it can't have been far from this same spot. 'Abu Christo' occupies an Ottoman building dating back to the eighteenth century and has a commanding view of the Crusader-era Pisan port. Behind the tavern, along an ancient stone alleyway running parallel with the stone-faced harbour, I spied a series of old stores and shops that must have once housed ships' chandlers and merchants. I peered through rusted iron grilles into their dark, vaulted interiors and imagined Baba Yannis sorting through boxes of brass ships' hooks, coils of lanyard and sheets of sailing canvas. I even imagined him marking the hours using a pocket watch similar to the one I carried with me, the one my father left in his will. Looking out across the empty harbour, the choppy waters of the Mediterranean slapping noisily against the ancient stone pier, it wasn't hard to imagine the busy port of the late nineteenth century, a profusion of masts and rigging swaying on the swell, the sound of sailors and shoremen calling out to one another in a medley of languages, Italian, Greek and broken Arabic. The pungent smells of cargoes of fresh fruit waiting to be loaded. Oranges and lemons were a valuable export from these parts.

Strangely, nineteenth-century accounts by travellers from Europe and the United States paint Palestine as barren and desolate. Mark Twain described the Palestine of the period as a 'hopeless, dreary, heartbroken land . . . living in sackcloth and ashes'. In fact, the land was fertile and well watered by mountain aquifers. However, reports from the period also speak of roving bands of Bedouin from the Jordan Valley stealing crops and imposing heavy demands on local peasantry. Organised agriculture, particularly of cereals, citrus and olives, was starting to flourish, especially in coastal areas with access to ports like Acre. The penetration of European traders looking for produce to export, hand in hand with Ottoman reforms initiated in the 1830s to modernise administration and foster social equality, meant that Baba Yannis arrived on the coast of Palestine at a time of comparative political stability and commercial opportunity. If anything, he was part of the wave of foreign settlement that drove a wedge in Palestinian Arab society between more prosperous, heterogenous coastal towns such as Acre and the less developed mountainous and desert interior, a gulf the Palestinian sociologist Salim Tamari describes as the 'Mountain against the Sea'. 'The cities represented foreignness (a popular Palestinian saying claimed that "nothing comes of the West that pleases the heart"), innovation and political subjugation, as well as what the peasant desires most: freedom, escape from ruthless nature, and material advancement.'

The 'push factor' for Baba Yannis would have been the poverty of the newly liberated former Ottoman territory that became the newly minted Kingdom of Greece. How ironic that Greeks who had fought the Turks for independence in the 1820s, as had the Vatikiotis clan from Hydra, ended up leaving Greece in search of work in Ottoman lands. Squalid factional squabbling overtook the vaunted notion of nation-building in Greece. Eventually order was imposed in the form of a Bavarian: King Otto (r. 1832–62). And though cast as a modern European kingdom, Greece after Ottoman rule was divided and destitute. An account from the 1830s describes 'naked rocks, dry bush and uncultivated fields. Roads and bridges were nowhere to be seen. People lived either in caves or little huts, sometimes made of dirt and other times of rocks simply placed on top of the other. You not only looked upon deserted houses, but whole villages and towns. Athens, which numbered 3,000 houses before the struggle for liberation, now contained barely 300.'

By contrast, the Ottoman Empire in this period, even in its state of decline, had started to revive. Economic reforms in the mid-nineteenth century saw roads and bridges built, and telegram services as well as railway lines established across the Levant region. Among other things, these reforms, known as the *Tanzimat* (reorganisation), offered additional freedoms to non-Muslim subjects of the empire – triggering more immigration and fostering a spirit of enterprise. This 'reorganisation' of the empire was a reaction to encroaching European power, which used Ottoman insistence on Muslim primacy to justify attacks on Ottoman lands. In response, the Ottomans promoted equality and non-discrimination between Muslims and non-Muslims, hoping to fend off European intrusion. The Ottoman Constitution promulgated in 1876 supported the idea of the equality of all Ottoman citizens.

Even so, there would have been little culture shock for Baba Yannis in Acre. Greeks have peopled the Levant for centuries, as traders, mercenaries and priests. The Greek Orthodox Church was well established, and the Holy Land was after all the cradle of the Christian faith. At the time, Greek identity was closely linked to the Greek Orthodox Church, which considered all adherents, even if they were Arabs, as Greeks. This was rooted in the notion of a mixture of religious and nationalist dogma some scholars have termed 'Helleno-Orthodoxia'.

Accordingly, the Christian Orthodox Arab populations of Syria and Palestine were regarded as Greeks who were 'chosen people' because they were members of a Church held to be the 'true faith'. Long before the Christian era, Greeks and Romans colonised the region, leaving folk memories, knowledge of Greek philosophy and a palimpsest of their culture, as well as ruins.[1] For Baba Yannis, therefore, settling in Acre was not really a venture into terra incognita. As my father wrote of the Greeks in his diary:

> What Englishmen have never understood is that Greeks constitute basically an Oriental society of the late-eighteenth-century variety. In part, their failure to realise this is due to their Public-School image of a Greece which combined a classical tradition with a nineteenth-century struggle for independence and liberation from

> Ottoman rule. Byron and ancient Greek classes fostered this idealized English image of Greece, especially among public-schoolboys and dons in Oxbridge.

Indeed, nineteenth-century nationalism drew on notions of Greece as the source of occidental Western civilisation purveyed by North European romantics such as the British poet and adventurer Lord Byron. What this tended to neglect is that Greece and much of the Balkans had been under Ottoman rule for centuries, and that the Greeks of the classical period had long migrated across the Mediterranean to southern Italy. The focal point of Greek identity at this point in the nineteenth century was if anything the Greek Orthodox patriarchate in old Constantinople.

Given this cultural ambiguity, seafaring Greeks like Baba Yannis were mobile, unsettled and probably better off plying trade between the Levant ports. It turns out that Baba Yannis might have started a trend: the Vatikiotis family had mostly migrated from Hydra by the end of the nineteenth century. When I checked at Hydra's town hall, situated in the grounds of the main Orthodox church at the harbour front, I was told that the last Vatikiotis born on the island was in 1895. Yet as I walked around, talking to locals, I found that many could remember the name – and the branch of the family named Bikos as well. In the 1960s, my father met two old Bikos spinsters who showed him family papers pertaining to Vice-Admiral George. 'A well-known family, made Hydra proud,' Panayiotis the archivist declared, slapping me on the back. Later, he directed me to a tiny church situated high above the harbour, where the well-to-do lived – apparently to avoid attacks from pirates – and where my forebears probably worshipped. The church was locked. In the patch of scrub grass around its perimeter I picked up remnants of a crystal chandelier that had once hung by the altar. The Vatikiotis-Bikos clan on Hydra were relatively well off and proud of their contribution to the revolution, so it must have been something of a come-down for Baba Yannis to make a meagre income in Acre and support five children, all of whom except for the youngest son, my grandfather, Jerasimous, and his elder sister had died by 1913.

What he did and how well he fared is not really the point of the story about Baba Yannis. Far more interesting is that, in the context of cosmopolitanism in the Middle East, and like the Sornagas of Egypt, Baba Yannis was fiercely loyal to his homeland. The Ottomans were happy to accept Greeks, Italians, Christians of any kind as subjects of their empire. As Nicolas Pelham writes in his absorbing account of pluralism in the Middle East: 'When Europe was locking in ghettoes what minorities it had not annihilated, Islamic scribes recount how on their holy days Christian patriarchs and Jewish dignitaries led their flocks through the Middle East's cities dressed in finery that rivalled the caliph.' Thus, the Orthodox Christians of Acre – whether Greek or Arab – were all looked after by the Greek Orthodox Church, as a *millet* of the Ottoman realm. The Greek Orthodox Church of Saint George sits in the centre of Acre, a few paces from the port. This is the church where Baba Yannis worshipped, and where his children went to Sunday school. On the Sunday I attended morning service, the church was filled with Arabs, half a dozen Russians and Rita, the last Greek in Acre. I joined the service late, though not without being noticed by Salim, the graveyard caretaker, who gave me a friendly nod.

Outside Saint George's Church in Acre today

Yet for all this tolerance and temptation to assimilate, not to mention the possibility of Ottoman citizenship, Baba Yannis remained very much a flag-waver for Greece. He renewed his Greek passport fastidiously. I have a copy of one of these passports issued in Beirut in 1874. His domicile is given as Hydra, but the passport records him receiving the document in Jaffa, which was the administrative centre for Acre under Ottoman rule. There were other Greeks in Acre, most of them from Asia Minor, who had settled as Ottoman subjects. Many of them were Arabised; they spoke Arabic and adopted Arab manners and customs because they intermarried with the sizeable Arab-speaking Greek Orthodox community.

A recent genetic study by the Sanger Institute in Cambridge suggests that despite thousands of years of invasion and settlement by peoples of different origin and faiths in this region of the Middle East, DNA analysis indicates limited biological mixing. This suggests a common misunderstanding about the meaning of cosmopolitanism, which people take to mean intermarriage and intermingling. In fact, cosmopolitanism in the Middle East context comes closer to the classical definition of pluralism, as defined in Southeast Asia by the colonial-era British economist John Furnivall, who observed that people of different races and religions 'mixed but did not mingle' in the marketplaces of the Dutch East Indies and British Burma. The imperative for mixing was commercial, people's proximity a product of migration facilitated by conquest and imperial domination. My mother talked about mingling in Egypt, but the only intermarriage in her stable Jewish Italian family was between Catholic and Jewish Italians – apart from her British father. On my father's side in Palestine, it was different. His grandmother was a Nazarene Arab, but in the Greek Orthodox setting mingling and intermarriage was a product of common religious identity – an Arab in the Orthodox Church was considered Hellenised and therefore Greek!

Yannis did not, like many Levantine Greeks, seek the protection of other foreign powers, as allowed under the Capitulations. His Nazarene wife Evmorphia had been Hellenised, in that she had lost her Arab culture and spoke Greek. According to my father, Baba Yannis spoke no Arabic: 'he simply refused to learn the language.' I can only assume, given his family background, that Baba Yannis must have felt loyal to the newly independent Greek nation – less than half a century old by the time he had settled in Acre. Yet Yannis paid a price for this loyalty: when the Ottoman Turks once again fought the Greeks in 1897, Yannis chose to go into exile instead of renouncing his citizenship; he did the same in the Balkan War of 1912. In the first instance, there was no evidence of anti-Greek prejudice; in fact, Greeks continued to prosper in the empire. Yet on both occasions, Baba Yannis went to Cyprus. According to a conversation my father had with an

Arab Catholic priest who knew them well, 'friends in Acre tried in vain to stop my grandfather Yannis from going into exile. When they pressed him about leaving a wife and young family behind, he retorted: "Would you change your faith? This is what I am being asked to do by the Ottoman Authorities when they offer me *rayya* status. I refuse to change my faith."'

My great-grandfather's reluctance to accept Ottoman citizenship is at odds with the ease with which he was able to settle in Acre, embrace the protection of the Greek Orthodox Church and marry a native Orthodox Christian Arab. Here lies the key to one of the mysteries of Ottoman-era cosmopolitanism, which can be hard to fathom when regarded through the lens of modern nationalism. For despite the pronounced European nature of modern Greek identity, the perception of Greeks in the Middle East was coloured by their long history of influence in the region – first during the classical Greek period of conquest and occupation of Arab lands led by Alexander the Great and the Hellenised Ptolemies, which left a legacy of science and knowledge that passed into the early Islamic civilisation. So much so that the ninth-century Arab philosopher Al-Kindi translated the works of Aristotle into Arabic and argued that Arabs and Greeks were closely related. Greek influence then survived through the Byzantine Empire, the Orthodox Church and latterly under Ottoman rule, as influential administrators and bureaucrats serving the Ottoman caliph. As a result, the Arabs of Palestine would have made almost no distinction between Greeks and the Ottoman establishment – both were regarded as *Rum*, a label derived from the word 'Roman' coined in Byzantine times after the founding of Constantinople in the second century AD. In this context, Greeks and Turks were seen as coming from *Bilad al-Rum*, the country of the Romans, and the Orthodox Church is still referred to in Arabic as *Al-Rum al-Orthodox*.

This narrative of Greek affinity and integration with the Orient, so to speak, is at odds with the modern Europeanised Greek nationalism that developed after the War of Independence in the late 1820s and determined the patriotic inclinations of Baba Yannis and others like him. For while Greeks increasingly regarded themselves as Europeans, their Arab hosts continued to distinguish them as more familiar, as the acceptable *Rum*, rather than the alien, infidel *Franj*, as Northern Europeans had been referred to from the times of the Crusades. These *Franj* established the Latin kingdom in Jerusalem at the end of the eleventh century, and were led by a family of French noble descent. Although they survived nearly two centuries, these Latin rulers, drawing on the ranks of pious mainly French knight-crusaders, were never well integrated into the fabric of society, huddled as they were behind great stone walls and treating native Greek and Arab Christians as an underclass – although they did manage to introduce the French language to the Levant. They were finally expelled by the Mamluks after the Siege of Acre in 1291. The Greeks remained.

The Greek diaspora, one of the world's oldest and largest, is known for being uncharacteristically patriotic for such a far-flung people. In Sydney, the sizeable Greek community closes down the city centre when it marches on Greek National Day, in a colourful parade of blue-and-white-flag-waving schoolchildren, incense-swinging priests and young men dressed as Greek Evzones. It's the same in New York, and other major cities in the USA, Canada and Australia, home to the majority of diasporic Greeks. Some 5 million Greeks are thought to live outside the country – that's half the population of Greece today. And at the heart of this identity lies the Greek Orthodox Christian faith; it was this tradition of orthodoxy that Baba Yannis passed on to his children. (In 1953 my grandfather wrote to the *Jerusalem Post* in high dudgeon, after the newspaper mistakenly misidentified a Church figure as Greek Orthodox, when in fact he was Greek Catholic – the letter was published.)

Jerasimous Vatikiotis as a young man

Baba Yannis died penniless in 1913. He was seventy-three years old. All the travelling to and from exile to honour and protect his sacred Greek identity had taken its toll and his lungs had been scarred by pleurisy. Soon after, his son – my grandfather Jerasimous – was sent to study in Jerusalem at Saint Dimitri's School, which sits within the Old City walls near the Greek Orthodox patriarchate.

I knew Jerasimous well, for he died in Athens at a ripe old age in 1993. Sadly, I don't recall him telling me anything of his childhood, other than enthusing about Palestine in a lost era, his bright, lively eyes, deeply set in his long, Arab-looking face, lighting up as he showed me timetables of the Palestine Railways he had compiled as a clerk.

During my stay in Acre, I noticed busloads of Israeli tourists visiting at the weekend, encouraged by the bright winter weather. They came to imbibe the history and enjoy the seafood, or roam the walls and beach below. They trotted around the narrow streets in horse-drawn *gharries*, illuminated at night with gaudy arrays of LED strips. They took mad joyrides in powerboats driven by local Arab studs with swept-back hair and wraparound shades, riding the waves expertly and churning up a turbulent wash that ricocheted off the ancient sea walls. In Crusader times, the harbour was closed at night, and protected by chains. It would have been filled with boats from the Italian ports of Pisa, Genoa and Venice, reflected today in the city's street names – Pisan Port and Amalfi Square. I sat and watched the weekend jollies from the terrace of 'Abu Christo', as the moon rose in the blood-red afterglow of the setting sun.

Later I strolled over to the Khan al-Umdan, a square built around an Ottoman-era inn, whose arched recesses shelter cafés serving ice cream and coffee and, of course, shisha. With a population of around 48,000, and approximately a quarter of those members of other faiths – Christians, Muslims, Druze and Baha'is – around 95 per cent of residents within the Old City walls today are Arabs. Most of the original Arab inhabitants fled in 1948; the current population is comprised of internally displaced Palestinians who were forced off their land after 1948 and arrived as refugees.

Sunday morning service at Saint George's Greek Orthodox Church was conducted in three languages: Greek, Arabic and, to my surprise, Russian. The priest intoned the liturgy in Greek and switched every now and again to Arabic. The chanters, elderly women with their hair covered, sang their responses in Arabic. There were specific cues for the Russians, two rows of elderly men and women in front, to read from their own liturgical crib sheet.[2] Although Greek formed the core of the liturgy, it was washed out by the Arab majority in the congregation of perhaps fifty, mostly elderly, people. Rita, the last Greek in Acre, was near the front.

The previous day I had also met Wafer, who sells Druze handicrafts in the old Turkish bazaar. She's an Orthodox Arab with two children: a son who is married with children, and a daughter, an architect, who is single. 'It's hard to find good Christian husbands,' she told me as I studied the silver trinkets and woven Druze bags she had on display. She looked at me with piercing dark eyes and asked: 'Do you know any?'

On Sundays the noisy Israeli weekenders have gone, and the Arab residents of the Old City go about their business with an air of composed insouciance. The clack-clack of backgammon counters emanates from inside small coffee shops, and the sweet smell of dried sage and tahini wafts around the Ottoman marketplace, filled with people shopping for groceries amid stalls selling mounds of olives and nuts and citrus and dried fruits.

I had an appointment to keep before I left – with As'ad Ghanem, a gentle native of Acre who teaches political science at nearby Haifa University and who is actively involved in politics. 'I took your father's course when he was a visiting professor here,' he declared after we had ordered coffee. His tone seemed almost neutral, but I gathered he didn't agree with everything my father had to say. 'I don't remember his lectures too well, but they were interesting,' he added, perhaps sensing injured filial pride. I began to explain my quest.

'Look,' he said, leaning forward over a table made of an old barrel on which sat our coffee, bitter and dark and flavoured with cardamom. 'I'm not sure exactly what you're looking for, but let me tell you this: the elites that grew out of the colonial heritage are responsible for the misery of the Arabs. Nasser, the Syrian and Iraqi Ba'ath Party. The collapse of the Ottomans and the colonial legacy – this created an artificial type of elite, a political culture and society that is false and which has misled us.'

Throughout my journey I was met with angry outbursts like this when I broached the subject of cosmopolitanism, mostly from Arabs. I sensed a mixture of two sentiments: the loss of an era that was secure and prosperous, if neither just nor fair; and at the same time, anger about the legacy of that era and its modern states which offered only fleeting security and prosperity, but mostly interminable inequality and injustice for the majority. All the same, I was startled by As'ad's candour. We had only just met, and had not even touched the coffee. It seemed that everyone in Acre liked to put their cards on the table immediately, which somewhat unnerved my more reserved sensibilities, having been tempered by years living in Southeast Asia.

'You can read it in my book.' He cited a recent publication.[3] 'In fact, everything I say you can read. I like to tell everyone that because it saves a lot of time.'

Despite how abrupt he seemed, I liked As'ad. Born to a Muslim family near Acre, he now lives in Haifa. Ahead of the 2019 elections in Israel he launched a new political movement that was controversial in Palestinian nationalist circles: the Popular Unity Party, which campaigned on a platform to get more Palestinians elected to the Israeli Knesset (parliament).

As I listened, I realised my first instinct had been wrong: that perhaps after all he did like my father's lectures. I recalled my father's diary entries from the mid-1960s, when he knew then – as we know now – that Arab nationalism as it emerged in the 1950s shamelessly rode on the back of the catastrophe that befell Palestinians after partition in 1947; that – as he argued – Arab leaders pounded diplomatic tables, spilled the blood of Egyptian, Iraqi and Syrian boys and then ultimately betrayed the Palestinian cause, never in fact intending a serious fight with Israel because they knew they could not win.

As'ad's epiphany was to see through the flimsy veil of pan-Arab nationalism, to recognise the selfish accumulation of power and privilege, and decide that the future of his people would be vested in the success of their communities.

'The most powerful group of Arabs are right here in Israel – the 1.5 million Arabs who live here,' As'ad said, clutching the table and making the coffee cups rattle. 'Why? Because we have education, we are well off, make good incomes and enjoy services, even as we lose recognition and our identity. This makes us powerful. Why? Because we are a source of power in the wider Arab world – through our use of language, our culture which is Arab, and the Palestinian diaspora. So, if we can survive as Israeli citizens we can be influential – we can succeed.'

I pointed out that going against this grain is an increasingly virulent strain of Israeli nationalism that defines Israel as a land for Jews only, as if the Arabs – almost 20 per cent of the population – don't exist. 'The Israel your father knew is dead,' As'ad said in another hail of rhetorical bullets. 'The two-state solution is also dead, so we must find a way to survive as a single state.'

I admired this man's pragmatic recipe for peaceful co-existence in a land riven by generations of loss and simmering hatred, and I found the germ of something I had been looking for: hope. One of the frustrations stemming from my own battle with identity is the distinct hopelessness of the Middle East, rooted in interminable conflict. This made it hard for me to wear my Middle Eastern origins when I was growing up. Quite apart from the inevitable confusion over which part of me was Jewish or Arab, there was the stigma of claiming a landscape of perpetual strife as home.

CHAPTER SIX

Brother Maximos in a Cave

'Here inside the Old City of Jerusalem the great are small and all come and go.'

John Tleel, Greek dentist, 2007

The entrance to the Greek Orthodox patriarchate in Jerusalem's Old City can be found down a narrow alleyway leading away from Jaffa Gate and under a modestly sized stone archway adorned by a small iron cross. It is easy to miss. But its modesty belies the wealth, spiritual power and deep sense of privileged belonging inherent to the Greek Orthodox Church, particularly in Jerusalem. For my family in Palestine, the Church was not just central to their spiritual lives, it also guaranteed their physical well-being and security. As much as my great-grandfather Baba Yannis wrapped himself in the Greek flag and took pride in his newly minted nationalism, after he died it was the Church, with its peerless ancient heritage and considerable wealth, that provided his son, Jerasimous, with shelter and schooling. And it was the Church that took in my paternal grandmother, Paraskevi Meimaraki, and her four siblings when, at the age of sixteen, they were left fatherless.

The story of the Greek Orthodox Church in Jerusalem, the extent of its power and privilege and how it fostered and promoted Greek welfare and identity in a land increasingly divided between Arab and Jew, is so closely entwined with that of my own family that I feel ashamed of how little attention I paid to this sizeable piece of my identity-jigsaw growing up.

Worldwide, the Eastern Orthodox Church claims around 300 million adherents – most of them today living in Russia and Ukraine. The chief patriarch, the equivalent of the Roman Catholic pope, sits in Istanbul, which the Greeks still call Constantinople after the Roman

Emperor Constantine who ruled from AD 306 to 337 and established his new imperial capital on the Bosporus. The Greek Orthodox Church, in essence, evolved from the Roman Empire. After seeing a vision of the cross before a battle, Emperor Constantine believed the Christian faith was helping him defeat the Gauls in northern Italy, so he became the first Roman emperor to embrace Christianity. For this reason, the Greek Orthodox Church reveres him as an important saint. Constantine sent his domineering Greek mother, Helena, to Jerusalem on a mission to locate Christ's tomb and other holy relics. After Helena is said to have discovered three crosses under a demolished pagan temple, Constantine had the Church of the Holy Sepulchre built in the exact spot, over the ruins of the Roman site. No one is certain if the relics were real, or if the site where they were found accords with sacred Christian geography. That being said, the church, completed around AD 330, encloses both the alleged tomb of Jesus and the presumed site of his crucifixion. It is the principal focus of Christian pilgrimage to Jerusalem to this day.

Possession of the holiest of holy Christian sites and the fact that they were there first gives the Greek Orthodox Church a commanding sense of primacy. This was not something I recognised when I was sent as a five-year-old to Sunday school in Bloomington, Indiana. It was here, in the USA, where my father made the first and only attempt to teach me Greek or, rather, have someone else tutor me. I was a reluctant pupil. America in the 1960s was hardly a paradise of pluralism. In the Deep South, the KKK were burning black churches, and in mainly white and Protestant 'Hoosier' Bloomington, Greek language wasn't exactly the way to win friends – at least not for a kid playing by the neatly trimmed curbside of the aluminium-sided housing development we lived in, where I sported the same crew cut, wore the same striped-cotton T-shirt and rode the same red tricycle that every other kid on the block rode as well.

All the same, there were ways to be Greek in Bloomington. Somehow my father found a Greek Orthodox church to baptise us in, and Greek godparents to boot. My godmother could barely speak a word of English, but she tried hard, corrupting all the English words so that 'automatic' became '*arimari*'. Her husband, Pete Costas, ran a popular diner downtown called the 'Book Nook'. It was famous as the place where Hoagy Carmichael composed the hit song 'Stardust' in the late 1920s.[1] I must have visited the diner, which the family sold in 1968, but all I remember was their rambling house, lemonade on a generous porch, slamming screen doors, huge smiles and large hands pinching my cheeks and tousling my hair. In 1966, when I was nine, my family boarded the SS *United States* and sailed for the United Kingdom, where my father would take up a job as a professor at the University of London. I promptly turned my back on those Hoosier roots. Had I stayed, I might eventually have felt more Greek among the strong community there. Instead I had to adapt myself to England, which was, at the time, even less friendly towards alien cultures than it is now, and very much a bastion of Anglo-Saxon Protestantism.

Imbued as I was with the more accessible narrative peddled by liberal, scone-munching Anglican prelates from their oak-panelled pulpits, I remained unaware of the institutional power of the Greek Orthodox Church, especially as it is exercised in the Holy Land, and how it was the key to my family's welfare and survival in Palestine. Of particular significance was the role the Church played in bringing my grandmother, Paraskevi Meimaraki, from Lindos, the ancient town on the island of Rhodes where she was born, to Jerusalem. For it was in Jerusalem that she met my grandfather Jerasimous, and where they married in 1923.

'There is little peace within the gates of Jerusalem,' wrote a perceptive British journalist on a visit to the Old City in the early 1930s. 'It is a city of disturbing influences, of the exploiting of faith, a hotbed of superstition, idleness, avarice and ill-will, where Christianity is marred by unchristian rivalry.' Not much has changed since Walter B. Harris, a *Times* correspondent, remarked that in Jerusalem, 'envy, hatred and malice walk hand in hand. The air breathes distrust and the very dust is permeated with suspicion.' He was referring to the relations between the various faiths that crowd Jerusalem's ancient alleyways with shrines, and the holy places overlapping and competing for sacred space and priority. 'The Catholic and long-haired Orthodox priest and the Protestant missionary look askance at one another when they meet, and keep count of each other's flocks.' They continue to do so, even today, in an archaic contest of faith that embraces geography and demography in one of the most divided places on earth.

To illustrate how this works, take the Church of the Holy Sepulchre. The Greek Orthodox Church, jointly with two prominent Palestinian families – the Judeh and Nuseibeh – holds the keys to this holiest of churches. It was the great Arab conqueror Saladin who, after seizing Jerusalem from the European Crusaders in 1187, decided to hand the church back to the Greek Orthodox patriarchate and conveniently blocked up the second entrance, in Simon Sebag Montefiore's words, 'to control the movement (and profits) of pilgrims more easily'. Until recently, the door of the church could only be opened from the inside and only by a Greek priest, after members of the Judeh and Nuseibeh families had unlocked the outside – and only with the help of a ladder provided from inside, again by the Greeks. The arcane ritual is not about security – in one of the most heavily policed cities in the world – but does ensure that Greek control is absolute. On the first few visits I made I found impossibly long queues outside the sepulchre itself, which sits under the main dome, dimly lit by oil lamps provided by each denomination. Then, on another visit, I was asked what religious denomination I belonged to. Upon declaring myself Greek Orthodox a supervising priest ushered me to the front of the queue to observe the sacred shrine where Christ is said to have been entombed.

Beyond the preservation of strict ritual boundaries, the principal advantage of the Greek Orthodox Church has been that it owns the ancient stones upon which these rituals are performed: the patriarchate has held the title to large tracts of land in Palestine for centuries. Originally, this land was mainly in the vicinity of holy sites and monasteries, most of which were built in the early centuries AD. In the second half of the nineteenth century, religious men of means – including members of my family – used their own money to acquire more land around these holy sites to enhance their security and to ward off Christians from other faiths who were also in search of sacred real estate. There was something of a religious land grab. The Greek Orthodox Church's land holdings also expanded under the heavy weight of Ottoman taxation, as many in the Orthodox community turned their land over to the patriarchate to avoid being taxed; thus by the early twentieth century, as much as a third of the land in Palestine was owned by the Greek Orthodox Church. Today, both the Knesset and the Israeli prime minister's office sit on Greek patriarchate land, leased for ninety years, as does perhaps a third of the Old City of Jerusalem, and the nearby upscale suburb of Rehavia. Land is valuable currency in a country where contestation over possession of sacred space has become a critical issue for preserving religious tolerance and diversity. Having cornered the best real estate, the Greek

Orthodox Church then had another problem: there weren't enough Greeks.

The lifeblood of the Church is the liturgy in the Greek language. The patriarchate in Jerusalem treads a fine line between Greek nationalist identity and its claim to primacy as custodian of Christian holy sites. Yet embracing Arabs and other adherents to the faith who don't speak Greek has meant a gradual dilution of the congregation's Greek identity and therefore the language of worship. The answer was to persuade more Greeks to come to the Holy Land, a call that members of my paternal grandmother's family answered. This quest for land and souls lies at the heart of how one half of my Greek family arrived in Palestine. If the Vatikiotis side of the family settled in Acre on the back of commerce and trade, the Meimarakis went to Palestine on the wings of prayers.

With the help of a friend I was fortunate to secure an audience with the current Greek Orthodox patriarch, His Godly Beatitude Theophilus III. I wanted to ask him about the status of the Church and its relationship with Greeks – past and present. And, of course, I wanted to learn more about my family's life.

As modest as the entrance to the patriarchate is from outside, once inside I was led up a grand, balustraded staircase and ushered into a spacious marble-floored hall dominated by a carved wooden throne upon which sat Theophilus. A short man of around sixty years old, the patriarch made up for his deficit in height with the length of his grey beard, the sparkle of mischievous eyes and a magnificent icon of the Virgin and child framed in diamond-studded silver that hung by a heavy chain around his neck.

'We are the only religion and Church institution that is authentic,' declared His Godly Beatitude, as the patriarch is formally addressed. 'That's because the Greek Orthodox Church is built on the righteous stones – the blood of the righteous – as opposed to other religions, which base their creed on the word of the apostles, written subsequently.'

These precise, carefully chosen words weighed heavily on me. I was baptised in the Greek Church, and had little exposure to it apart from those Sunday-school lessons back in Bloomington. Although much later I was married in a Greek church and later had our two children baptised Greek Orthodox, I grew up in England, where churchgoing was all about belting out fancifully written Victorian hymns from the

Anglican hymnal and reading Anglicised passages of the King James Bible during compulsory chapel every morning at school. Blood and righteousness were veiled, intangible concepts to me. Yet I remembered enough about religious protocol to kiss the patriarch's hand when I met him.

'Our Church is the continuation of the first patriarch, Abraham,' Theophilus went on, after inviting me to drink a tiny glass of sweet red wine poured by one of his attendants. The Prophet Abraham is the first man of the monotheistic world. But Theophilus went further: 'The Jews lost their priesthood with the destruction of their Temple by the Romans in the second century. The Greek monks are the original Christians, and have managed to guard over the prayers and rituals of earliest times. These were lost to the Jewish people. Spiritually speaking we are far more Jewish than the Jews.'

This startling assertion speaks to a strong sense of Greek identity with the Holy Land. Alexander the Great conquered the region, then lost it to the Persians before the emergence of the independent Jewish kingdom that the Romans eventually subjugated during the time of Christ. In fact, according to some historians, the council of the earliest Christians saw themselves as part of the Jewish establishment. Yet the Greek sense of historical continuity was reinforced by the Greco-Roman culture of the early Byzantine rulers, in particular the Emperor Constantine and his determined Greek mother, Helena. This endowed Greeks with a sense of belonging or, more precisely, a right to belong to what was already a hotly contested land. There were periods during the Crusades of the eleventh to fifteenth centuries when the Church was supplanted in Jerusalem by the Roman Catholic Church. But during the long periods of Arab rule that followed the Crusaders' defeat, the Greek Orthodox Church, *Bilad al-Rum*, survived by blending with and accommodating each of Jerusalem's successive invaders from Saladin and the Mamluks to the Ottoman Turks. It was the Ottoman Sultan Suleiman the Magnificent, who had married an Orthodox Christian and whose grand vizier was an Albanian Greek, who in the early sixteenth century rebuilt the walls of Jerusalem that stand today.

The Christian quarter, with its churches, schools, homes and shops, was therefore filled with Greeks. And it was here that my grandmother Paraskevi ran as a teenager through the little lanes and alleyways of the Old City, all of it owned by Greeks, speaking Greek with almost anyone she encountered. It was where my grandfather Jerasimous attended Saint Dimitri's school, located next to the patriachate, where lessons were conducted entirely in Greek. He arrived in Jerusalem as a boy after his father died, leaving the family penniless. The church offered him shelter and an education. After their marriage, Jerasimous and Paraskevi's children, including my father, were born in Jerusalem. Today the louvered shutters of Saint Dimitri's are firmly shut – the Greek school has moved a little way down the road past the Armenian quarter on the west corner of the city walls. Apart from a fluttering Greek flag here and there and the occasional passing priest in billowing black robes, there is little to mark this area as the bastion of the Church of the righteous blood and stones.

How my grandmother Paraskevi left Lindos and arrived in Jerusalem as a child is a story of two bearded Greek monks who answered the call of religious duty towards the end of the nineteenth century and went to serve the Greek Orthodox Church in the Holy Land. Armed with assurances and the support of His Godly Beatitude, I went in search of my grandmother's forebears in the monasteries they helped rebuild in the Judean Desert east of Jerusalem.

On a bright day in September that promised to be hot, I boarded a morning bus to Bethlehem at Jerusalem's Hanevi'im station. The air-conditioned coach was filled mostly with Muslim Palestinian students studying at Bethlehem University, a Catholic institution established in 1973 for Palestinians under Israeli occupation. We wound through the city's complex series of underpasses, past Jaffa Gate (the entrance to the city's Christian quarter, where I was staying), and eventually on to the Bethlehem road. The students, mostly women wearing hijab, were quietly going over their assignments and otherwise checked their smartphones.

Half an hour later the bus arrived, and I found myself looking for a taxi to take me to the Monastery of Saint Theodosius, which one of my great-uncles, Leontios Trochalaki, spent the best part of sixty years rebuilding with his own hands.

I went in search of evidence that my family were not just parvenus or opportunists passing through the Middle East simply to make good; but that they toiled for greater purposes, put down roots and contributed to the shaping of the landscape, in secular and sacred space. The story of Brother Leontios and that of another great-uncle, Maximos Meimaraki, who was ordained as a monk and lived in caves in the

Judean Desert, explains how my grandmother Paraskevi Meimaraki arrived from Greece to live in Jerusalem, in the Christian quarter of the Old City. Their story also sheds light on the important role of the Church in the cosmopolitan era and was an eye-opener for someone like me, raised in the typically secular context of the mid-Baby Boom generation.

My taxi driver, a Bedouin with fleshy hands, large brown eyes and long, full eyelashes, grinned amiably as we set off. His car, an ageing black Mercedes sedan, had a timing problem and the engine took a while to start. He came from Beit Jala, one of the three villages that constitute Bethlehem. His Bedouin forefathers had migrated up from the Hejaz some seventy years ago in search of pasture for their goats. He drove a hard bargain for the cost of my ride, which I was sure could have been agreed for half the price, but for the Bedu, as the great desert traveller Wilfred Thesiger remarked, 'It was impossible . . . to provide for a morrow when everything depended on a chance fall of rain.' I was a passing shower.

We drove through a heavily built-up area towards Beit Sahour, the eastern component of the city that has grown substantially since I last visited in the mid-1980s. The area looked more like a post-industrial wasteland than the once-proud and wealthy birthplace of Christ. Shoddily built apartment blocks with unfinished masonry and rows of commercial properties, mostly housing shabby *shawarma* restaurants and grease-stained tyre shops, obscured a more pleasant view of the undulating limestone Judean Hills dotted with ancient olive trees. In Ottoman times, Bethlehem, perched on the edge of the desert, was known for its bountiful olive harvest, expansive vineyards and fertile grazing pasture. The town's grand, pink-hued and yellow-stone mansions were a symbol of the rich merchant class who built fortunes on the back of the trade in religious artefacts and who were among the first Palestinians to travel as far as America. 'They carried their wooden, pearl-embellished handcrafts to the Philadelphia exhibition of 1876. They returned to their country with an abundance of wealth, and prompted others to follow in their footsteps.'

Today, much of the occupied Palestinian territories is a maze of regulatory and physical obstacles to conventional communal life. The untrained eye doesn't see the extent to which the bitter years of conflict between Arab and Jew have altered the landscape to divide villages from the land their residents once farmed; to make it impossible for the people of one place to visit those of another without passing through checkpoints manned by heavily armed security, and the menacing nature of the observation and scrutiny all the people of Palestine are subjected to if they are not Jewish. And even if they are, signs warn Israeli citizens that they are barred from entry to certain areas. No one talks about the situation very much, because the system has been in place for decades, which makes for a greater tragedy – that of resignation. The Palestinian lawyer Raja Shehadeh, who lives in nearby Ramallah, has written several books with detailed descriptions of the area's partitioned geography. His colourful, personalised accounts offer detailed documentary evidence of what it means for Palestinians and Israelis alike. Here he is driving along a back road trying to reach his home in Ramallah: 'There was hardly any mention of Arab towns, nor could any be seen. There was nothing to indicate to an Israeli driving along the road that there was an Arab presence in this land. It was as if the Israelis had painted a reality for themselves, shielding all other realities from sight.'

One of the most effective ways in which Israel has divided the area has been through the construction of its own settlements. Israel has used the settlements as barriers and buffers to enhance the security of Jerusalem and the surrounding areas under their control. Usually perched on hilltops, these block-like piles of apartment buildings tumble down the slopes occupying terraces planted with ancient, gnarly olive trees, under which sheep and goats once grazed. The Palestinians are therefore forced into new areas – but only those where they can afford to buy or build, like Beit Sahour. They can't move too far into the high-security zones of the self-governing West Bank because they would risk losing the right to move about freely and work in Israeli-controlled Jerusalem, which is where all the jobs are. This is why the students at Bethlehem University have to make the half-hour commute every morning.

As we climbed the winding road and approached the village of Ubeidiya, about eight kilometres from where the bus had left me, my driver recalled an earlier era when the population had been mixed. There were once many Greeks living in the area, he insisted. Indeed, historical records show villages inhabited by Greeks, and that Beit Jala, home to my driver's Bedouin tribe, had a thriving Greek community of 2,000 inhabitants in the 1830s.

The presence of Greeks could explain why my great-uncle Leontios came this way at the end of the nineteenth century. Just as plausibly, given the relative success of the Roman Catholic Church (particularly the Franciscan Order in Bethlehem), Leontios, along with other Greeks, might have been sent to the area to shore up the authority and sway of the Greek Orthodox Church. At any rate, Leontios arrived from the island of Crete in 1890 as a young monk in search of a holy mission. Back then the village of Ubeidiya served as a waypoint for pilgrims to the nearby fifth-century Monastery of Saint Sabbas 'the Sanctified', established by the eponymous Cappadocian-Syrian. Mar Sabbas, as it is known locally, is a magnificent stone-walled edifice perched atop a ravine and was a magnet for the devout, ascetic priests who preferred to live in caves and ponder the wonders of their faith. Today Ubeidiya is exclusively Muslim and Arab, as evidenced by recently built mosques. The Palestinian Christian community has shrunk considerably across the occupied territories. Having comprised more than 10 per cent of the population in 1922, today it is estimated that the Christian component of Palestinian society is less than 2 per cent. Many have left because they feel squeezed between an increasingly intolerant Muslim Palestinian community and the hostile intransigence of the Jewish state.

Great-uncle Leontios discovered that Ubeidiya was situated near the ruins of another fifth-century monastery established by Saint Theodosius, and with that he had found his mission. A photograph dated 1899 shows a group of monks and Church notables, Leontios among them, posing as the foundation stone is laid for the rebuilding of the monastery, which had been destroyed during successive Persian and Arab invasions after the eighth century, rebuilt as a convent and then abandoned again in the sixteenth century.

We approached the monastery on the rise of a hill overlooking stony pastureland and nearby villages gleaming in the mid-morning sunlight. I had expected to see rows of cypress trees waving gently in the breeze, trees my father told me Leontios had planted. Instead, disappointingly, there was a broad, roughly paved gash along the side of the road where several tourist coaches were parked outside a high concrete wall, behind which a bell tower was just visible.

The place looked more like a high-security prison, or a commercial truck stop. A firmly shut, heavy iron gate appeared to be the single entrance. Coach-drivers gathered in the shade of one of the buses and drank tea steaming from small paper cups. Nonchalantly, one of them indicated a bell to press. After a short while the unsmiling face of a grey-eyed, bearded priest appeared behind a small grille opening. He was reluctant to let me enter.

'No group?'

'No, I'm alone,' I said in English.

His eyes narrowed further. He was about to close the grille and back away.

Then I repeated myself in broken Greek: '*Einai monos mou.*' The change of language did the trick; his beady eyes relaxed and after a few moments' rattling of keys he opened a smaller door cut into the gate. I stooped through and into a courtyard scorching in the dazzling sun. Off to one side a wilting, wandering grapevine cast a sparse shade and under it sat a group of Greek pilgrims fanning themselves and listening to a lecture delivered in sonorous tones by their guide, a corpulent man wearing a black robe but without a priest's hat.

The Monastery of Abba Theodosius

There was something crass and commercial about the scene that, along with the coach park and the difficulty in gaining entry, had already shattered my expectations. When I was very young, no more than ten, my father and I had visited a Greek monastery perched on a mountain on the island of Hydra. After an hour or so on the back of a donkey, we were welcomed – warmly – by the berobed monks, whose beards smelled of rosewater and sandalwood and who served us sweet wine and spoonfuls of quince. As a boy, my father had visited this very same monastery, where his uncle Leontios helped him make walking sticks out of the wood from almond trees that had then shaded the courtyard.

'Hurry up now,' barked the spotty-faced priest who had only reluctantly let me in a few moments ago.

His name, I later learned, was Brother Michael. Up close his matted beard and oil-spotted tunic reeked of neglected hygiene. With his hands perched swaggeringly on his hips, he harangued the group of pilgrims thirsty for the shade.

'You have to leave soon,' he said, pointing at his large watch, loose as a bracelet on his wrist. Meanwhile, another group of pilgrims was just emerging from the church – mostly pot-bellied men in cheaply patterned polo shirts and stout women wearing garish headscarves. They were Russians, engrossed by what their own guide was telling them and energetically crossing themselves over and over again. I dived inside before another group had the chance to take their place.

Built of local, pinkish-yellow limestone, the exterior looked recently refurbished. The frescoes of icons depicting various saints were luminously vibrant. A nun wearing a simple black habit asked me in Greek where I was from and I told her I was of Greek origin. My command of the language could not stretch to explaining about Leontios. Fortunately, a Greek-language pamphlet I found lying at the entrance beside a tray of devotional candles helped me: 'The Monk Leontios from Crete, who built the central monastery building, discovered and restored the cave of the Magi and bought 400 acres of land around the monastery and spent his life working for it.'

Around me I was looking at a life's work.

The small church is situated next to a cave where the three Magi are said to have spent a night after paying homage to the infant Jesus. The cave was the main reason why Theodosius 'the Cenobiarch', famous for pioneering the cenobitic tradition of monasticism (whereby monks lived together in a community rather than as hermits), established the monastery in the early sixth century. Eventually there developed a thriving community of some dozens of monks and nuns.

My great-uncle Leontios hailed originally from the city of Hania on Crete. His mother was a Meimaraki. The first Meimaraki to move to Palestine was Maximos, who had studied at Greece's remote monastery complex of Mount Athos. Maximos arrived towards the end of the nineteenth century and joined the exclusively Greek Order of the Holy Sepulchre, tasked with staffing and protecting holy sites. A photograph of Maximos later in life depicts a well-built man with piercing dark eyes, bushy eyebrows and a full white beard that obscures most of his mouth. He looks intelligent and pugnacious; not someone to trifle with. At the end of the nineteenth century, as the Church was expanding to cope with and serve a growing number of pilgrims and keep up with the expanding network of competing faiths, monks like Maximos and Leontios took to the desert to the east of Jerusalem, where they found and began rebuilding the remains of Byzantine-era monasteries destroyed during earlier periods of invasion. They were often alone; others opted to live as hermits and strict ascetics, following the tradition of Jesus's fasting and meditating for forty days and nights in a cave somewhere near Jericho in the Judean Desert, when he was supposedly tempted by Satan.

Maximos spent time in a cave in the desert near Mar Sabbas Monastery, a short drive from Saint Theodosius. As an anchorite, or religious recluse, Maximos had food sent up daily in a basket. But in addition to meditating in the search for inner peace, the role of the monks was essentially that of caretakers. 'They guarded churches and shrines,' my father explained.

'They quarrelled and brawled with Armenians, Roman Catholics and other denominations over who had the right to which corner of what holy shrine.' And every once in a while, my father wrote, 'Maximos would be called upon to help defend a holy site – with his fists.'

Brother Maximos Meimaraki

I emerged from the dark, small church into the blindingly bright courtyard, the heat breathtakingly intense. I wanted to speak to the custodians, and asked to see the superior, Father Erotious. Brother Michael hesitated and again pointed to his watch. It wasn't yet noon, and the monastery was not due to close until 3 p.m. I stood my ground. Brother Michael then placed his palms together and rested his head against them, indicating that the superior was having a nap. I didn't budge. Brother Michael shrugged his shoulders and led me under the trailing vine to the dim interior of the monks' quarters.

Father Erotious had indeed been napping, and emerged from his room rubbing his eyes. His priestly robe was partially undone and he wore no hat; his oily grey hair had been hastily tied in a bun that looked like a steel-wool washing pad. He was ancient but sprightly, and told me that he had been living in Saint Theodosius for more than half a century. Brother Leontios, about whom he could remember stories, had died two decades or so before he had arrived. Erotious, also from Crete, joined the Greek army and had promised to devote himself to the Church after demobilisation. Once home he forgot his promise until a series of blinding headaches prompted him to reconsider. He spoke Greek and broken English, so we just about managed a conversation. He began by complaining about the heat. Then he started to complain about the pilgrims.

'All I see is tourists – Russians and, yes, a few Greeks, but mainly Russians. They come every day. They use our water, our electricity – it's so expensive, you know.'

I gently pointed out that at least the church was being used. That's not the case for many churches in England.

'Yes, but every day, they come,' he insisted. 'And there are only two fathers and three sisters. We are only five!'

As if on cue, a sister emerged out of the gloom with a cup of coffee and a cake. Hospitality at last! I asked if young priests still came to study and stay.

'Not any more,' he said, emitting a deep sigh and patting his knees, as if to make sure they were still there. 'Just the buses with the Russians – and Romanians, by the way. Many, many Romanians.'

The old priest waved his hands and pursed his lips with exasperation and sighed again. At this point the sister indicated that Father Erotious needed to rest. Our conversation was over.

Before leaving I visited the cave of the Magi that Leontios had restored. The grotto is also the last resting place of John Moschou, a sixth-century Greek monk who wrote the 'Spiritual Meadow', a foundational text of the Eastern Church. An ancient stone staircase led me down. Once inside, I barely had a moment to reflect on my great-uncle's achievements before another group of pilgrims, Russians again, tumbled down and flooded the sacred space. They immediately set about bobbing and weaving between the different icons, paying special reverence to the mummified body of John Moschou, who lies below an altar. Hands whirred, making signs of the cross as they kissed various icons like birds pecking at crumbs. Earlier in the church I had paid a few coins for a candle, and before leaving I planted it alight in a little tray by the main altar. A thought for Brother Leontios.

I was both surprised and proud to see the extent to which these ancient holy sites, which my family played a role in renovating, remained in business, so to speak. And that the arduous sacred exertions of my two great-uncles were good investments; the church thrives, even if now thanks to the piety of Russians, Ukrainians and others from the Eastern Orthodox Church. But what motivated my two great-uncles to strike out into the Judean Hills, live in caves and then rebuild ruined monasteries at famous holy sites? The answers were to be found back in Jerusalem.

Maximos had a brother, Manolis, who had also left Crete and worked as an itinerant pharmacist selling medicine from the back of a mule. Manolis eventually settled down on another sizeable Greek island, Rhodes, and married a local beauty called Zoe. Manolis abandoned his mule-borne pharmacy after marrying and became a teacher in the ancient town of Lindos. He and Zoe had two sons and four daughters, among them my grandmother Paraskevi. When Manolis died prematurely in 1902, it was to Brother Maximos that his widow Zoe turned for help. The Church took in Zoe and her six children when they arrived in Jerusalem in 1904. Maximos, apparently a man of means, assumed full responsibility for his brother's family and supported their education, mostly in Church-run schools. They lived initially in accommodation provided by the Church close to Jaffa Gate. And like my grandfather's family in Acre, the Meimarakis felt at home in Jerusalem, where the Christian quarter was dominated by Greeks.

Zoe later built a spacious home in the Katamon quarter near Saint Simeon's Monastery, a quiet spot ringed by pine trees away from the bustle of the Old City. I have a grainy picture of the ground-breaking ceremony, which must have been sometime before 1920. The Church was generous. Paraskevi received more formal schooling than was common for girls of her age on the Greek islands, and several of her siblings studied at university and went on to have good jobs. Her eldest brother, Markos, was a financier in Europe and became something of an adventurer, growing rich off of selling grain and animal feed to the Greek army during the First World War. Later, according to my father, Markos operated out of France, the Congo and Djibouti in French Somaliland, where he died as an enemy alien in a concentration camp in 1943. Another one of my grandmother's siblings, Agapitos, whom I met when I was a teenager, became chief cashier at the Ottoman Imperial Bank in Jerusalem and travelled as far as China on business. My aunt Artemis recalled that he drove around Jerusalem in a red MG sports car that he had imported from Britain.

The story of my paternal grandmother's family, the Meimarakis, illustrates the close relationship Greeks had, and still have, with Jerusalem and the surrounding Christian holy sites mainly through the agency of the Greek Orthodox Church. But as much as the Church offered security and fostered a rich community life, they grew up in Jerusalem at a time of great upheaval and change in the political order as the Ottoman Empire collapsed around them and a completely new and ultimately disruptive dispensation evolved under British rule.

During my stay in Jerusalem I based myself at the tired but friendly New Imperial Hotel, built for the patriarchate in the 1880s to house the growing number of pilgrims. The rooftop terrace affords a sweeping view over the Old City: the Tower of David, the ancient citadel, built over the remains of King Herod's palace and its fortifications, which date from the first century BC; the Old City gently sloping down towards the Temple Mount, where Abraham offered his son Isaac for sacrifice, where the Prophet Muhammad rode to the heavens astride a winged horse, and where today armed Israeli police maintain control over access to the Al-Aqsa Mosque, the third-holiest site in Islam.

At just past six in the evening peals of church bells ring in the setting sun, dipping behind Notre Dame, the hilltop headquarters of the Roman Catholic Church outside the city walls, the yellow stone glowing more deeply in reflection off the Dome of the Rock, the gold-sheathed Islamic shrine built in the seventh century over the foundations of the Jewish Temple. A flock of pigeons rises up and darts across the sky. Sirens scream from nearby Rehavia, one of the city's modern areas, built on Greek Orthodox Church land outside the walls.

Paraskevi Meimaraki c.1923 (seated right)

Just below me is Jaffa Gate, one of the seven entrances to the old walled city. Precisely here, a little more than 100 years ago on the morning of 11 December 1917, Edmund Allenby, a stocky British general, dismounted from his horse and walked through the gate towards crowds of people anxiously awaiting him, and with him the end of 400 years of Ottoman rule over Jerusalem. The Turks, who had been fighting on the German side of the war, had surrendered to British forces two days earlier, a haphazard affair involving a makeshift white flag ripped from sheets waved at a handful of British soldiers unsure of what to do or who was in charge.

People lined the streets five deep and stretched themselves out of windows along Allenby's route. They cheered the British troops and those of other Allied forces that had already congregated inside, waiting. This being a city of multiple faiths, leaders of all religions were there – rabbis, sheikhs, priests, monks – each of them wrapped in colours and robes particular and distinct. Allenby dismounted before entering the city in a deliberate gesture of respect, in contrast to Kaiser Wilhelm's extravagant and ill-judged mounted entry through the same gate in 1898 (for which the entrance was widened). Nevertheless, and adding a martial flourish, trumpets blared to announce the arrival of this khaki-uniformed king, adorned not with a crown but with polished brown-leather belts at his waist and across his chest, his brass pips gleaming. Passing the offices of Thomas Cook's tours on the left, just after the New Imperial Hotel, Allenby turned right and walked towards the Ottoman police headquarters, known then as the *Qishle*, where, beneath the Tower of David, he read out a declaration:

> Since your city is regarded with affection by the adherents of three of the great religions of mankind, and its soil has been consecrated by the prayers and pilgrimages of devout people of those three religions for many centuries, therefore I do make known to you that every sacred building, monument, holy spot, shrine, traditional site, endowment, pious bequest or customary place of prayer, of whatsoever form of the three religions, will be maintained and protected according to existing customs and beliefs of those to whose faiths they are sacred.

Allenby reading the Jerusalem Declaration

My grandmother Paraskevi, then aged twenty, was in the crowd that day. She watched Allenby walk through Jaffa Gate and heard him make the declaration. Well educated, she understood English. However, I doubt she would have recognised T.E. Lawrence, who joined Allenby on his walk, having discarded his flowing white Arab robes in favour of a borrowed British officer's uniform. She might, however, have noticed the brief effort to fly the future flag of the yet-to-be-established State of Israel, its Star of David stitched by a prominent Jewish family from Egypt, the Cicurels, who had it smuggled into Palestine by a Jewish subaltern from New Zealand in the British army. It flew for twenty minutes atop the Tower of David, which overlooks Jaffa Gate, before the British took it down.[2]

Few moments in modern Middle Eastern history are as celebrated as Allenby's entry into Jerusalem. And, like everything else in this part of the world, its meaning is contested. The Palestinian chronicler of Jerusalem, Wasif Jawharriyeh, wrote in his diary of the time that the British occupation 'freed the Arab people from the despotic Turks; we were all nurturing great hopes for a better future, particularly after what we had been through – the miseries of war, famine, diseases, epidemics and typhus that spread throughout the country, and we thanked the Lord who saved all our young men from the damned military service.'

Allenby's taking of the city marked the end of a long, harsh winter, with food so scarce that grains of barley were salvaged from donkey droppings. The war years had been hard on the Palestinians, nostalgic for plentiful harvests and prosperous trade. My grandmother and her family lived well under the Church's protection and welfare; they built a family home, found good schooling and prospects for work. But as the Ottomans geared up for war, there was hardship and a sudden decline.

'Ottoman rule was good until the First World War began,' recalled Warda Simha, a ninety-three-year-old resident of Bethlehem whose family were farmers: 'but when the locusts came they destroyed everything and this was followed by the drought; military conscription and how rich people were able to pay to not be recruited.'

The immediate years after the British arrived heralded some stability, enough for my grandparents to make plans for a life together in Palestine. They met at a branch of the Savvides photo studio where my grandmother worked adding touches of colour to portraits taken in black and white. Her elder sister, Elizabeth, had married into the Savvides family, whose studio was on the road outside Jaffa Gate, its signage apparent in photographs from the time. Paraskevi and Jerasimous married in August 1923 at the Greek Community Centre, which had been established in 1902 and still serves the remnants of the community in Jerusalem. Soon afterwards they left for Kantara on the banks of the Suez Canal, where my grandfather had obtained a lowly but promising job in government service with the Palestine Railways. But the dark clouds of sectarian conflict that would soon overshadow their lives and ultimately make them refugees were already gathering.

PART II:

THE RUPTURE

CHAPTER SEVEN

Philby's Batman

'Never doubt Great Britain's word. She is wise and trustworthy; have no fear.'

Sharif Hussein of Mecca to his son Faisal, May 1917

General Allenby's entry into Jerusalem marked the turning point after which Palestine – and much of the rest of the Middle East – would never be the same. For Allenby's triumphant ejection of the Turks and promise of protection for all faiths in Jerusalem masked a more complicated and contradictory set of imperatives for Britain. These set the stage for the drama to come and presented another member of my family, my British maternal grandfather Richard Mumford, with an unreconcilable set of challenges when he reached the Middle East in 1922.

The First World War tugged at a string that has been unravelling in the Middle East ever since. Richard Mumford was witness to the immediate aftermath of the war in the Middle East as the victorious British and French arrived as the region's new overlords. Having miraculously survived the trenches in France as an infantryman, he joined the Colonial Service and was sent to the Middle East in 1922 as confidential secretary to Harry Saint John ('Jack') Bridger Philby, father of Kim Philby, the notorious double-agent who spied for Soviet Russia. Richard was twenty-eight years old. Jack Philby, nine years his senior, had just been appointed as the Chief British Representative or Resident of a piece of desert wedged between the borders of Palestine and Syria, which the British called Transjordan and which later became the modern Kingdom of Jordan.

From the outset Richard Mumford, straight-laced and uncomplicated (and who had worked as a journalist before the war broke out), saw the whole British enterprise in the Middle East as doomed to fail.

It must have been clear not only to him, but also to others: the hubris of the British and French playing chess with the discarded pieces of the Ottoman Empire using a board of their own design, with rules they made up mostly as they went along. They paid scant regard to the various and intrinsic natures of Middle Eastern societies or their complicated, interwoven histories, and failed to replicate in any shape or form the stern, sometimes harsh stewardship of diversity and dependency that had held the region together somewhat stably if not always peacefully over six centuries under Ottoman rule.

At the start of the First World War in 1914, Britain had almost no presence, let alone interest, in the Middle East. The central focus of empire was India, where the British Raj was an enduring source of wealth and power for Britain. It was only after the Ottomans entered the war on the side of Germany that London decided to confront them: already weakened by internal ructions, the old Ottoman Empire seemed ripe for the picking. But when initial Allied military assaults on Anatolia through the Dardanelles and in Mesopotamia in 1915–16 were repulsed, the British needed a back-up plan. Meanwhile, the Arabs to the south had developed a distaste for Ottoman rule.

Modern forms of communications – the railway and telegraph – plus political reforms at the start of the twentieth century imposed more effective taxation and central authority upon the empire's distant provinces than the Arabs were accustomed to. The Hejaz railway, completed by 1910, may have been inspired by the Ottoman sultan's pious goal of facilitating easier access to the Holy Sites of Mecca and Medina, but the Arab princes who claimed descent from the Prophet Muhammad and ruled the region were afraid the railway would also bring Turkish troops and tax collectors; they were anxious to preserve their princely power and privilege.[1] An Arab alliance with the British offered a useful way to push back against Ottoman power by attacking the Turks from behind. To encourage them, a small group of Arabists based in Cairo (among them T.E. Lawrence), engineered a set of promises to the Arabs that in return for support against the Turks, Britain would endow them with independent kingdoms. It wasn't a bad plan, and was consistent with the practice of British imperial policy elsewhere, which routinely offered to prop up weaker princely states in order to undermine more powerful ones that stood in the way of British objectives.

The flaw was that while one group of British officials was promising the Arabs self-determination, another was plotting to give a sizeable chunk of Arab territory to the Jews. At the same time that Lawrence was busy stitching together his Arab Revolt, Zionist activists and their supporters in the British government successfully lobbied Prime Minister Asquith to promise a national homeland for the Jews in Palestine, which was outlined in the Balfour Declaration of 1917. Arthur Balfour, who had made the declaration as foreign secretary, had previously been Secretary of Ireland, where he was known as Bloody Balfour after ordering police to open fire on a crowd of protestors demanding land reform in County Cork. Many of the officials who oversaw the establishment of the British Mandate in Palestine had experience of trying to put down the Irish rebellion, often using brutal methods. Meanwhile, both the Jews and the Arabs were horrified to learn later that, in spite of promises made to them, the British and the French had agreed to carve up the Middle East between them in a secret agreement reached by British diplomat Mark Sykes and his French counterpart François Georges-Picot in 1916.

When the Arabs saw both the Balfour Declaration and the text of the Sykes-Picot Agreement (revealed after it was discovered among government papers in Moscow and published by victorious Bolsheviks after the fall of the Russian tsarist regime in 1917), they understandably felt betrayed. Therefore, to Palestinians, who had cheered Allenby's entry into Jerusalem because of promises of a United Arab kingdom, it soon became obvious that the British meant to oversee the displacement of Arabs by Jews. For the Jews, Allenby's arrival was the first evidence that Britain meant to enforce the recently made Balfour Declaration.

When Richard Mumford arrived in Palestine from London in 1922 the British government, concerned by the increasing numbers of Jewish settlers and friction with their Arab neighbours, had partitioned the region by excluding the area east of the River Jordan from Jewish settlement. The area was renamed Transjordan and given to Abdullah, the son of Hussein bin-Ali, the Sharif of Mecca. Hussein, a direct descendant of the Prophet Muhammad, was one of the prominent Arabs the British had supported in the uprising against the Ottoman Turks instigated in 1916 by T.E. Lawrence. Transjordan had never been anything other than an area used by caravans of trade and pilgrims moving back and forth between Syria and the coast of Palestine and the Arabian Peninsula. The British never intended the place to become anything much. According to Sir Alec

Kirkbride, a senior British diplomat who was serving in Transjordan when my grandfather arrived, the British simply needed a place to resettle Palestinian Arabs once the national homeland for the Jews in Palestine, which Britain had pledged to support, became an accomplished fact. 'There was no intention at that stage', said Kirkbride, 'of forming the territory east of the River Jordan into an independent Arab state.'[2]

Amman in 1922 was hardly worthy of being called the capital of a new state. The main street was lined by dowdy, single-storey shops, mostly owned by blue-eyed, fair-haired Circassians, the Muslim, non-Arab people from the Caucasus and the Black Sea region deported to Ottoman Lands by the Russians in the mid-nineteenth century.

My grandfather Richard described a rough and rustic setting, Philby's official residence being just a 'two-story [*sic*] house and the office a couple of wooden huts in the courtyard'. The cars were Model-T Fords, 'almost the first Fords made, I imagine, but very suitable for that country owing to their high clearance'. A ruined tenth-century mosque served as the main place of worship for Muslims. Towering above the town and a second-century Roman amphitheatre stood the walls of the citadel, a pile of stone ruins on a site continuously inhabited since the Bronze Age and which in Greek and Roman times was known as Philadelphia.

Transjordan was a typically British afterthought, conceived after the lines of imperial domain had been drawn. To establish who owned what, an understanding between the British and the French was negotiated in secret by Mark Sykes, a former conservative MP and Yorkshire squire turned intelligence officer, and François Georges-Picot, a suave French diplomat whom many regarded as the better negotiator. The Sykes-Picot Agreement reached in 1916 drew a line in the sand extending from Acre on the coast of Palestine, cutting across the old Ottoman province of Syria, all the way to Kirkuk in Iraq near the Persian frontier. North of the line lay French-controlled Syria; south lay Palestine, and east beyond the River Jordan was what became Transjordan, eloquently described by Philby's graceful and rather charitable biographer Elizabeth Monroe as 'a floating particle, half desert, half cultivated, the ownership of which had not been decided by the peacemakers'. Further to the south lay the Hejaz, the western littoral region of the Arabian Peninsula and home to the Muslim holy cities of Mecca and Medina, as well as Arab leaders clamouring for their reward for helping the British defeat the Turks. Britain struggled to reconcile its conflicting promises to Arabs and Jews.

The Arabists, led by T.E. Lawrence in his post-war role as a Foreign Office advisor, urged the British Colonial Office, then led by Winston Churchill, to consider Transjordan part of the kingdom that had been promised to the Arabs in return for the British-backed Arab Revolt against the Turks that Lawrence instigated and helped lead. Churchill was leery, influenced by his formative years in South Africa, a patchwork of tribes Britain had tried but failed to turn into a confederation. Lawrence's grand visions of a pan-Arab kingdom also struggled against the views of powerful colonial officials in India, who, although far off, feared that independence for Muslim Arabs would inspire revolt in the far bigger Muslim population over which the British ruled in the subcontinent.

Meanwhile, Jews arriving in Palestine under British protection claimed the territory east of the River Jordan as part of their own homeland, arguing that it belonged to the ancient Jewish tribes of Reuben and Gad. Since no one could decide what to do with Transjordan, wedged as it was between Arabs and Jews, the British reverted to imperialist habit and consigned its administration to a group of inexperienced public-schoolboys such as Kirkbride and later Philby, with vague instructions to encourage self-government and keep costs at a minimum. The Colonial Office policy generally was to make the colonies pay their way: parsimony was the rule for Palestine, as Elizabeth Monroe put it. Or as Kirkbride nicely summed it up, it was the old problem of making bricks without straw: 'They [the Arabs] were told that it would be a waste of time their asking for assistance in the form of money or troops, but that any expert advice available would be placed at their disposal.'

But roosters were coming home to roost: the Hashemites, the Arab dynasty led by Hussein which governed Mecca and ruled over the Hejaz, were in a desperate dynastic struggle against the aspiring Al Saud family, backed, as it is today, by the conservative Islamic Wahhabi sect. The Wahhabis were and always have been purists with a literal view of the Muslim faith; they abjure all forms of idolatry and saint-worship and believe in the absolute sovereignty of God. To the Wahhabis, physical symbols of religion, including tombs and monuments, are heretical. The rich diversity of Islam, suffused from the various cultures it has embraced, are considered contaminations.

Much like the Spanish Inquisition, the Wahhabis offered the Al Sauds a dogmatic rationale for suppressing those who opposed them. The more urbane Hashemites needed security, so they turned to the British, whom they had also helped fight the Turks, and demanded thrones in the territories the British were carving out of Arab lands. To press his case, Abdullah, the clever and charming son of Hussein, marched on Amman and established himself there in 1921. According to the British diplomat Julian Huxley, Abdullah possessed a 'peculiar shrewdness, sometimes rising to wisdom'. He also burned with ambition and persuaded the British to let him prevail and preside over the new, rather undefined and provisionally named state.

Into this confusing clash of deadly Arab tribal politics and clumsy British line-drawing stepped my maternal grandfather Richard Mumford. His arrival and eventual settlement in the Middle East in the early 1920s coincided with the point at which the region began to pivot away from almost a century of stability and growth, presided over by modernising rulers making the most of flexible arrangements of autonomy under Ottoman rule. In fairness, not all of the empire's troubles were brought on by the subsequent intrusion of European powers; greed and ambition had landed some of these rulers in debt and, in the case of Egypt, precipitated bankruptcy. Ottoman efforts to modernise and reform at the start of the twentieth century bred instability and opened fresh fissures, mainly because they involved levying higher taxes and insisting on conscription in areas that were once left largely alone. All the same, the First World War significantly weakened the Ottomans' grip on power, and brought British colonial rule to Iraq, Palestine and Egypt. And so began to fray the richly woven carpet providing a cosmopolitan base of opportunity and security for my Greek and Italian family.

I have often wondered how the son of Welsh Catholic farmers who had moved off the land to London ended up working by the Suez Canal and marrying into a large family of Italian Jews. Richard Mumford was, by all accounts, a man of moderate views and ambitions, and a typical example of an Edwardian middle-class education and upbringing. Yet, like so many of his generation, the life he thought he might lead – as a journalist – was diverted down a completely different path by the outbreak of war in 1914, which over the next four years killed 18 million men and women and maimed millions more in a horrific frenzy of organised violence masquerading as modern warfare. It created fateful intersections of people and places, and affected all of their destinies. Richard died in 1960 when I was barely three years old. He was sixty-four. The only photograph I have of the two of us shows a chubby-cheeked toddler perched on his bony, tweed-clad knees; his face, hollow and drawn, is barely smiling. By then he was ravaged by chronic emphysema and a weakened heart.

Richard's parents had emigrated from the Welsh countryside to London in search of work, like so many other farming families in the Edwardian era. His mother, Elizabeth, was the daughter of a gamekeeper on Lord Raglan's sprawling, seventeenth-century Cefn Tilla Court near Usk in Monmouthshire;[3] his father, Alfred, was a farmer's son. They were typical of the proto-middle class, moving away from the patronage of squires and landowners to emerging professions and property of their own. My great-grandfather Alfred rose swiftly from a position as a lowly solicitor's clerk to manager of the Coliseum Theatre in the West End of London, with enough money to send Richard, who was born in 1894, to Wimbledon College in Edge Hill, a secondary school founded by Jesuits in 1892, a natural choice for his Catholic parents.

Richard Mumford aged twenty with his mother Elizabeth, c.1914

After leaving school, Richard found work as an apprentice with Lord Riddell at the *News of the World*, the original tabloid newspaper for the working classes established in 1843. Its motto was 'all human life is there.' The *News of the World*'s offices were situated in Bouverie Street, just by Temple Church behind Fleet Street. By the time of Lord Riddell's death in 1934, *News of the World* was, according to an obituary published in *Time* magazine:

> as common a phenomenon of the British Sunday morning as church bells. Full accounts of the nation's latest divorces, accidents and murders were devoured downstairs by goggle-eyed scullery-maids. Upstairs in her boudoir the lady of the house was feasting on the same spicy journalistic fare, for to the upper crust the paper's selling point was that it presented the week's scandal news in toto and in one lump.

In the same article Riddell is described as: 'an insatiably curious man, with a reputation of being able to bewitch a stranger's life story from him in ten minutes'. Riddell golfed with Prime Minister David Lloyd George every weekend and served as press liaison for the government when the war broke out.

Richard's apprenticeship must have proved fertile to his continuing education, to his urban identity, and to the expansion of his own network of contacts both personal and professional. He moved from his mother's home in Kingston as soon as he could. His father had died of tonsillitis in 1908 when Richard was just fourteen, and he had been closer to his father than to his imperious, domineering mother. His new lodgings, at a boarding house at No. 4 Steeles Road in Hampstead, north London, saw him living with a collection of up-and-coming, like-minded young men trying to make their way in the world. They were engaged as clerks in the Civil Service, banks, stockbrokers and at a shipping firm.[4] The war that erupted in 1914 crashed in on all their futures.

Today it is hard to understand the moral pressure imposed on young men to join up and fight for king and country, and how men out of uniform could be taunted and handed white feathers, an emblem of cowardice, by passers-by.

My own memories of war from the Vietnam era are of protest and resistance – and then the wave of patriotism that followed the attacks on New York and Washington on 11 September 2001 as colleagues of mine signed up to serve in Iraq and Afghanistan. For my grandfather, and others of his generation, if they had doubts, they were buried deeply. Richard decided to take 'the King's shilling' on 8 September 1916, though as an only son he was not obliged to do so.

Enlisting as a private, he served first in a reserve squadron of the 2nd King Edward's Horse, then went for a spell of training with the 6th Battalion of the Royal Fusiliers. He subsequently saw action in France with the 3rd Battalion of the Royal West Kent Regiment, a unit of light infantry. His unit was designated in reserve and not recorded as having 'very special opportunities of distinction', according to regimental history. But its divisional commander spoke of 'the fine spirit shown by the battalion in everything it had been called to do, and the casualties it suffered, nearly 200 in all, were some indication that it had not a little to endure'. At any rate, Richard was shot, bayoneted and gassed before he was discharged on 10 March 1919 for being 'surplus to requirements' and due to suffering 'impairments since entry'. He had fought at the bloodbath of Passchendaele, one of the war's defining and most senseless battles, which lasted from July until November 1917 and left as many as 600,000 killed or wounded on both sides.

Richard never left an account of his wartime experiences, although he did confide in my mother the horror of seeing his best friend killed next to him in the trenches. My great-grandmother Elizabeth, a widow and with her only son away fighting, probably couldn't bear to stay behind and wait for the usually inevitable notice of death in action. She enrolled as a nurse and went to France herself. As nurses during the war were mostly members of the Queen Alexandra's Imperial Military Nursing Service (QAIMNS) and with about 100,000 regular and reserve QAs serving in countries such as France, India, East Africa, Italy, Palestine, Egypt, Mesopotamia, Salonika and Russia, Elizabeth was posted to a hospital near the château at Baye, working for the French Red Cross in the Marne-Ardennes region. Here, this formidable, domineering Welsh woman was confronted with the horrors of war – men with no faces, missing limbs and infected wounds. The death and unspeakable suffering were a shock to the Edwardian women who had led sheltered lives in the relative comfort of gas-lit suburban parlours. The experience would have marked her, especially knowing that, with her husband gone, her only son was on the front line. She met Richard once when he was on leave in Paris, perhaps thinking that with the attrition rate as it was she might never see him again. Later, Elizabeth stayed on in France to work with wounded soldiers and their rehabilitation, and was there nursing when Dick was posted to Transjordan.

After the First World War and by then only twenty-five, Richard, like countless other demobbed and discharged servicemen, was at a loss, and likely suffering from what we now recognise as PTSD. For want of anything better, and with a view perhaps to putting the nightmares of the recent past behind him, Richard signed up with the P&O Line to work his way around the world as a steward on a passenger ship. On his return to London he took the Civil Service exam and, upon passing, was assigned to the Colonial Office in Transjordan. It was a welcome posting: as a victim of mustard gas, Richard had been advised to move to a hot, dry climate to help strengthen his lungs.

To reach Amman, Richard travelled by ship from Southampton to Port Said and from there he took an Egyptian train to Lydda, a port on what is now the Israeli coast. Here he changed trains and rode along the Hejaz railway to Amman, the same line my paternal grandfather Jerasimous worked on as a railway official under the British Mandate of Palestine. 'What a surprise!' he recalled in a brief written account of the journey:

> . . . the train consisted of a very old engine, a few wagons and the first-class passenger coach which was the back half of the guards' van fitted with two wooden benches. Owing to a coal shortage, the engine was fuelled from dumps of wood and naturally the steam kept dropping. When we crossed the Yarmuk Valley we had to get out and walk while it climbed the gradient. It took all day to get to Amman and a Greek trader saved me from starvation by sharing his bread and hard-boiled egg.

Richard arrived to find Philby busy trying to define the boundaries of the new state. This was no easy task. The Arab tribes, as Richard put it in a written recollection of his stay in Jordan, 'were not prepared to respect artificial boundaries which interfered with their age-long habit of raiding each other'. Amman, still essentially a village in 1922 with fewer than 4,000 inhabitants, was growing fast, swollen by refugees fleeing conflict in neighbouring Syria – much as it is today. The town was connected to the outside world by the railway branch line to the port of Haifa in the west, and several caravan routes to the east, into the Hejaz. An unmetalled road connected Amman with Jericho to the north. Situated on a high plateau above the river valley, the city was hot and dry in the summer. In winter it rained regularly, with temperatures plunging close to freezing.

Amman in the winter months is a cold, rainswept place. On one of my visits in blustery, near-freezing March I sat in a poorly heated café watching couples bundled up in puffa jackets playing backgammon and smoking shisha, a chill wind blowing through cracks in the windows. The city has ballooned in size since Richard was there in the 1920s. Buildings stretch up and down the rocky hills that were once barren scrub used by the Bedouin for grazing. A few of their ragged tents survive on the outskirts, ringed by cheap housing for refugees, who have poured into Jordan since its establishment. The latest wave, from Syria, number more than 2 million.

In addition to the physical hardships of life in Amman in the 1920s, no one seemed to know quite what to do. The British, as they were in other colonies, were few on the ground. The Colonial Office was preoccupied with events closer to home in Ireland, where an uprising in 1916 grew into a full-fledged revolution and an eventual transition to Irish independence in 1921. The local population in Transjordan, in this case Abdullah and his tribal followers plus a motley crew of merchants and refugees, were restive and impatient, unsure of their future. Threatened with the loss of the Hejaz and exclusive stewardship of the Muslim holy sites to the Al Sauds, they felt estranged, suffering from a loss of prestige; they were prone to random acts of violence. 'All the Arabs were armed,' Richard wrote, 'and a favourite trick of theirs was to take pot shots at anyone walking along the road to see if you would duck. In any case they are a rotten bad shot. I got used to it and took no notice.'

Emir Abdullah, despite his talents and warmth towards the British officers he worked alongside, was never Britain's primary champion; that privilege fell to his elder brother, Faisal, who had led the Arab Revolt with Lawrence. The British tried to make Faisal king of Greater Syria, to include Lebanon, Jordan and Iraq. But the French, concerned about his British backing, successfully ejected him, and left him with a rump kingdom in Iraq. All the same, Abdullah turned out to be a capable administrator who ruled what would become known as Jordan after it became a formal state. He was assassinated in 1951 by a Palestinian who suspected that he was about to make peace with Israel.

The first British official residence in Amman was 'a four-roomed house with no fireplace, no sanitation, and floorboards so thin that every movement of the servants below could be overheard'. Philby himself described a house that 'exuded peculiar smells with a basement reported to be insanitary and infested with vermin'. The original residence in Jebel Amman, near the current El-Rainbow Street area, was eventually abandoned after an earthquake and a larger building erected behind the Raghadan Palace in the east of the city. In addition to Philby and Richard, there was one other assistant, a Syrian and a Lebanese clerk, and a Circassian guard. A small Royal Air Force outpost carried mail between Cairo and Jerusalem and there was a fellow called Peake, a British soldier in charge of a small force tasked with border security.[5] Richard, who did not initially live at the residency, eventually moved in: 'At first, I was in a house in the village, rented by the government, but shortly after Mrs Philby and the two children returned to England. Philby then asked me to move in and take charge of the house, servants and catering. It sounded OK and I thought my experience at sea would be useful.'

It might have been useful, but it wasn't easy. Philby entertained regularly and was spending money he did not have, as British colonial officials were expected to fund their own parties. There was a procession of notable Arabists, journalists and wealthy travellers, including Elizabeth Titzel, an American archaeologist of captivating beauty, whom Philby made a considerable fuss over.

Richard's duties included preparing briefs for the colonial secretary, Winston Churchill, and for Sir Herbert Samuel, High Commissioner in Palestine. Samuel, a Jew, frequently visited Amman, and on one occasion Richard had to stop the staff serving him eggs with bacon. Philby was often away on inspections, leaving Richard to deal with some rather hairy situations. One night he was roused by Arab officials from the Transjordan government with news of an attack:

> Philby was away on inspection in the Dead Sea area. Batten had returned to the army and Kirkbride was on leave, so I was alone in Amman. About 4 a.m. Salamah woke me and said that members of the Transjordan government were in Philby's office and wanted him. I got up and went to see them and explained that Philby was away. They told me that a large invasion by the Wahhabis was in progress and that they were advancing on Amman, and would I

> arrange for the RAF to bomb them out. There was no love lost between Philby and Group Captain Gordon O.C. RAF Amman, so this latter request was a ticklish job. However, I got on the telephone to RAF and told the Duty Officer the position. He said he would not take the responsibility and would call the Group Captain. Gordon listened to my report and then asked me, 'What do you want me to do?' I replied that I was merely reporting what the TJ Government people had told me, without responsibility as to its accuracy, as I felt he should be informed as he was responsible for the territorial safety of the country. He replied 'All right, a ration plane will be going out to Ma'an and I will ask the pilot to have a look round.' Accordingly, I told the TJ Ministers not to worry as the RAF were flying out and they went off quite happy. Later Assad and Elias arrived scared stiff and asking for arms. I let them have a rifle and 50 rounds each from our store. During the morning Peake Pasha turned up and on hearing the position arranged for a mobile column of the TJFF to set out. So, Amman was saved and as far as I know casualties were confined to a border settlement.

This culture of unflappability, and what might have seemed a lack of concern and commitment, must have infuriated the Arabs. These Englishmen were intruders, with no real stake in the future of this barren land. They tended to consider what they were doing as transient and were more concerned with pay, conditions and a better posting. The stark Arab way of life and flat, featureless desert were no match for the manicured lawns and tennis courts of Delhi and Calcutta, which remained the privileged centre of the British Empire. For all the romanticism subsequently woven around Lawrence and the exploits of other Englishmen in the Arabian Desert, at the mundane level Transjordan was a backwater, and my grandfather Richard appeared to have no illusions about his modest posting.

Shortly before his death, and urged on by my father, Richard wrote an account of his time in Transjordan. The twelve-page document, which he typed out in 1960, is cautious and conservative, reflecting his modest and correct character, and also mindful, as he says, of the Official Secrets Act and the danger of libel: Philby was at that time still alive (but died shortly after my grandfather). From the outset it seems he was aware of the contradictions of British policies rooted in the Balfour and then McMahon commitments: 'I have never heard that any

British statesman has been able to reconcile the two pledges,' he wrote. He recorded that his superiors seemed to think the same way. Philby and his immediate boss, Sir Herbert Samuel, a Jew but no Zionist, were of the view that 'the mandate of Palestine was unworkable and was becoming more difficult in carrying out as Jewish immigration increased yearly.'

It's revealing but not necessarily comforting for me to know that many British colonial officials had their eyes wide open and weren't all fanning themselves on their verandas, whisky and soda in hand, with their backs to the 'subject people' they governed, so to speak. It is hard enough, given the rise and fall of my family's fortunes under colonial depredation, for me to reconcile my own feelings about how badly the British wrecked the Middle East with the fact that my maternal grandfather was a serving colonial official. Yet it seems that Richard Mumford was sensitive to the damage that was being done, and it troubled him:

> As far as I can remember in pre-war days the Arabs and the Palestinian Jews managed to get on together by a kind of mutual toleration. It was not until the mass immigration of Jews from central and Eastern Europe after the Balfour Declaration that the real trouble started. And it was largely the fault of these European Jews. They adopted an arrogant attitude to the Arabs and outrages on both sides occurred, many too obscene to print. To try and maintain order, the British government sent out a lot of Auxiliary Police, commonly known as the Black and Tans. They did not improve matters at all. In fact, as in Ireland, their conduct was brutal and finally they aroused the passions of Arab and Jew alike. Some of them were sent to Amman and on one occasion when I had been in to meet the train and collect our supplies, one of them, blind drunk, slashed Issa with his whip and I was only just in time to snatch Issa's gun from him to prevent shooting. I reported the incident to Philby and within a week the Black and Tans had left Amman.[6]

Richard's account of this period is scattered with reminiscences and opinions that suggest he was wide-eyed and impressionable, but at the same time not all that taken with the job or the environment, and still wounded physically and psychologically by the war. He kept a pet hedgehog and gazelle and had few friends. One of them was the manager of a new branch of Barclays Bank by the name of Forder, the son of a missionary to Palestine who spoke Arabic fluently: 'He was a decent chap and good company for me.' And for a while Richard shared digs with a man called Powell, who was sent to collect specimens of local birds. 'Quite a nice man, but stuffing the birds was a smelly job and I was not sorry when he moved out.'

Memories of the First World War hovered, and there was enmity for those who had sided with the Germans, as well as flashes of how cool one learned to be under fire. Among the staff Richard oversaw was an Arab driver, Suleiman: 'a troublesome type. He had been employed during the war by the Germans, and he had a working knowledge of both German and English. I had suspicions that he was doing a bit of petty thieving of petrol and oil.' One day Richard confronted him and threatened to report him for theft of a missing spare tyre. 'His hand flew to his pistol and for a moment I thought he would shoot me. I would have stood little chance in a struggle so I ignored him and went on with my work. After a couple of minutes, he left the room and duly returned later with the spare tyre. I had no further trouble with him.'

Richard writes about an excursion to explore an old Roman amphitheatre in the nearby ruins of Philadelphia, where he finds the remains of a British soldier 'evidently wounded in 1918 and crawled here and died'. He often visited the RAF base, where the commanding officer, a veteran of the Battle of Loos, '[gave] us a party on Loos night (15th September) . . . as there were no women available, some of the RAF boys used to dress up as girls and they made quite a good job of it'.

While serving in Amman, Richard met T.E. Lawrence and the other famous Arabist of the period, Gertrude Bell. 'A fanatical pro-Arab,' he wrote of her. 'The first thing she asked me was: "What do you think of the Arab race?" I took the line of tact and replied as she wanted . . . [she] was a Victorian "Blue Stocking", no make-up, clothes apparently bought off the peg, and thrown on. She had pince-nez glasses and was entirely devoid of sex appeal.' He might have thought differently of Lawrence. They shared similar backgrounds: fathers who died prematurely and stern Welsh mothers. And almost certainly they shared the psychological trauma of losing close friends in the war.

The British colonial world in the Middle East was populated by effete products of elite boarding schools and Oxbridge, groomed to foster imperial interests. Philby was a Queen's Scholar at Westminster, the best public school in London at the time, where he 'marched up the school all the way – determined to be top'. As a boy, writes his biographer Elizabeth Monroe, he would wake a friend at 6 a.m. to read Greek plays 'because he said they were easier to appreciate if read in company'. He went on to read Classics at Trinity College, Cambridge, where he took a First Class degree. Being brilliant as well as dedicated servants of the realm, these men – and they were with rare exception men – often combined eccentricity with high ambition. The strictly Catholic Richard Mumford, with his farmer's heritage and grammar-school education, must have felt somewhat out of place, and perhaps outgunned intellectually, surrounded as he was by socialists, idealists and people of ambiguous sexuality, most of them with their high-flying Oxbridge educations. Richard told his children later that the major source of his unhappiness in Amman was Philby, whom he grew to dislike intensely. There might have been a gulf between them because of their different war experiences: Philby, unlike Richard, had spent the war in the comparative safety of India, then Mesopotamia. Yet, as an Indian civil servant, his was deemed a vital position, which prevented him from joining up. His brothers had all enlisted and were killed in France.

Philby had a habit of working late into the night, expecting my grandfather to stay up with him and take down his dictated memos. And he was extravagant. Like Lawrence, Philby was fond of engaging the Arabs in their garb and in accordance with their customs. One day Philby gave a party for some forty tribal chiefs. Richard had the job of making the arrangements: a midday meal, Arab-fashion, in the garden: 'Mainly mutton and rice on large platters and finger bowls of water for each man, followed by fruit.' What annoyed him most, though, was Philby's lack of funds. For this particular feast, Richard had to foot the bill with his own money, as Forder, the Barclays Bank man, 'refused to cash Philby's cheque because his account was nearly dry!' These financial problems constantly weighed on Richard, who was forced to beg and scrape to fulfil his duties, either by spending his own money or borrowing from others. And at one point, Philby refused to allow Richard to purchase a portable typewriter for travelling on official missions; he was forced to lug around a heavy, cast-iron standard-sized machine.

There was something stiff and inflexible about the way the English conducted themselves in the Middle East. While fond of riding camels across the desert in flowing Arab robes, Philby insisted on a strict and rather impractical dress code for staff. 'We were not allowed to wear shorts even in summer and we all had to have a moustache,' Richard complained. As Lawrence wrote in his memoir *Seven Pillars of Wisdom*, 'We English who lived years abroad among strangers, went always dressed in the pride of our remembered country, that strange entity which had no past with the inhabitants, for those who loved England the most, often liked Englishmen the least.'

Philby was high-minded and broke; Richard was a practical man of little pretension. Throughout his account of the time he spent in Amman Richard is critical of Philby, but he was not the only one who found Philby difficult. Whitehall did, too. When he had clashed once too often with his superiors, they began bypassing him in favour of communicating directly with his subordinates, including Richard, and also with Emir Abdullah. One of Philby's contemporaries in the Foreign Service described him as 'exasperatingly contrary, consistent in his inconsistency . . . a champion of the Arabs who advocated Jewish immigration into Palestine, a British patriot who was interned during the war as a danger to his country, a rebel against the establishment who loved the Athenaeum, *The Times*, the cricket scores and the Honours List . . . He was selfish, irritable, stranger to humility, a difficult subordinate, an impossible colleague.'

Richard – no doubt fed up – applied for a transfer and travelled to Cairo to lobby for the move. His colonial masters, while sympathetic, told him to stay put. Frustrated, he resigned. And so, with a promising Civil Service career over, he moved initially to Alexandria, where he took up a position with Savon and Co., a job that took him to Port Said within a few months. Here, alongside the Suez Canal, my grandfather embarked on a new chapter of his so far not very happy, not very fulfilling life.

Port Said, a city perched on the very edge of Africa, recently severed from Asia by Ferdinand de Lesseps's canal, would have been an exciting change from sleepy, flyblown Amman. The port, established while the canal was under construction as a new settlement in 1859 to house the men who worked on building the waterway, was named after de Lesseps's friend, Said Pasha, whose signature on the proposal made the dream into a reality. The city wasn't as grand as Alexandria or what Ismail Pasha had built in the new downtown area of Cairo, yet in the late nineteenth century it was such an important port that all the major maritime powers had consulates there.

In the mid-1920s Port Said had grown to 100,000 inhabitants and possessed all the facilities of the modern Levant – complete with Greek doctors, Italian engineers, a well-tended European quarter, recreation and social clubs, first-class hotels and white-linen restaurants. It was a comfortable if not terribly cosmopolitan place, a bit of a provincial backwater by contemporary Levantine standards. All the same, Port Said must have been a pleasant change of scene after the rigours of truculent Bedouin society in Amman. Far from the risks of Wahhabi raids and errant snipers, photographs from the period depict bathing cabins along a sandy stretch of beach and boulevards lined with palms and casuarina trees. Richard lodged at the fashionable Grand Hotel de la Poste at 42 El-Ghomirya Street, where I later stayed when I embarked on this journey. And where at a tea dance he met his future bride, Lidia Sornaga, who was holidaying with her sisters. Richard and Lidia were married in Cairo a few months later on 29 January 1927 but settled in Port Said, where their twins, John and Josie, as well as my mother, Patricia, were born.

Richard had escaped from the tragic contradictions of Palestine and the clutches of a suffocating bureaucratic environment populated by ambitious servants of empire. He surrendered himself to his new and relatively exotic Jewish Italian in-laws. He was at once relieved, but also very much alone: he spoke no Italian; he was a Catholic; and, compared to the Sornagas, he was poor.

Richard left no letters, and there is no mention at all of his yearning for home in England or worry for his mother, who must have missed him terribly – after all, she had followed him to France during the war years. It was said that she had desperately wanted to see her son in Egypt, especially after the twins were born in 1928. Elizabeth, who was alone but still working as a nurse, wrote and suggested she join them. The prospect alarmed my grandfather: he worried that she would quarrel with his in-laws. 'She was the kind of woman who bossed people around and demanded that things were done her way,' my mother recounted, based on what she heard from her father. I can only conjecture why Richard would have been less than enthusiastic, but, at any rate, being told by your only son that you were not welcome, especially now that you had grandchildren, must have been a crushing blow.

Elizabeth died by suicide on 14 September 1928. A death certificate issued at the Royal Surrey Hospital in Guildford records the cause of death as Lysol poisoning. A painful end; and a surprising one for a devout Roman Catholic. Elizabeth was just fifty-one years old. This happened before my mother was born.

Soon afterwards, the Mumford nuclear family moved to Cairo, where Richard found work as an administrator with the British Air Ministry. The British had occupied, but not formally acquired, Egypt as a colony. The military occupation lasted seventy years – from 1882 until 1952 – spanning almost the entire period during which my grandmother Lidia's family, the Sornagas, lived in Egypt. An air command for the Middle East was established in 1922 with its headquarters in Cairo, its operational areas including Sudan, Palestine, Transjordan and Iraq as well as Egypt, with its 'uniquely central geographical position *vis a vis* the empire [which] made it a natural "Clapham Junction" for the new post-war imperial air routes'. Taking off in 1938 from Ismailia, 'the city of beauty and Enchantment' located on the west bank of the Suez Canal, a flight of newly designed Vickers Wellesley bombers made the first non-stop flight to Darwin in Australia, a distance of more than 11,000 kilometres. It was the dawn of air power and Richard Mumford, wounded veteran from the trenches of France and disillusioned former colonial official, found himself at the centre of its emerging bureaucracy, and in Egypt on the brink of another war.

CHAPTER EIGHT

Among Arabs and Jews

'As to the reconciliation between the two races, nobody makes any attempt to bring it about.'

Lord Peel, 1936

I was barely ten minutes in Haifa, Israel's northernmost and principal port city, when Johnny Mansour called to say he was on his way to meet me. I had just checked into a small but tidy guest house run by an Orthodox Christian Arab called George, who later confided in me that he may have once been a Greek. My Greek name brought out the residual Greek in Arabs of the Orthodox Church. 'Come,' said Johnny, as soon as he arrived and after shaking my hand for the first time, 'we're going for a walk.'

I had been introduced to Johnny – a local historian with a friendly round face and warm smile – by a mutual friend from the Palestinian Liberation Movement. I needed a guide to Haifa, where my father Panayiotis had lived with his parents and three siblings from the age of five until he left for university in Cairo shortly before the end of the Second World War. Despite the troubled times, his was a happy childhood. He told us of long, hot summer days on the beach, or of wandering with friends through scented pine forests in the hills behind the eponymous bay. I find it vicariously intimate to imagine his childhood: a triumph of perseverance and adaptation to the onset of communal strife and eventual war. He lamented that, just as he came of age, he confronted the end of an era.

It took me less than three hours to reach Haifa from Jerusalem by train, yet I felt as if I had entered a different world, and immediately at home. Jerusalem, an ancient city carved out of sacred rock, is built like a fortress; Haifa, in contrast, slopes gently to the sea, the mellow aquamarine and turquoise hues of the Mediterranean softening the harsh contours of the mostly modern, built-up areas. Haifa, though, like Jerusalem, has its own ancient roots. There is evidence of settlement around Mount Carmel, the 520-metre limestone escarpment that overlooks the city, dating back at least 3,000 years. And though high elevations were often places of worship in ancient times because they were regarded as closer to the heavens, in the case of Mount Carmel it seems the wooded scrubland on its slopes was considered a place to escape from God – quite unlike Jerusalem. It was only in the twelfth century AD that the Catholic Order of Carmelites established itself on the windy summit.

Haifa's medieval past belongs to the Arab community. Zahir al-'Umar al-Zaydani (1689–1775) was a Palestinian warlord from the Galilee area who properly established Haifa in the eighteenth century. Al-Zaydani led an autonomous Palestinian state that grew under relatively weak Ottoman rule, and which thrived, like Acre to the north, on growing exports of cotton and citrus fruit to Europe.

In the twentieth century under British rule, Haifa became Palestine's principal port, and the location of an important oil refinery built in the 1930s to process oil piped in from the fields of Kirkuk in Iraq. The British developed the port and established a refinery close to the train station built by the Ottomans as a major stop along the Hejaz railway that carried pilgrims to the holy cities of Mecca and Medina from all over the empire. Haifa became the headquarters of the Palestine Railways established under the British Mandate after 1920, for which Jerasimous, my grandfather, worked as a clerical officer and later manager. And with the commercial development and industrialisation that occurred after the First World War, the city expanded rapidly and became home to a sizeable population of workers, mainly poorer Arabs who left the tight-knit farming communities of nearby villages. Palestinians called Haifa *Umm al-Gharib*, meaning 'Mother of the Stranger'.

'Where did you say your father lived?' Johnny asked as we started to walk briskly up the hill along the old Carmel Avenue.

'Five, Mosul Lane.'

'That's just around the corner,' he said, his owlish face grinning with enthusiasm.

Late-afternoon light danced off the ochre stones of the nineteenth-century buildings of the German Colony, so called because this residential area of Haifa was built by the German Templars in the

1870s. The stout buildings constructed of neatly trimmed blocks of stone looked ageless and indestructible. The street that runs through the colony, straight up from the harbour, once named Carmel Avenue, is now called Ben Gurion Avenue, after Israel's first prime minister. We had set off towards what used to be called Vine Street, now Hagefen. Not five minutes into our walk, shortly after turning left off Carmel Avenue and passing the Greek Consulate, Johnny stopped, turned to me and said: 'Wait, did you say five?' He slapped the palm of his hand theatrically on his bald forehead. 'That's where I was born.'

Not for the first time on this journey did I feel that the gods of coincidence were walking beside me.

5 Mosul Lane as it is today

No. 5 Mosul Lane is nestled in three clusters of L-shaped, four-storey, yellow-stone apartment buildings built around a cul-de-sac. The buildings glowed golden, their warmth pulling me towards them. In style they maintained a sense of art-deco modernity; built in 1937, such residential buildings were rare at the time. The whole block was owned by a family of Arabs from el-Jesh, a mountainous region near the Lebanon border populated by Christians of the ancient Maronite Church. The family rented the second-floor apartment to my grandfather Jerasimous in 1938, when my father was ten years old. The apartment had a veranda looking out to the harbour and northwards across Haifa Bay. 'On a clear day we could see as far as Acre,' my father recalled. Having a view of the town further up the coast where he was born and grew up must have pleased my grandfather. According to my father's youngest sister, Artemis, the 'old man', as we all called Jerasimous in later life, hated moving, and any kind of change: 'He would get physically sick when he was about to move,' she recalled. 'If he could, he would have gone back to Acre.'

By the 1930s Haifa had become a very different place to the medieval walled city my grandfather knew in Acre as a child. My father described the Vine Street neighbourhood – with Mosul Lane part of it – as a foreigners' no-man's-land: a kind of twilight zone wedged between the Jewish area and the poorer Arab quarter, inhabited by 'a few Mandate officials, well-to-do merchants, a few professionals and foreigners'. When my father's family moved there, the neighbourhood was new and up-and-coming; it was a considerable improvement on their first place – an apartment along the busy Jaffa Road.

Haifa's growth spurt attracted all kinds of people from the surrounding region; as a result, the city acquired layers of social complexity and a modern look. Contemporary photographs depict commercial buildings with streamlined trimmings set along broad avenues, almost a facsimile of townscapes in the United States of the era.

The ground-floor apartment of 5 Mosul Lane in my father's time was occupied by another Maronite Christian from Lebanon and his wife. The couple were well off, had relatives overseas and spoke French at home. My father remembered their parties, where everyone spoke European languages, no Arabic: 'One could say these people represented the swinging set of those days.' Other neighbours included a Catholic Arab businessman and his family; a senior colonel in the Palestine police force; and a Bahai Persian who was a senior official in the Land Registration department. Haifa is home to a sizeable Bahai community, an ecumenical monotheistic faith that originated in Persia. The Bahai are by definition cosmopolitan, their networks stretching from the Middle East across to South Asia and beyond. My father's Bahai neighbour was married to a relative of the founder of the sect, whose children married into a Pakistani Bahai family. The politics was mixed as well: some of the Christian Arabs supported the European fascist movements of the 1930s; and Haifa was also home to one of the region's first communist movements, built on the back of the labour unions of refinery, dock and railway workers.[1]

Most of the neighbourhood was Arab- and French-speaking – they were, in my father's words, 'Levantines enjoying the prosperity offered by the British Mandate'. This speaks to the close nexus between these Levantine 'others' and the colonial administration, which was British and therefore required no knowledge of Arabic, or even much mingling with Arabs and Jews.

Johnny arranged for me to meet the current owner of the building: Saleem Isaq, a retired lawyer, who turned out to be the grandson of the man who had built the block and rented the second-floor apartment to my grandfather. Saleem, who was then a young boy, remembered the Vatikiotises because of the musical instruments my father and his siblings had to practise. My eldest aunt, Zoe, had a beautiful voice, he recalled; my aunt Artemis played the cello. My father also learned the cello and his older brother, Yanni, played the violin. 'I was something like three or four years old then. I was just listening to the music.' We were sitting in Saleem's modest living room. His wife served us coffee and cinnamon-infused cake. 'Music,' he said, 'when it is played well, stays with you.'

I knew what he was talking about. When I was about ten I heard my aunt Zoe practise piano in my grandfather's tiny flat in Athens. She had a beautiful soprano voice and trained as an opera singer in Rome during the 1950s. My uncle Yanni also became a professional musician, and played viola in the State Orchestra of Athens. I used to wake from long siestas in his apartment listening to him practise before a concert, and on warm summer nights I would sit in the cheaper seats of the ancient Herodes Atticus arena below the Acropolis, listening to the orchestra play a medley of classical favourites, the air scented with eucalyptus and rosemary. Of all the tenants the building has seen come and go this past seventy years, Saleem said he remembers the Vatikiotis family best of all. 'I can hear your grandmother calling from the balcony to the children playing below: "Children, do you want *labneh* and *zaatar*?"'

In 1918, as the British arrived in Palestine, Haifa had a population of just 22,000, only an eighth of whom were Jews, who migrated slowly but steadily to the city over the next decade. Initially Palestine wasn't a popular place for Jews from Europe to settle, especially when compared to the United States. But after the USA implemented tougher immigration policies in the mid-1920s, the steady trickle to Haifa became a flow. By the mid-1940s the city's population was 140,000, half of them Jews. Yet for all the ingredients of healthy cosmopolitanism in Haifa – including the pot pourri of educated Levantines who were civil servants, like my grandfather, employed by the British Mandate – the mixed population provided tinder for the fires of sectarian polarisation, prejudice and hatred. Rising unemployment in the 1930s and the start of segregation in the workplace between Arabs and Jews generated unrest and violence. All of this was set against the gathering clouds of fascism and war in not-so-distant Europe. Haifa in this period was a harbinger of things to come for Palestine as a whole.

With everything that has happened in Palestine and then Israel since 1947, the turbulence of the mid-1930s is often overlooked. Yet this period was instrumental to the decline of the region's cosmopolitanism. It also set the stage for the dark decades to come of conflict between Arab and Jew. The Palestinian sociologist Salim Tamari points out that by the 1930s the inclusive diversity of cultures that drew on a composite of religious influences began to be disrupted by notions of nation and territory. First, the British and the French drew lines in the sand that established notions of sovereignty far more definite and geographically fixed than the Ottomans ever did. Then the Arabs grew unhappy about the liberal way in which the British authorities encouraged Jewish immigration. There were two aspects to this: first the basic policy supporting a Jewish homeland in Palestine enshrined in the Balfour Declaration of 1917, and then the rise of anti-Semitism in Nazi Germany that turned what the British hoped would be a steady flow of Jewish migrants into a flood.

Neither the French nor the Americans could understand why the British, normally prudent about managing complex societies for profit, were so willing to set Arabs against Jews in what was clearly a prelude to conflict. Perhaps that's not what they intended. British colonial policy could be confoundingly haphazard and un-meticulous in places, compared to the fastidious mercantile minds of the Dutch, for example.

It has been widely believed that no one bothered to ask the locals what they thought about the matter of Jewish immigration. But this is not quite true. Now consigned to an almost forgotten footnote, a commission established by President Woodrow Wilson in 1919 embarked on a month-long consultation with the people of the region, to establish what they thought of the mandates Britain and France were proposing to establish under the terms of their otherwise secret carve-up. The King-Crane Commission, led by two Americans, Henry King, a prominent theologian, and Charles Crane, a wealthy businessman and noted Arabist, was imbued with Wilson's idealistic notions of self-determination, which is why the British and the French were reluctant to participate in the exercise. With remarkable prescience, the commission concluded that a Jewish state wasn't viable because the majority of the region's inhabitants were not in favour; thus, it would need to be established by force of arms. The report proposed instead something like the Greater Syria governed by the Ottomans, with all constituent ethnic and religious communities granted rights, much as the Ottoman *millet* system allowed. But with Wilson's failing health and the vehement determination of the British and the French to proceed along the lines agreed by Messrs Sykes and Picot in 1916, the commission's final report was buried.[2]

The trouble started almost as soon as the British Mandate was established. The Jews, emboldened by the Balfour Declaration, demanded rights and access to their holy sites and attacked Arabs to make their point. Jewish immigration generated demand for land, and poorer Arab farmers came under pressure to sell their land cheaply to alleviate debts incurred to their landlords. The resulting evictions and homelessness among Palestinians generated still more anger and resentment. In retaliation, the Arabs agitated against the British government, and attacked the Jews. In 1929 as many as 600 people were killed in a general uprising that started with an argument between Arabs and Jews over access to the ancient wall of the Jewish Temple in Jerusalem, forcing the British to bring in added military support from Egypt. By 1930, some British administrators started to realise, in the words of Sir John Chancellor, High Commissioner to Palestine, that London's policy of supporting Zionist aspirations was a 'colossal blunder'. Chancellor predicted further unrest: 'both parties are now smuggling arms into the country, the outbreaks will be organised, and the Palestinian Arabs will almost inevitably have the material support of Arabs from the neighbouring territories and certainly the moral support of the whole Moslem world.'

To counter the sense that they were losing control over their land with increasing Jewish immigration, the Arabs demanded self-government. And, as they did in other colonies, the British responded to demands for representation with the idea of weak elected local councils. But the Jews were outraged: how dare the British promise the Arabs self-rule in the land promised to them alone? Similarly, efforts to limit Jewish immigration were viciously attacked from Zionist quarters and the weak British government of the time, which under Prime Minister Ramsay MacDonald lacked a parliamentary majority, hurriedly withdrew the idea of Arab councils and reluctantly continued to permit Jewish immigration.

The Jews, especially the Zionists among them, grew more arrogant and assertive. When the British built the modern port of Haifa, the Jews demanded a percentage of jobs and higher wages than Arabs, arguing that Jews had a higher standard of living that needed to be maintained. Amid rising insecurity, the British proceeded to arm and train a Jewish police force, which became the basis of the paramilitary *Haganah* (Hebrew for defence), from which the Israeli army of today evolved. The British were caught in an ever-tightening noose of their own making. As my maternal grandfather Richard Mumford recognised in nearby Transjordan in the mid-1920s, it was impossible for the British to reconcile their promises of both a Jewish homeland on Arab land and new Arab kingdoms. While London made no effort to prevent Jews from settling in Palestine, the effete Arabists in Cairo fretted about betraying their Arab allies; the pressure needed a valve. It came in the form of an all-out Arab rebellion in 1936. What later became known as the Great Revolt was the first major challenge to British rule anywhere in the Middle East and the most significant anti-colonial insurgency in the Arab world since the First World War.

Nevertheless, these rising sectarian tensions coexisted alongside remarkable economic development, with demand for labour and immigration transforming this small strip of land between the River Jordan and the sea. In the decade from 1929 to 1939 the population of Palestine nearly doubled, reaching 1.5 million people, a million of them Arabs. Haifa's population more than doubled from 30,000 to 65,000 in the same period. Much of the migration to Haifa was from surrounding Arab villages, where higher birth rates and poor farming methods drove people away, looking for work and opportunities. At the same time, Jews arrived in greater numbers, including those with premonition and gumption enough to escape from Germany during the rise of the Nazi Party. In 1936 more than 60,000 Jews arrived, the highest number in one year since the establishment of the British Mandate.

My father, then eight years old, was unaware of ominous developments in Europe, but he noticed the changes around him:

> We simply saw and heard new things – shops, factories, more and more doctors' shingles outside doors and buildings with strange central and east European names, better music over the wireless, fabulous (in local terms) Jewish soccer elevens, splendid swimming pools and beach resorts. Rents went up, and whole families of five and six souls lived 'happily' in one room. Buxom girls clad in short-shorts, and boys with short khakis, heavy field boots and sporting knapsacks over open-necked denim blue shirts crowded the trains, getting off at kibbutz stations. Good public transport – Leyland and Thorneycroft buses – littered the main roads and avenues from the Bay to the Carmel. The Egged Bus Company made it possible for all of us to travel by road to practically any part of the country. Europe, and with it modernity, had really come to Palestine in force.

As much as Haifa began to look and feel like a modern city by the mid-1930s, it was also becoming a seething cauldron of angry Arab sentiment. The working-class Arabs of Haifa were susceptible to political foment and polarisation. Early efforts by left-wing activists to bind Jewish and Arab workers together in communist-inspired unions floundered on the rocks of Zionist-inspired efforts to keep Jews and Arabs apart. This in turn made Arab workers more responsive to Palestinian nationalist sentiment, which grew more virulent with the increasing level of Jewish immigration. As elsewhere in the Muslim world, a leadership vacuum was emerging: the Ottoman caliphate was in its death throes and the Hussein family was losing its control over the holy sites of Mecca and Medina in the Hejaz. The Arab cause in Palestine intensified, much as Sir John Chancellor predicted, after its leadership tied their grievances to the banner of Islamic struggle. One particularly effective Arab Muslim leader, a Syrian cleric called Izz ad-Din al-Qassam, happened to live in Haifa, which helped make the city the crucible of the Arab Revolt.

Al-Istiqlal Mosque, one of the most important in Palestinian modern memory, was at the heart of the revolt. Built in 1924, the mosque served the burgeoning Arab community, and in addition to its religious role also provided community services: housing the Shariah court and Islamic *Waqf* (a charitable foundation) offices. The dull, municipal design of the building, complete with an Ottoman-style, copper-roofed minaret, and today sandwiched between the threadbare flea market and the railway museum in lower Haifa, reflects this duality. It was here, in the late 1920s, that Al-Qassam started preaching. The charismatic cleric developed a popular following, especially among the poor working men and boys eking out a fragile existence. He established a youth movement and developed a name for himself as a firebrand nationalist, having already dabbled in the anti-colonial struggle before leaving his native Syria.

As regional registrar of Muslim marriages, Al-Qassam travelled to Arab villages in Galilee and south towards Jaffa, and everywhere delivered rousing sermons encouraging anti-British sentiment. Helped by wealthy Arab businessmen, he arranged the purchase of weapons and established small bands of armed men who began to launch sporadic attacks on Jewish settlers. These popular and near-spontaneous outbreaks of violence were, in the words of the Israeli historian Tom Segev, 'expressions of social unrest, national rage, and the dark mood of a generation that had matured under British rule'. Emboldened, Al-Qassam called for a jihad against the British, but failed to get wider support from the Palestinian establishment, his efforts foundering on the disparate self-interests of rich families, who could never quite put the concerns of people whom they considered their tenants above the security of their wealth and privilege, which depended on currying favour with the authorities. Nevertheless, in November 1935 Al-Qassam and a few other men took to the hills to raise the flag of rebellion, only to be killed soon after in a British police operation. The manner of his death and the movement Al-Qassam built inspired later generations of Palestinian fighters and the military wing of Hamas. The contemporary Palestinian Islamic movement bears his name – the Al-Qassam Brigades – as do the locally built rockets that periodically rain down on Israeli suburbs.

Al-Qassam's death lit a touchpaper; at his funeral procession, the huge crowd of his followers roared, 'Revenge! Revenge!' The rising tide of anger forced vacillating Palestinian notables in Jerusalem to establish an Arab Higher Committee, which in April 1936 backed calls for a general strike, sanctioned violence against the British and the Jews, and sparked the Great Revolt. Lasting until 1939, the Arab uprising involved marauding bands of rebels, some led by bandits and opportunists rather than ideologues or genuine religious leaders. They attacked Jewish settlers and the British army or police, sabotaged the oil pipeline from Iraq to Haifa and cut telegraph wires. But many Arabs were also killed in vicious efforts by their leaders to settle scores and impose loyalty. There was an accompanying strike by Arab workers and traders, disrupting the markets that had otherwise been places where Arabs and Jews had mixed and interacted peacefully, and where now there was the risk of bombing and sniping.

These were the first signs of the separation of Arab and Jewish society that would eventually become the template for the modern Israeli state. Contemporary accounts recall that the strikes went on for months, curfews for days, and that boisterous demonstrations became a daily way of life: 'The Arab population was fighting for its independence from British rule,' wrote John Tleel, a Greek from Jerusalem who lived through the era. 'Excess vegetables and fruit decayed in the streets and markets, for there were no Jewish buyers. The Arabs were banned from selling anything to the Jewish population. He who defied the ban was considered a traitor and would be treated as such.'

The British authorities were initially complacent, unaware or at least unconcerned, about the development of guerrilla hit-and-run tactics used by the Arabs (with greater effectiveness in later decades). 'It was all good clean fun,' recalled a senior British policeman. 'We chased them and they did their best to get out of the way.' And for the Vatikiotis family, living on relatively quiet Mosul Lane, the only manifestations of rebellion were the presence of larger contingents of British troops and tighter police security: their apartment overlooked the military police barracks, from which my father said emanated 'occasional screams of the difficult inebriated trooper while police were trying to sober him up or discipline him.'

Eventually, however, the sabotage and the artful use of IEDs prompted a sterner British response: 25,000 extra troops were shipped in and airpower was used against the marauding rebel bands. The British huddled behind fortified police posts known as Tegart Forts, and raised and trained a Jewish military force. A young British officer who later made a name for himself fighting the Japanese behind the lines in Burma used rather unconventional tactics. Riding into skirmishes with a Bible and giving no quarter, Captain Orde Wingate would sit quietly afterwards, stark-naked, reading his Bible and munching on raw onions. Wingate once floated the idea of blowing rams' horns to scare the Arabs, citing the biblical story of how the prophet Joshua brought down the walls of Jericho. Meanwhile, the rebels melted into the rocky hillside and were able, with tacit acquiescence, to find refuge in French-controlled Lebanon and Syria – the French had never forgotten British efforts a few years earlier to destabilise French-controlled Syria using the Hashemites. Over three years, several hundred Jews were killed and between 2,000 and 5,000 Arabs, many in internecine feuding.

Sir Alec Kirkbride, who after leaving Transjordan was posted as British District Commissioner in Galilee, and oversaw Acre, Haifa and much of the area affected by the revolt, describes the situation in terms that foreshadows the manner in which the Palestinian Liberation Movement operated after the partition of Palestine in 1947 and in the modern period:

> The troops brought the armed bands of Arabs to battle on several occasions and trounced them thoroughly, but experience proved that warfare of this kind did not act as a deterrent but encouraged younger villagers who were attracted by the prospects of honour and glory . . . The hanging of Arabs for the illegal possession of firearms was equally ineffective as a means of checking the revolt. The more martyrs were killed, the more Arabs there were willing to take their place.

The Great Revolt set the stage for, and established, many of the tactics and methods of conflict used in the longer struggle between Arabs and Jews that would follow the Second World War. More importantly, the revolt convinced the British government that there was no viable way for Arabs and Jews to live together peaceably and, after a short review, a Royal Commission led by Lord Peel recommended in 1937 the partition of Palestine into Jewish- and Arab-held areas. The Peel report drove a final nail into the coffin of Ottoman-derived cosmopolitanism, and buried forever the notion that Arabs and Jews could coexist in the same land under the same government. It began to fossilise the society my father and his family had known for three generations, albeit with the outbreak of the Second World War in 1939 effectively ending, or at least pausing, this first Arab Revolt in Palestine.

The day after we visited my father's old house on Mosul Lane, Johnny Mansour picked me up from the German Colony for a tour of the old Arab heart of the city known as Wadi Salib. The quarter, which first sprung up in the mid-nineteenth century, was clustered around the Ottoman Pasha's Palace, which still stands forlorn and half ruined adjacent to the hammam the pasha built for his family's and public use. Wadi Salib tumbles down the hill in a cascade of dressed stone and elegant ogee arches towards the port. The elegant neighbourhood, with its columned, marble-floored homes, was once the heart of the city, home to merchants and civil servants and the workers who were drawn to Haifa's new port at the start of the twentieth century. The old quarter finishes up adjacent to the railway station where my grandfather Jerasimous worked, and which had been built in 1905 by Germans for the Ottoman sultan's project for carrying pilgrims along iron rails from Damascus to the holy cities of Mecca and Medina in the Hejaz. Haifa was one of the first modern Arab cities in the Middle East, more Arab than the cosmopolitan entrepôts of Beirut and Alexandria, and with modern industries and facilities then lacking in Damascus. Today, the old stone homes of the bourgeoisie who once lived in Wadi Salib are mostly deserted, their inhabitants forced to flee after partition in 1948, mostly north across the Lebanese border, where the Christians among them (according to some Palestinian sources) were immediately naturalised to bolster the size of the Maronite Christian community. What is left of Wadi Salib stands like a silent sentinel awaiting redevelopment, its grand arches and porticoes daubed with graffiti.

As we descended through the old quarter towards the Ottoman-era railway station, following in what might very well have been the tracks of my grandfather's daily commute, we stopped for a hearty breakfast of mashed black-bean *foule* and garlicky hummus in a café occupying the ground floor of Al-Istiqlal Mosque. At nearby tables young Arabs sat preoccupied with their smartphones. As we dipped our warm flatbread into the oily beans and creamy hummus, Johnny reflected on the significance of the floor above. Al-Qassam, he noted, was buried outside of Haifa – the British were afraid his tomb would make him a martyr.

'Today the people of Haifa see only what is visible, not the invisible history,' he reflected forlornly. Outside, the physical ruins of Wadi Salib are under a preservation order and cannot be demolished. The wind blows through the gaping holes in the walls of old homes and their courtyards and gardens, which are used now as public car parks. The rich and diverse society that had lived here is gone. A flash of anger welled up from deep within Johnny's soul. 'They have taken the city from us, our city of Haifa,' he said, 'without asking us.' 'They' being the Israelis. Haifa's population of more than a quarter of a million people today includes only some 35,000 Arabs, or around 12 per cent of the population; half of them live in the Wadi Nisnas quarter, just up the hill from where we were sitting.

We finished our breakfast with a sweet cup of steaming-hot Turkish coffee and set off for Wadi Nisnas, a vibrant neighbourhood filled with the bustle of family life and an air of normality. We walked through a maze of narrow streets where children skipped past, their mothers calling after them and hanging out laundry to dry in the heat. Johnny pointed out the ground-floor apartment where he had grown up, after moving from Mosul Lane in the mid-1960s. Most of the inhabitants, he said, are Christian Arabs – in fact, more than 65 per cent of Haifa's Arab residents are Christian. Many moved from villages in rural areas afflicted by intolerance inspired by the more orthodox ideas of Islam infiltrating the Palestinian community in recent years. In 1948 Wadi Nisnas was the only safe space for the Arabs of Haifa, though they had been corralled there by the Israeli Defense Forces. It remains a safe space, and one of the most vibrant Arab communities in Israel.

And then, slap bang in the middle of it all, we came across a building festooned with red flags. 'The communist party,' Johnny said. 'They're successful here . . . They have two elected members on the municipal council, and four members in the national parliament.' I asked why. 'The communists are the only party that works on the inside of Palestinian society and gives voice to Arab civil society,' he replied without hesitation, then took me to a news stand where he pointed out the communist newspaper *Al-Ittihad*, no longer funded by the Soviet Comintern.

Later in the day, we drove up the hill to the ritzy Carmelilyya area at the top of Mount Carmel. Here the European or Ashkenazi Jewish elite have built themselves a small-scale version of Bel Air or Beverly Hills, complete with strip malls and retro 1960s-era hotels including the Dan Carmel. Near the top sits perhaps the oddest community in Haifa, a district called Kababir, home to around 1,500 members of the Ahmadiyya sect, a branch of Islam not recognised as mainstream and widely persecuted across the Muslim world, graced here by an imposing new mosque with its twin minarets – although legally only one is allowed. We met the imam, amiable but intense, who hailed from Kerala in southern India. He tried to entice us for tea, and presumably a missionary pitch.

The Haifa I saw guided by Johnny Mansour would have been familiar to my father – even today – and, like my father on his frequent visits back to Israel in the 1980s and 1990s, I was relieved to escape the suffocating manifestations of religious identity and contested sacred space of Jerusalem. During my father's time, in a land where no one could decide after the First World War who had primacy, Arab or Jew, Haifa developed as a kind of cosmopolitan neutral ground populated by a dazzling variety of people: Armenians, Greeks, Muslims, Christian Arabs and European Jews. Its inhabitants spoke English, French, Greek, German, Yiddish, Arabic or Hebrew. Today, Haifa is known as a liberal, tolerant place, especially by Israeli standards. My father's old neighbourhood is littered with galleries and theatres that declare themselves 'Jewish-Arab' cultural centres. 'Mostly Arab, really,' said Johnny, a Catholic. There is an upbeat and upmarket air to the place, its restaurants offering global cuisine and fine wines, its bars serving up craft beer and techno music. The old British Military Police barracks opposite 5 Mosul Road is being renovated as a boutique hotel. Apart from the abandoned Arab quarter, the city remains an island of cosmopolitanism in a country increasingly besieged by notions of orthodoxy and intolerance.

When the Vatikiotis family moved into 5 Mosul Lane in 1938, Haifa was a thriving modern port city, albeit bruised by the revolt and uprising of the 1930s, after which daily contact between Jews and Arabs grew problematic. In June 1938 the Irgun, a radical Zionist terrorist group, planted a bomb at the city's central Arab fruit market, killing eighteen people. A few days later my father, who was travelling on a Jewish-owned bus, saw an Arab boy emerge from an alley and hurl a home-made bomb in his direction. The explosion caused little damage, though my father, then barely a teenager, was shaken. Over the next seven months another 120 Arabs – and some Jews – were killed in Irgun attacks on public markets in Haifa. And when violence between Jews and Arabs intensified, my grandfather Jerasimous was sometimes offered a ride to work in a British armoured car, to avoid the snipers that infested many of the city's neighbourhoods. The Arab nationalist roots of the rebellion became entwined with the fascist anti-Semitic narrative in Europe, as Arabs targeted Jews and Jews started to defend themselves.

As the Second World War commenced, communities took sides: the Arabs, eager to get rid of the Jews, generally sympathised with the Axis powers; the Italians, and by extension Roman Catholics, identified with the strong state that emerged under Mussolini. Religious and state identity began to merge.[3] The Muslim Arab community were generally pro-German and pro-Nazi. Adolf Hitler invited the Grand Mufti of Jerusalem, Amin al-Husseini, to Berlin. Some Greeks began sympathising with the Jews, especially after the Nazi occupation of Greece. Jerasimous, when asked by an Arab colleague how the Greeks could possibly resist the German army, replied: 'We will mobilise our women to resist the Italians and our men to fight against the Germans.'

Then, one fine day at the end of July 1940, the Italian air force bombed the refinery and port facilities in Haifa. My twelve-year-old father was swimming on a nearby beach. He and his friends had no time to get out of the water, so they hid underneath a diving platform while the sea around them was churned by bombs and shrapnel – a close call. During another raid – this one by the German air force on a Friday – Muslim Arabs streamed out of their mosque to applaud the bombers only to be strafed by a diving Stuka. The effect on the Arab population, according to my father, was immediate: 'No more strutting about proclaiming how the Axis would fix us all – Greeks, Jews and British.'

Despite the bombing, the coming of the Second World War was in many ways a respite for the people of Palestine. It wasn't really their war. Europe, and later on North Africa, were the main battlegrounds. Yet Greeks like my father and his family, for whom the war was something of a watershed, highlighting an emerging and increasingly bitter divide between Arab and Jew, became 'acutely aware of how alien they were in that passionately contested Holy Land'. Sure, my father continued to play soccer with his Arab friends, take cello lessons from a Jewish teacher and enjoy the modern music halls and cinemas owned by Jews – European tastes and styles were attractive to a Greek kid born in Palestine. But the Arab grocers grew less friendly, the Jewish music teachers more nervous about their security, and among the families and friends in the Vine Street neighbourhood allegiances based on race and religion were being drawn.

The Vatikiotis family in Haifa, 1944

The onset of war may have forced Arabs and Jews to limit their skirmishes, but the ideological currents generated by the war attacked the already frayed sinews of communal harmony. Nazi anti-Semitic sentiment infected the Palestinian elite – most famously that of Amin al-Husseini, whose support of the Great Revolt in 1936–39 forced him to flee to fascist Italy and Germany, from where he allowed himself to be used by the Nazis to propagate anti-Semitic hatred. Meanwhile, mistrustful of Arab loyalties, the British authorities turned to the incipient Zionist military underground for help with the war effort, and many Jews signed up to fight in the North African campaign and in other Middle East theatres. These twin ideological thrusts – Zionism and Nazism – punctured the great cosmopolitan society confected by the Ottomans below the waterline.

At the outbreak of the Second World War, my father was attending Saint Luke's School for Boys, built by the Anglican Church of Scotland in 1920 and still run by them today. It was here, as the war raged elsewhere and Arabs somehow managed to coexist with Jews, that he met the friends he would hold close for the rest of his life. Many were Protestant Arabs. The Protestants made deep inroads into the Arab Orthodox Christian community in the first decades of the twentieth century, riding on the back of British imperial presence. For many, it made sense to cross the aisle to the modern church, with its well-funded schools and the promise of access to favoured jobs in the Mandate administration.

Among them was a bright kid called Wadie Haddad, whose father taught my father Arabic at the school: 'our fierce Arabic master who named his first-born son . . . Caesar'. Wadie, the younger son, sat a couple of desks from my father in class. 'I remembered Wadie in the track and field events on the school's sports day, his veins showing through his skinny face and wiry frame, warming up for the races. I remembered him as tense and secretive, but always a smiling model pupil.' The boys' friendship survived the upending of their happy world of weekends on the beach and football in the early evenings. It survived even the partition of their land, which saw them separated because they went to different universities – my father to the American University of Cairo, where he studied the liberal arts, and Wadie to the American University of Beirut, where he studied medicine. And then, later, when my father took up his pen and started writing about the Arab world, Wadie took up the gun. He became one of the leaders of the emerging Palestinian Liberation Movement, and an architect of the violent militancy we have come to know as global terrorism.[4] Their lives would continue to intersect, as you might expect of close school friends. What I only found out much later, long after my father died, was just how close they were during the period of foment and struggle after the partition of Palestine.

Walking down the hill towards Saint Luke's at sunset, I found Canon Hatem, who looks after the church and its attached school. He was leaving his office, and led us to the church just next door. Inside he pointed to the baptism font, its wooden lid carved with a Star of David.

'The Anglicans were ambitious,' said Canon Hatem. 'They thought they would be converting the Jews.'

'It reminds me of a British village church,' I said. With its nod to the Gothic I could almost hear strains from the English hymnal echoing in the wooden rafters.

'The Anglican Church was quite successful, though,' he continued, interrupting my reverie. 'We converted a lot of Arabs, but today congregations are shrinking.' He looked up, then around. 'The situation is terrible. That's why I now preach the Jesus of Palestine, not the Palestine of Jesus.'

There was an edge to his voice. Canon Hatem struck me as a man of otherwise gentle disposition, but candid with his criticism of the weakness and failure of his fellow Arabs. As we walked out into the playground, he gestured towards a mural of smiling faces on one of the walls: 'We teach peace here,' he said, 'we have to.'

CHAPTER NINE

Rommel at the Gates

'Today we . . . have the gates of Egypt in hand, and with the intent to act!'

Field Marshal Erwin Rommel, October 1942

Field Marshal Erwin Rommel, the charismatic commander of the *Panzerarmee Afrika Korps*, was entrusted by Adolf Hitler with the task of driving the British out of Egypt, seizing the Suez Canal and linking up with German forces marching down through the Caucasus to take the British-held oilfields of Iraq. Had Rommel succeeded, it is doubtful that Britain and her allies could have so quickly turned the tide of the war, and the history of my mother's family in Egypt, as well as that of my father's in Palestine, would have been very different.

In 1942 the British government led by Prime Minister Winston Churchill was under immense pressure at home. The Allies had by then lost France, Greece and Singapore to invading Axis forces which, led by the Germans, thrust across North Africa towards Egypt, threatening the lifeline to Britain's empire via the Suez Canal. According to the British author and broadcaster Jonathan Dimbleby, Churchill fought the Second World War 'as much to save the global reach of the British Empire as to destroy Nazism'. Egypt, which Britain controlled but no longer directly governed after 1922, had to be defended at all costs. Facing a likely no-confidence vote in the House of Commons, Churchill flew to Washington in the early summer to plead with President Franklin Roosevelt for American intervention. No sooner had Churchill arrived than the critical forward British base at Tobruk in present-day Libya fell to Rommel's hard-charging tank divisions. Churchill received the news on 21 June 1942 while standing with Roosevelt in the Oval Office. He later wrote that it was 'one of the heaviest blows I can recall during the war'. The British military historian Niall

Barr described the fall of Tobruk as representing 'Britain's complete military humiliation'.

The way was clear for Rommel to strike at Alexandria and drive on to Cairo. German propaganda radio broadcasts were chirping that the women of Alexandria should 'get out your frocks; we're on our way!'

The Second World War carried a conflict between European powers to the shores and deserts of the Middle East. The principal protagonists – Nazi Germany and the Allied powers led by Britain – cared not a jot for the local population, whose towns and cities they trampled over in battle tanks or pounded with artillery. They cared only somewhat for the region's European residents, the Levantine Greeks and Italians, in so far as they represented useful expatriate supporters or could serve as administrators of a future occupation. This toxic brew of war, and its underlying nationalist impulses, destroyed a delicate society, and set the stage for the expulsion of all foreigners from Egypt.

The war had already disrupted the comfortable lives of my mother's Italian family, the Sornagas. When Italy declared war on Britain in June 1940, the British ordered the Egyptian authorities to round up all Italians between the ages of fifteen and sixty-five. Around 8,000 Italians were sent to internment camps, established near the Suez Canal and close to the Nile Delta, which consisted of sparsely equipped tents fenced in with a high-wire perimeter. Visits from dependants were allowed, but security was strict. Even before then, the halcyon existence of Egypt's sizeable Italian community was irreversibly altered by the rise of fascism in Europe.

There is perhaps no better monument to Italian fascism on the African continent than the Casa d'Italia in Port Said; it is a testament to Italy's fleeting effort to revive the Roman Empire. Built in 1937 by Clemente Busiri Vici, a Roman architect who specialised in expressions of fascist grandeur, the three-storey, art-deco buildings served as the centre of Italian social life until the defeat of Mussolini, who had travelled to Egypt to preside over its inauguration in 1938. The bold declaration carved into its façade in Italian reads:

> IN THIS HOUSE OF ITALY BUILT ON THE FAITH AND LOVE OF THE HOMELAND THE MILLENARY ESSENCE OF THE COUNTRY THE CULT OF DANTE LIVES ON WITH THE WORK OF ITALIAN INSTITUTIONS THE SHINING TRADITION OF

THE TRIPLE VICTORY UNDER THE GLORIOUS
SHIELD OF SABAVDO
IS THE ANIMATING POWER OF ROME ONCE
AGAIN AT THE HEART OF AN EMPIRE XXVIII
OCTOBER MCMXXXVIII – XVI REIGNING
VITTORIO EMANUELE III
LEADER OF FASCISM AND HEAD OF THE
GOVERNMENT BENITO MUSSOLINI
FOUNDER OF THE EMPIRE

Benito Mussolini, a socialist turned fascist, became Italy's youngest ever prime minister in October 1922 after marching on Rome with 30,000 supporters. King Victor Emmanuel II, fearing civil war, sacked the incumbent liberal prime minister, Luigi Facta, and caved into Mussolini's demand to seize power. Within a decade Mussolini was ensconced as dictator and had launched an ambitious bid to rekindle the Roman Empire, starting in North and East Africa. Having invaded Libya, Ethiopia, Eritrea and Somalia, the Italian dictator had Egypt in his sights. He declared his intention to reclaim overseas Italians, to 'Italianise' them and use them as an overseas spearhead of a new imperial Rome. In doing so, he tugged at the feelings of the Italians in Egypt, by then the country's second-largest foreign community.

Many of these Italians were outwardly loyal to their homeland; even the majority who had been born in Egypt and who rarely ventured to Europe had close ties with the Italian state, either through consulates, community associations or schools. For the basis of those mechanisms of extraterritoriality, the Capitulations of the Ottoman era, was foreign citizenship, no matter where you were born or how long you had lived under Ottoman rule. Compounding this tug of loyalty was the fact, as the Levantine writer Anouchka Lazarev points out, that the Italians had begun to feel like second-class citizens in British-controlled Egypt. The Italian elite might have 'nibbled pistachios and sampled the vol-au-vents along with other Levantine notables', she writes, 'but they were still part of a national community of Italians' – a sizeable one at that.

The significance of foreign nationality for the Levantine community, once a convenient way to evade legal action in their adopted homelands, altered after the First World War. States like Italy and Greece began demanding a greater degree of fealty from their overseas citizens as ideological polarisation and political mobilisation intensified at home. In Greece, the struggle between royalists and the fiercely liberal prime minister, Eleftherios Venizelos, and the subsequent invasion of Anatolia in 1919 galvanised Greeks of the Levant who had been, until then, rather remote from their homeland. This was especially the case after the Greek army's defeat at the hands of the Ottoman Turks in 1922, when the majority of Anatolian Greeks were forced into exile. In the Ottoman Empire's death throes, confronted by aggressive European intrusion, the rising Turkish nationalist movement inspired hatred against Christian Greeks and Armenians. The resulting killing of perhaps a million or more of them in 1915 greatly inflamed Greek nationalist sentiment.

After the 1920s, news from Europe was carried more effectively by radio broadcasts and newspapers fed by telegraphed wire reports, which helped create more awareness of global events. In Italy the rise of fascism and revival of imperial Roman ambitions, and for Jews the growth of Zionist consciousness, contributed to what the Alexandrian Greek Ilios Yannakakis describes as a process whereby 'community identity gave way to one of nationality, surreptitiously modifying the relationship between foreign nationals and their homeland.' Quite simply, after almost a century as a community detached from Europe and grounded in an oriental setting, Levantine society became affected by Europe and its volatile discontents. It wasn't all jingoistic hot air. Mussolini's fascists set up active programmes for the Italian community in Egypt: they built sports clubs and old people's homes, and organised excursions to their newly colonised settlements in Libya and Somalia.

As Levantines of European descent were being drawn closer to their countries of origin and in the process divided, so Egyptians were becoming more aware of their own national consciousness. A movement for independence from increasingly effective British rule grew after the end of the First World War and the collapse of the Ottoman Empire. The nationalist Wafd Party, led by the lawyer turned nationalist leader Saad Zaghloul, helped lift the veil of Britain's so-called protectorate and exposed it for what it was: colonial domination. Egyptians were no longer notionally part of the Ottoman domain but, as Lord Cromer put it, a 'subject people' of the British Empire. The straw that broke the camel's back, so to speak, was the Convention of Montreux, which in 1937 abolished the Ottoman-era Capitulations, meaning that all foreigners were required to abide by Egyptian law.

Egyptian nationalists resented the protection that had been given to foreigners by the Capitulations, which were often used to evade taxation and cover up criminal activity.[1] And although those medieval Ottoman devices of extra-territoriality might have been useful to protect the foreign community a century earlier, when it was helping to build and run modern Egypt, the reality by the 1930s was that foreigners were too numerous, and too privileged. The protection granted under the Capitulations that most irked the Egyptians was the one preventing their government from imposing direct taxes upon foreigners without the consent of all the relevant powers. The security of the Levantine community was threatened further when, in February 1922, the British government was forced to recognise Egypt's independence in a bid to appease the nationalists and calm the situation.

The declaration was carefully negotiated by Britain's High Commissioner to Egypt, Lord Allenby – the same Allenby who had marched into Jerusalem in 1917 with his promises of protection. As with his foolish decision to partition the Old City, the 1922 declaration included a clause that fundamentally undermined the independence of the Levantine community and – again – helped deepen the divide between them and Egyptian society. It stated that the 'protection of foreign interests in Egypt and the protection of minorities' was a matter 'reserved to the discretion of the British Government'.

Allenby had no choice but to end the 'veiled protectorate' that had been in place since 1882. The pressure from nationalists was intense and, after a popular uprising sparked in 1919 by the arrest and exile of Saad Zaghloul, there was a menacing increase in violence against the British. Even after notional independence was granted in 1922, nationalist-inspired strikes and demonstrations grew in frequency throughout the 1930s, disrupting commerce and education. Protection of foreigners was deemed one of the 'reserved subjects' that Allenby felt was important for the security of the empire, particularly the canal. His fawning biographer, Viscount Wavell, wrote with the arrogant flourish of many biographers of the late imperial age that, after forty years of 'moral predominance' in Egypt, Allenby expected that Britain's views, and therefore interests, would have a 'penetrating influence'. This was a delusion, typical of a liberal mind trapped in what it believed to be the logic of imperial rule.[2] Accordingly, with their resentment of British domination, if not direct rule, Egyptians started to see the Ottoman-era Capitulations as directly benefiting the imperial European powers, rather than those detached Europeans and Levantines whom the legal status protected.

The loss of extra-territorial protection after 1937 set Italians in Egypt adrift and rendered them susceptible to nationalist impulses, even if, given the rather fluid notion of belonging characteristic of Levantine society, their flag-waving may have been motivated by convenience rather than conviction. It was some time before they realised that the world they had lived in so comfortably for almost a century had vanished.

My mother was twelve in the scorching-hot summer of 1942 as Rommel's forces advanced towards the Egyptian border after the fall of Tobruk. The family was divided. Her father, Richard Mumford, was working for the British Air Ministry in Cairo, and as the German army made progress in July and the British Eighth Army fell back, he was issued with a British army uniform and told to be ready to evacuate by railway across the Suez Canal to Palestine. Special trains were laid on, and many British residents began to install themselves in Palestine, boarding the train at Kantara East. There was by then a shortage of basic goods and commodities such as flour and fuel in Cairo. The British were accused of hoarding supplies for military use, which generated even more resentment, spurring angry crowds to the streets shouting, 'Forward Rommel!' and 'Long Live Rommel!' Anti-aircraft guns and searchlights raked the night sky in anticipation of the occasional German air raid. At one point the British Embassy started burning documents and its ambassador urged King Farouk and his court to make plans to decamp to Khartoum.

My mother's cousin, Giorgio Eberle, then five years old, remembers the enforced blackouts: 'In our apartment selected electric bulbs were coated with a transparent blue film and . . . wooden shutters were covered with dark-blue packing paper held closed with drawing pins. One had to let sunlight enter rooms during the day and avoid electric light leaking out at night. It was quite a job. Guards would whistle from the street if one did not comply.'

For my mother's other Italian cousins, the situation was rather different. Despite being Jews, they were pro-Mussolini fascists: 'They shipped their wives and children to Italy in the firm belief that the theatre of war in the Middle East would engulf Cairo as the Germans advanced towards victory . . . As indeed did many Egyptians,' my mother recalled. The plan was to call them back once Mussolini had galloped across the desert to victory. My mother described members of her family as patriotic Italians and fervent monarchists, partially explaining the segue to Mussolini and fascism. In mid-1942 it seemed that the Italian and German armies would win and, besides, it was only after June 1942 that news started to seep out – initially from a Warsaw newspaper – of Hitler's genocide of the Jews.

Even if my mother's Jewish Italian family were blinded by the imperial grandeur – and therefore to the dangers – of Mussolini's Italy, they were not immune to the general sense of insecurity that gripped Egypt at this time. Giorgio Eberle relates that 'as far as possible, many Italians resorted to remedies, turning to trusted friends of another nationality. The most valuable objects were mostly hidden, as was the car, radio, furniture.' There was a collective atmosphere of ambivalence; everyone was fearful of the disruption invasion would bring, but at the same time they were ready to welcome the invaders. The divide between the Levantine community and Egyptians was further deepened by the arrival of so many Allied troops, who bulked up the European presence. 'The Strangers in the land wore khaki, steel gray, blue and tan,' wrote John Rogers Shuman, an American teaching English at the American University. 'Their eyes were clear – the blue of iris, the brown of goldenrod, the gray of rocks; many Egyptian eyes were diseased with trachoma, or squinted, were red-lidded or simply shrivelled.'

Surrounded by a throng of Italians, Richard Mumford had reason to worry: as Tobruk fell it hardly looked as if the British army would prevail. And, living as they were in leafy Heliopolis, which was where the majority of British troops were billeted in several large camps, the family could hardly expect to remain unscathed: German air raids had started targeting the camps.

'Expecting the worst,' my mother recalled, '[my father] persuaded my mother to take us children to El-Wedy [to the Sornaga factory] for the duration of the crisis, thinking we would be safe there because my uncle [Samuele Sornaga, the founder] knew some Egyptians in high places he could depend on to protect us.' Many of King Farouk's inner circle and close advisors were in fact Italian Jews. And so my mother and her two siblings, together with my grandmother, decamped to El-Wedy, where fascist members of the family had managed to evade internment because Sornaga's brick and ceramic tile production had been deemed vital to the war effort. My mother's cousins, Guido and Paulo, were key engineers. And there was Mario the accountant.

Giorgio Eberle's family was less fortunate: 'Like all Italians aged between sixteen and sixty-five, my father was a civilian interned, first in the Italian schools of Bulacco and then in some fields [former rice paddies] of Embabeh, next to the Nile, which were very humid. The housing was in military tents with four or six camp beds.' The Italians were generally treated well, though, and as Giorgio recalls, it seemed 'just a bother':

> The guards were not cruel, they observed the rules and were aware they were dealing with civilians who deserved respect. This does not mean relations were not tense at times. Interned people could get visits from a family member around once a month. I remember visiting my father and his tent mates. They could receive and send mail subject to censorship and engage in a number of social activities and artisanal hobbies. Life must have been a torture for jealous guys with a pretty wife in town, particularly if there had been rumours concerning her. I was told a story of someone who tried to escape from the camp to verify one such rumour but who was 'gently' shot in the arm. It was certainly harder for women staying back in Cairo and Alexandria having to care for themselves and the rest of the family, dealing with local authorities, problems of food rations, subsidies received through the Swiss Consulate or the Red Cross, children's education.

At the factory, the situation was bizarre. 'So there we all were,' my mother wrote in her brief personal recollection, 'my mother, aunts and cousins all glued to the radio listening to the latest bulletins to follow the progress of the war. In the evening after dinner the men sat at the piano singing patriotic fascist songs like the popular ditty 'Faccetta nera bell'Abissina':

> Little black face, beautiful Abyssinia,
> Wait and hope,
> Because the hour is drawing near
> When we shall be near you.
> We shall give you a different law
> And a differing king!

As the Germans advanced, the priorities and loyalties of the Levantine elite started to realign like iron filings near a magnet. Egyptians, who had no love for the British, started learning German and preparing portraits of Adolf Hitler fringed with red, white and black bunting to welcome Rommel's triumphant arrival. Allegedly, the Egyptian government drafted a letter to Rommel stating that Egypt's sympathies lay with the Axis powers and that only circumstances were forcing Egyptians to work with the British. Rumours, probably seeded by German spies, suggested the British were planning to assassinate King Farouk and that he would seek refuge with Rommel's army. 'Strangely enough,' my father wrote in his *Modern History of Egypt*, 'the public was both terrified at the possible coming of the Axis occupation, and at the same time pro-Axis in their sympathies.'

As the Germans continued their advance, some of my mother's relatives boasted of the property they would take over once the troops arrived. In fact, the Germans were in contact with the Egyptian government as their army neared Alexandria, and asked for help identifying the residences of prominent Jews, promising that Jewish property would be theirs for the picking once they – the Germans – were in charge. Some sympathisers even took to emulating *Il Duce*'s infamous black shirts, and dressing accordingly. British intelligence discovered detailed preparations within Italian circles in Alexandria for a post-war government of Italian-occupied Egypt as early as 1940; meanwhile, the British tried to maintain an aura of calm, describing the situation in a characteristic understatement as 'a flap'.

There was indeed an air of unreality about life in Cairo – both the sad delusions of some Italian Jews about what an Axis occupation would mean for them, and a remarkable obliviousness on the part of the British. Rommel was within striking distance of Alexandria, yet the belly-dancing dens, the night clubs, Groppi's and the long bar at Shepheard's Hotel were full every night. Literature and writing from the period conveys a sense of fun and foppery, at least for the British, who careened between the possibility of death at the hands of Panzers in the desert and a cold beer in Alex, as Alexandria was fondly known. As Noël Coward noted with typically biting wit in his *Middle East Diary*: 'The place is the last refuge of the *soi disant* "international set". All the fripperies of pre-war luxury living are still in existence here; rich people, idle people, cocktail parties, dinner parties, jewels and evening dress. Rolls Royces come purring up to the entrance steps.'

Yet behind the façade of 'gaiety and glitter', as the novelist Olivia Manning described Cairo during the war years, the situation was precarious. The 'veiled protectorate' imposed by Lord Cromer after the 1882 invasion had become formalised with the onset of the First World War in 1914 and the need to secure the Suez Canal. After reluctantly granting independence to Egypt in 1922, British officials continued to exercise control over the country's bureaucracy and resources. The Anglo-Egyptian Treaty, signed in 1936 as Mussolini was invading Abyssinia, aimed to buttress the country's independence, but the canal remained under British control, as the treaty granted the right for British troops to be stationed there.

The royal court under King Fuad, and later his foppish son King Farouk, was decidedly anti-British. Farouk's retainers and confidants were in fact mostly Levantine – Italians and Greeks – and it was suspected that as Rommel advanced, Farouk was establishing contacts with the Axis powers through his Italian circle. Hitler went so far as to gift the king a Mercedes roadster convertible. The British ambassador, Sir Miles Lampson, described Farouk as 'a rotter . . . that if things go badly with us will be liable to stab us in the back'. By all accounts the feeling was mutual; and after Lampson's attempt in February 1942 to force Farouk into appointing a prime minister friendly to the Allies or else abdicate by surrounding his palace with British troops and tanks, the king made every effort to shun or insult his erstwhile nemesis.

The Anglo-Egyptian Treaty committed Egypt to supporting British troops along the Suez Canal. This enraged the nationalists, and despite the British army's efforts to defend the country from invasion, their presence was, in fact, regarded as one. In 1942 close to 750,000 Allied forces were stationed in Egypt. My mother remembers the knobby-kneed British and Commonwealth troops, sweating as they arrived on troopships, who were assigned billets in Cairo. The scramble to prepare for retreat and exodus revealed to the British more than they had ever cared to know about the country they had occupied for half a century, paying little heed to the plight of its ordinary citizens. The poverty and squalor of the environment – from which they had allowed themselves to be fenced off in the lush grounds of the Gezira Club, where they sipped gin slings and held perpetual summer fetes – now became apparent. Egyptians, sick of the British and ready for a regime change, prepared enthusiastically for German victory and put up signs to welcome the Nazi army. Lawrence Durrell described Alexandria at the time in the opening pages of his famous *Alexandria Quartet* as 'the incubation of human misery of such proportions one is aghast, and all one's feelings overflow into disgust and terror'. Egyptians were seething with anger and resentment. Keen outside observers, such as John Rogers Shuman, noticed their shoulder-shrugging: 'the impression they gave of patiently waiting for the event to be over and the strangers to be gone. They refused to assume any share of the responsibility, and because they were uninterested, and because they closed their eyes and spat, their indifference was monumental.'

Levantine families who could count two or more generations born and raised in Egypt were at best ambivalent about the British presence. Egypt was their country as well, and they were susceptible to Axis propaganda that painted the British and French as colonisers whom the advancing Italian and German armies would defeat, and with the implication – however evidently false in hindsight – that liberation was at hand. So while the Italians and Greeks diverged somewhat on which side they backed, especially after the Nazi invasion of Greece in 1941, they were nonetheless unified by the fact that Egypt was home, and not the beastly, hot inconvenience that the British author Artemis Cooper, paraphrasing Olivia Manning and Lawrence Durrell, described as 'the physical sensation of enervated liverishness, brought on by heat, which makes everything seem tawdry and insubstantial'.

The Italians, on the other hand, were delusional about fascist Italy, which was distant and therefore never quite seen in anything other than idealistic terms. Many Italians were profoundly nationalistic, given that their forebears had been pioneers and victims of the struggle for unified nationhood. As Black Americans in Harlem and Jamaicans in the West Indies signed up to defend Ethiopia as the last African country to be colonised, Italians in Egypt cheered on *Il Duce*, as Mussolini styled himself. They underestimated the feelings of their Egyptian friends and neighbours, who viewed Italy's colonial adventure in Africa as no better than the British. In the face of all this, the British tried to win the Italians over. The renowned travel writer Peter Fleming, brother of Ian and then working for British intelligence in Cairo, was part of an effort to propagate anti-fascist sentiment among interned Italians and turn them into Allied sympathisers. The operation, known by the codename 'Yak Mission', failed. Whose bright idea was it to try and turn a group of people interned at the hands of British authority? At the same time, my mother's Jewish Italian family seemed to have either missed or misunderstood the implications of Mussolini's Racial Laws, implemented after 1938, which restricted the rights and freedoms of Jews in Italy. This misunderstanding wasn't just foolish; it also had tragic consequences for the Sornagas.

One of a number of my mother's relatives who opted to return to Italy as the war closed in on Egypt was Alda, her second cousin. Once, as a very young boy, I met Alda's sister, Bianca, in London and have memories of a pretty but heavily powdered face framed by white curly hair and lips painted deep red. Alda married a man called Aldo Lusena, who was nine years her senior. Aldo was from Florence, where he ran a successful wholesale fabric business. In 1941, soon after the birth of their daughter, Bianca-Maria, he moved the family 'home'. Moderately prosperous, they lived in a property on the Via degli Artisti, not far from the Canto de'Nelli, near many of today's tourist attractions. Mussolini's fascism weighed less heavily on them, with its less pronounced stress on anti-Semitism; many of Alda's relatives in Egypt were in fact pro-fascist, despite being Jews. Their security was short-lived. German troops occupied Florence in 1943 and by September the advancing Allies bombed the city and killed more than 200 civilians. Fearing for their safety, the Lusenas moved to the city's south-eastern outskirts, living on the Via Belisario Vinta. Soon, it wasn't just the bombing the Lusenas were afraid of. The Germans, aided by fascist supporters, began rounding up Jews for deportation. To escape the dragnet the Lusenas moved further out to the village of Bibbiena, where they lodged in a small hotel. Sometime late in 1943, with the help of a man called Giuseppe Ferroni, a travelling salesman Aldo knew, the family ended up in an even more remote village called Biforco, in the upper Casentino area east of Florence. 'They met a profiteer,' wrote Enzo Gradassi, author of the book *Sesto senso* (*Sixth Sense*), which tells their tragic story. Gradassi, a native of the region, argued that Ferroni 'had an interest in getting his hands on the fortune of the family and, little by little, instilled in Aldo's mind the idea that the Germans had found them and were about to come and get them'.

One can only imagine the state of fear Aldo and Alda lived in by late 1943. In all, some 8,000 Italian Jews had died by then at the hands of the Germans, and almost 250 had been deported from Florence before the city was liberated by New Zealand troops in mid-1944.

And as much as the historical record shows that many Italians helped shelter persecuted Jews, there were also those willing to extort money from them, or who sympathised with the fascist regime's anti-Semitic agenda.

Aldo and Alda Lusena and baby Bianca-Maria

The fate of the Lusenas still haunts the village of Biforco. For it was here, sometime during the night of 17 December 1943 or in the early hours of the next morning, on the second-floor room of a medieval village house, that the couple smothered little Bianca-Maria with a cushion and slit their wrists with a razor blade, dying in a pool of blood as they lay on the bed beside their suffocated daughter. According to *Fuochi sui Monti dell'Appennino Toscanini*, a local newspaper that in 1957 published a report on the story more than a decade after their suicide: 'their persecutions continued in the most beastly and inhuman way to the point of reducing this honest and innocent family to despair.'

Aldo's sister, Ida, later investigated their deaths, and discovered that a man called Ferroni from Casentino opened a fabric shop with the same material the Lusenas had brought from Florence. 'Everyone in the village called that "the workshop of the Jew", she was told, even though there were no Jewish businesses inside it. But everyone knew where the goods that were being sold came from.' The three Ferroni brothers were eventually jailed for several years and fined for extortion. I never heard my mother speak of this tragedy, though she did tell me that some of her cousins – even after settling in Italy long after the war – continued to espouse right-wing views.

*

Egypt came within a whisker of occupation by the invading Axis armies. At one point in mid-1942 German forces were just a few hours' drive from Alexandria. There were fears that Rommel would direct his tanks straight past the city to reach the Nile, cutting off the substantial European community from Cairo and leaving Alex to the mercies of an occupying army. The trunk road and the train through the Nile Delta were a lifeline.

Alexandria was, as in Lawrence Durrell's famous novels *Justine*, *Balthazar*, *Mountolive* and *Clea*, a city of triangular relationships: between the many Greeks and Italians and other Levantines who had settled there for more than a century; the British 'occupiers'; and the patient Egyptians who had seen conquerors come and go and who now awaited another wave, mostly worrying about what this would mean for relations between Copts and Muslims. Durrell, in the opening pages of *Justine*, described 'a thousand dust-tormented streets' inhabited by 'five races, five languages, a dozen creeds'. Durrell, who lived in the city from 1942 to 1945, served as British press attaché.

Even though my family lived in Cairo, they travelled frequently to Alexandria for weekend breaks by the sea. To imbibe some of this atmosphere, I decided to take the train to Alexandria, which leaves from Cairo's main railway station in Ramses Square. There I joined the relentless human press streaming in and out of the neo-Moorish station built at the end of the nineteenth century. The original site was the terminus for the first railway line in Africa, between Alexandria and Cairo, finished in 1851. Around me people squinted in the sunlight with furrowed brows and perspiring faces, leaning forward at a slight angle, pulling or pushing their loads on their silent, urgent journeys. I joined them and made the transition from bright sunlight to the dimly lit interior clutching my printed e-ticket.

The modern-looking train left the dung-brown urban smear of Cairo surprisingly quickly and plunged into the delta, where in sharp contrast green fields of maize and other vegetables were punctuated by rectangular dwellings of four or five storeys built like Lego of rough concrete frames filled in with crude red bricks, finished – as much as they could be – with often very small, frameless windows, many of which lacked glass or even shutters, making do instead with thin curtains. Piles of rubbish were heaped at the foundations of these dwellings, the pathways between them strewn with the carcasses of cars. There seemed little relationship between the fecundity of the surrounding land and the poverty of its inhabitants. We stopped at Tanta, passing through a causeway of rickety apartment buildings, where laundry hanging out of glassless windows almost brushed the dusty windows of the train as it passed. We then trundled on through Kafr el-Zayat, the town my great-great grandfather Samuele Sornaga settled in to establish his cotton-ginning business, and at this point the train crossed the Nile on a steel-girder bridge, where Said Pasha's heir had tumbled into the river to his death, bringing Ismail Pasha to the khedival throne.

Water is the eternal blessing provided to Egypt by the Nile, and it was hard to believe the desert lay just a few minutes' drive away in either direction. The well-tended fields were bursting with domesticated plant life arrayed in a kaleidoscope of greenery. Livestock, tethered under makeshift shelters, shared their space with clouds of flies. Plump white ibis feasted in the shade of billowing willow and eucalyptus trees lining the canal Ismail Pasha built to connect Alexandria to the Nile in the mid-nineteenth century. Today, while much of the land is planted with rice and maize, there is only the occasional field of cotton, formerly the source of the Sornaga family fortune.

The air-conditioned carriage was neat and relatively clean. My business-class seat reclined generously. Opposite me a young army cadet with eyes the size of small saucers munched on an egg sandwich his father had handed to him after seeing him off in Cairo with a double kiss to both cheeks. In 1942, the train would have been filled with young British army officers off to a weekend jaunt along the beaches.

After three hours we pulled into the magnificent Italianate railway station in Alexandria, resplendent with its Doric columns and twin clocks. I took a taxi to the Metropole Hotel, which faces the corniche to occupy one of the many 'palaces' built by the Greek merchant community at the turn of the century. These were mostly designed and constructed by Italians like my mother's great-uncle Luigi Piattoli, who – as mentioned in Chapter Three – built the Okelle Monferrato in central Alexandria's Place des Consuls. Today, inside the building, the central gallery reveals the extent of neglect: the lattice-glass roofing has all but gone; the stucco peels off the walls; the debris piles up on makeshift corrugated-iron sheets that provide shelter for the space below, which is occupied by a café filled with Egyptians languidly drinking tea and smoking shisha.

Alexandria is one of the oldest cities in the world, first established in the third century BC on a site already occupied by a pharaonic settlement. Bits of this rich Greco-Roman heritage are preserved in a museum housed in the basement of the modern library built on the site of Alexander the Great's original, which Julius Caesar may have inadvertently burned when he took the city in 47 BC. For centuries Alexandria slumbered under Mamluk and later Ottoman rule until the early nineteenth century, when Muhammad Ali built his palace adjoining a Mamluk-era citadel erected on the site of the great lighthouse that was destroyed in an earthquake in the thirteenth century. Outside the monstrosity that is the recreated great library, I reflected on the audacity of the city's existence – from ancient Greeks to Romans and Tuscan outcasts, drawing on a rich cultural palette to create a dazzling waterfront landscape on the edge of the desert.

Walking through the centre of Alexandria is to experience two dimensions of urban morphology. At street level, shops and stalls selling mostly cheap shoes, clothes and appliances cram every available space. But one level up a glorious architectural past unfolds: elegant balustrades embrace arched windows in a variety of classical shapes and forms, ranging from extravagant Venetian curves to the chiselled rectangular of early Bauhaus. It was in these streets, eerily dark and empty after the imposition of a curfew in July 1942, that Lawrence Durrell strolled, noting the names of shops that had put up signs welcoming the invading German army – expected at any moment.

In those feverish, fearful summer and autumn months, before the German advance was finally stopped at El-Alamein in November, the British tried their best to act calmly and continue their lives as normal, in so far as they did lead normal lives. 'The English do become odd here,' remarks a character standing up the bar at the city's plush Cecil Hotel in Olivia Manning's evocative description of the period: 'Ordinary couples who'd remain happily together in Ealing or Pinner, here take on a different character. They link themselves to Don Juans or tragedy queens, and throw fits of wild passion and make scenes in public.' And in Manning's *Danger Tree*, the first part of her Levant trilogy, she captures the atmosphere in Alexandria as the Germans advanced:

> The moon was pushing up between the sea and sky, throwing a long channel of light across the water. The promenade was spectral grey in the moon glimmer. Not a soul, it seemed, had come out to enjoy the cool of evening, but when they pushed through the heavy curtains into Pastroudi's, they found the restaurant crowded, noisy and brilliantly lit. The Alexandrians were eating while there was still something to eat. Uncertainty and fear raised the tempo of chatter into an uproar.

As I pounded the pavements of the famous Rue Fuad, the ancient 'canopic way' that runs east to west, I found the skeletal remains of this period. The tramline that used to convey Alexandrians in their profuse diversity from their marble-lobbied apartments to the sandy beaches of Ramleh and Sidi Bishr. Many of the cafés that line the corniche declare their origins proudly, with dates at the start of the twentieth century. Here, in the cooling mid-September breeze blowing off the Mediterranean, Alexandrians sit drinking tea or coffee, an accompaniment to sticky cakes. The most popular chain, 'Brazilian Coffee', opened in 1929. The Santa Lucia Restaurant, with its ageing piano player banging out Henry Mancini tunes, and serving platefuls of chateaubriand on tables set with heavily starched linen, opened in 1932. The ancient iron-grilled lift in the Metropole was installed in 1906, its five greasy cables taking up to four people to the fifth-floor veranda, which offers a stunning vista of the corniche where unfolds, in the words of Alexandria's famous Greek poet, C.P. Cavafy, 'The morning sea and the cloudless sky a brilliant blue, the yellow shore: all beautiful and grand in the light.'

The city's heritage survives, but is poorly maintained – in contrast to Havana in Cuba, where, despite the anti-colonial revolution, the communist city authorities have meticulously preserved the historic centre of the city. Many of Alexandria's buildings will eventually collapse under the weight of neglect. At the main court, a remarkable example of *fin-de-siècle* grandeur, dishevelled lawyers in cheap suits and crumpled ties scurry in and out, ignoring lumps of plaster literally cascading off the building. When I tried to find the beautiful Italianate villa where Durrell wrote the first volume of the *Alexandria Quartet*, I learned it had been bulldozed three years ago. Yet here and there I saw bits of the city preserved with care: the grand, porticoed entrance to the Opera House is swept clean and the building, which Luigi Piattoli had a hand in designing, boasts a full programme. The façade of the nearby Catholic Cathedral of Saint Catherine's has been scrubbed and, within, the canvases Luigi Piattoli painted to decorate the altar and ceiling seemed to have aged well.

As for the cosmopolitan society so vividly sketched by Durrell, only sad traces survive – here and there a Greek or Italian name still graces a shopfront. At the Greek Club close to the university an old lady speaks to me in broken Greek, her face lined with sadness. At the little museum housed in the apartment where Cavafy lived, off the Prophet Daniel Street, the door is opened by an Egyptian called Muhammad who tries to engage me in Greek. It was as if they were trying to re-link a broken chain. Near the citadel, overlooking the marina, Ilyas – a Greek from Kalymnos – manages the Greek Club's popular seafood restaurant. Young Egyptian couples huddle over grilled fish and salad. The Zephyron Seafood Restaurant out in Aboukir Bay, where Lord Nelson defeated the French fleet in 1798, was run by Greeks when I enjoyed grilled fish and dry white wine there in the 1970s. Today it still serves marvellously fresh fish, but gone are the Greeks – and also the wine.

Despite this neglect, it is easy to see how Egypt has relished throwing off a past associated with the reckless extravagance of feudal royalty and the foreign domination that ensued. 'Our country has been plundered and looted. Its affairs are in the hands of weak fools,' declares a character in *Cairo Modern*, one of Naguib Mahfouz's early novels set in the 1930s. 'No matter how high we advance, it will always be less than we deserve.' With one in three Egyptians living in poverty today, this catharsis is hard to reconcile with what Egypt has failed to do with the gifts it was bequeathed.

The tide of the war in the desert slowly began to turn after August 1942. Rommel's supply lines were overextended and harried day and night by the Royal Air Force. His advance ground to a halt. Mussolini, fearing defeat, cancelled production of a commemorative medal that depicted him with the pyramids of Giza as a backdrop. General Bernard Montgomery, who assumed command of the British Eighth Army after August, insisted on a relentless push towards German lines and Rommel was eventually defeated at the Third Battle of El-Alamein in November 1942. American forces landed in North Africa the same month, and by January 1943 the Allied invasion of Italy was under way. By the end of 1943, the danger to Egypt posed by the Axis armies had passed. The flap of mid-1942 quickly became a distant memory as Cairo and Alexandria revved up as a rest-and-recuperation facility for Allied forces. 'There was plenty of booze and cheerful girls mostly in clubs,' Giorgio Eberle recalls. 'We used to get back home early in the evening to avoid problems.'

In the autumn of 1944, my father arrived in Egypt at the tender age of sixteen to begin his freshman year at the American University. He had travelled on the train from his home in Haifa all the way to Kantara East, and then on to Cairo from Kantara West. During the course of his three years' studying this became a regular journey – and one no longer possible today because of the security situation in the Sinai. He always travelled first-class, and always for free, on account of his father's position in Palestine Railways:

> Arriving from Haifa by train around midnight or just after, I used to be met by the local Medical Officer of the British Palestine Railways in Kantara, Dr Mebadda Bourdhosh, a Christian Arab of Polish origin married to a Greek. My father would ring him from Haifa that I was on the train. Year in and year out, there was the good doctor, with his beret Basque and an overcoat to guard against the chill of the desert night. He always carried a bag of peanuts. I used to take him into the dismal crowded buffet of the station. I hated the place yet was fascinated by it and its patrons. Most of them were not passengers, but local Berberies and other native railway workers and employees drinking black syrupy tea. I always had a brandy there. Then we'd cross on the ferry together to catch the Cairo train on the West Bank. Once on board the good doctor would bid me farewell and return to Kantara East.

By 1944 the war had ebbed away from the borders of Egypt, but this did not make living there any less exciting. For while the British had beaten the German and Italian armies, they had failed to quell the rising tide of nationalist sentiment. Egyptians, if anything, were more frustrated, angry and impatient. 'When the bugle sounded, and the last gun was fired,' wrote John Rogers Shuman, '[the British] would disappear in a cloud, disappear for some other field, and the moment would come soon, was coming, approaching, and must be reckoned with. Then all the angry young men would be left holding the bag.' Egyptians, especially in court circles and in the army, were still smarting with humiliation after the haughty British ambassador, Sir Miles Lampson, had ordered King Farouk's palace to be encircled by troops and armoured vehicles in February 1942. And despite the Allied victories, a feeling of impending crisis hung in the air. 'Those of us who had the slightest perceptiveness,' my father told an interviewer in 1973 during a visit to Cairo, 'could see that as far as the foreign communities were concerned in Egypt, the game was up for them.'

This impending sense of doom for the Levantine community was reflected in the American University of Cairo's intake that year of 1944, which included a large contingent of Greeks, many of them from Palestine, like my father. Many other Greeks came from the canal zone. Most of the European students were residents of Egypt, schooled in foreign institutions like the English school in Heliopolis, where my mother had been a pupil, or the French Lycée, or the Armenian school. Although well-off Egyptians sent their children to these schools, where they sat in classrooms and played with the children of Levantines, there was a pronounced social divide that limited this mixing. Dating and marriage were frowned upon across religious lines and so the older they got, the less they mixed. The Levantines of these later years mostly had a poor grasp of Arabic, and Egyptian universities were not an option; nor could they, in 1944, easily travel to Europe or elsewhere overseas.

The writing was on the wall for my father's generation. As my father put it: 'the accident of the Second World War forced people to be purposeful – they had to go do something and get out.' While the British officers wearing khaki shorts and breezy smiles relaxed and basked in victory by the Gezira racetrack, or downed gin slings on the terrace of Shepheard's Hotel, the great Levantine community upon which so much of Egypt's infrastructure and industry was built were conscious of the angry scowls of their Egyptian friends, and of the palpable rumours of violent revolt. This, then, was the moment when the whole process that had begun with the arrival of my great-great-grandparents in the late nineteenth century went vigorously into reverse.

Yet even if the coffee grounds foretold a bleak future, there was much life to be enjoyed, still, in Cairo. My mother, then a teenager, 'tangoed in night clubs to live orchestras under the stars, went to late-night parties, drank too much whisky, smoked Player's Navy Cut, flirted and played at being in love'. Things a teenage girl from a well-to-do background did in those days. 'We picnicked at the desert, stared in wonder at the stars, entered the dark bowels of the pyramids and the cool elegance of the Mena House Hotel.'

My father, however, was poor. I have seen correspondence with the university assuring my grandfather that, despite the shortage of funds, my father would not be sent home; they recognised that he was a gifted student. He claims to have lived on no more than three Egyptian pounds a month, and made extra money by writing essays for less able students and by working as an usher for the university's magnificent Ewart Hall, where he was fortunate to see a performance by Édith Piaf. He enjoyed what male undergraduates all over the world enjoyed: going out drinking with friends and looking for love. It was on one such outing, with a young American student, that he experienced another taste of the violence that would from now on punctuate the Middle East with depressing regularity.

The night of 6 May 1947 was the anniversary of King Farouk's accession to the throne. To mark the occasion, lights were strung along the bridges crossing the Nile. My father was seeing a young American sophomore student called Ann Sprague, a niece of the American University administrator Charlie Howard's wife, Muriel. She hailed from Sandy Creek on the shores of Lake Ontario in upstate New York and was spending a year abroad. Ann had asked my father to show her the lights. 'The Nile was magnificent that night,' he remembered in an interview he gave for the American University archive in 1973.

My father was then living in a cheap pension run by an Italian just adjacent to the Metro Cinema on Soliman Pasha Street, now Talaat Harb. Built in 1939, the Metro was an art deco monument to the glory days of Hollywood's MGM franchise. Naturally it was designed by local Italian architects, and was the first air-conditioned cinema in Cairo. Its opening-night film had been *Gone with the Wind*. My father's room-mate, a fellow Greek called George Illiades, was also dating an American – the daughter of a US navy captain. George asked my father if he and Ann wanted to join him and his girlfriend that evening at the Metro. 'I said, all right, get me two tickets.'

The only seats available were in the gods, the upper balcony of the lavishly decorated interiors. The film that evening was a B Western titled *Bad Bascomb*, starring Wallace Beery and Margaret O'Brien. Its producer was Orville O. Dull. Bad and dull is exactly how my father described the movie. He didn't have to suffer very long. Eight minutes into the film, a bomb exploded beneath the more expensive seats at the front:

> Fortunately, we were upstairs in the balcony. The chandeliers started falling. I was wearing a pair of blue slacks, which turned white with all the plaster. My eyeglasses disappeared completely. Fortunately, they were blown forward to smithereens. In those days no one could leave the cinema before a performance ended. Because of security regulations, you had to leave a passport and identity card. We went through the shattered glass doors, which were still locked. I took Ann out. She didn't know what had happened; never heard a bomb in her life in Sandy Creek. When she saw the bodies being carted away by ambulances, she fainted on me. The Brazilian Coffee store across the street was a magnificent place in those days. I bought her a brandy. She came to. George and this other girl were looking for us, and then I said I must take you back to Maa'di. She says, no, you don't have to. We'll go see the lights because Charlie, Uncle Charlie Howard that is, didn't know. She hadn't told him we were going to the cinema. It turned out Howard had been looking for us in every police station and every hospital in town.

The Muslim Brotherhood were held responsible. Apparently the American-owned cinema was targeted to protest against America's support for the partition of Palestine, which occurred subsequently, on 1 September. Then, as today, the Brotherhood, which was established in Egypt in the 1920s, was a spearhead of opposition.

Although later completely destroyed by a fire in 1952, the Metro was rebuilt and still stands. When I strolled past it one afternoon in September 2019, Cairo was on edge because of anti-government demonstrations. Police patrolled the streets and the *Mukhabarat*, dressed in their finest ostentatious casual, were everywhere. The streets were mostly empty in the centre of the city. People were warned to stay indoors. Columns of armoured cars patrolled the main thoroughfares. I felt a compelling symmetry about the time and place.

The last two years of my father's time at the American University were eventful, as Egypt continued to be rocked by nationalist agitation. Cairo experienced regular bomb attacks and massive demonstrations that carried heavy overtones of anti-foreign sentiment. My mother's uncle, Samuele Sornaga, grew sick with worry about the business he had built and succumbed to a stroke in 1951. Her father, Richard, and her brother, John, left for England in 1947 – booking passage on the HMT *Empire Windrush*, the same ship that famously brought the first group of immigrants to England from the Caribbean in 1948. Advancing illness and unemployment after the war forced Richard to leave his wife Lidia and his two daughters in Cairo. They were not exactly deprived or destitute: the Sornaga family enterprise looked after everyone. All the same, at sixteen my mother left school and found a job with the British Council after taking a shorthand and typing course. While employed at the Council she met my father at a party organised by the Arts Committee at the American University.

Metro Cinema in Cairo today

'By now the British had moved out of Egypt and those who remained for reason of their work were made to feel very unwelcome,' she remembers. 'Many Europeans sensed the changing political climate, the rise of nationalism, the increasing corruption of the monarchy and the wealthy ruling class, and the subsequent resentment of the oppressed poor. Those who could returned to Europe.'

The grand passage of Egypt from medieval backwater to strategic crossroads guided by enlightened foreign rulers schooled in the louche opportunistic politics of the Ottoman divan had lasted a century. It was over.

A year or so after the Metro Cinema bombing, my father was sitting in an English literature class. The professor was reciting William Wordsworth's poem 'The World Is Too Much with Us' when two rocks came flying through the window, thrown by angry demonstrators. Outside people were screaming: 'Help us; give us water.' Some had been killed. The professor, whose name was Morris, was, as it happened, partially deaf and continued reading. Wordsworth composed the poem in 1802 as a critique of the changing industrial world:

The world is too much with us; late and soon,
Getting and spending, we lay waste our powers;—
Little we see in Nature that is ours;
We have given our hearts away, a sordid boon!
This Sea that bares her bosom to the moon;
The winds that will be howling at all hours,
And are up-gathered now like sleeping flowers;
For this, for everything, we are out of tune;
It moves us not. Great God! I'd rather be
A Pagan suckled in a creed outworn;
So might I, standing on this pleasant lea,
Have glimpses that would make me less forlorn;
Have sight of Proteus rising from the sea;
Or hear old Triton blow his wreathèd horn.

CHAPTER TEN

End of Days in Palestine

> 'The Jew murders the Arab and the Arab murders the Jew. This is what is going on in Palestine now and it will go on for the next fifty years in all probability.'
>
> Field Marshal Bernard Montgomery, 1946

My grandfather Jerasimous told a story that when the Israeli army forced Palestinians in Haifa to flee across the Lebanese border after partition in 1947, two Palestinian Arab friends came to see him at Mosul Lane. They were carrying small travel bags. 'Come,' they told him, 'we're going to Beirut to sit out the trouble. We'll be away two weeks at the most.'

His friends were convinced that combined Arab forces would sweep into Palestine and rout the Israelis in a matter of days. My grandfather demurred, insisting that as a civil servant he was obliged to stay at his post. More than seventy years later, the descendants of my grandfather's friends are still for the most part sitting in Lebanon or other Arab states, having lost their homes and belongings.

As the threat of war with Germany loomed over Europe in 1939, the British worried that their brutal suppression of the 1936–39 Arab Revolt was storing up problems for them in Palestine; it was already obvious that their support for the Zionist cause and Jewish immigration had pushed many Arabs into the Axis camp. The British needed to secure Palestine and its majority-Arab population for the defence of Egypt, which commanded the Suez Canal, and Iraq with its vital oilfields. With little thought for the consequences, the British government sought a means to turn the tables on the Jews and, in February 1939, at a hastily organised conference, invited representatives of the Zionist Jewish and Arab communities to Saint James's Palace to discuss the future. The delegations attended, but refused to meet, thus preventing the conference from reaching a consensus. The government, led by Prime Minister Neville Chamberlain, nevertheless drew up a policy that stepped back from earlier promises of a separate Jewish state, imposed restrictions on Jewish immigration into Palestine, and protected Arab land from Jewish encroachment. It was hurried and contingent, both overestimating Arab sympathy towards Nazi Germany and underestimating the Jewish response, which was to promptly launch a revolt of their own against British rule in Palestine.

My father's family in Haifa had already endured three years of violent upheaval at the hands of Palestinian Arab agitators; now they faced the threat of violence at the hands of what the British started calling 'Jewish terrorists'. From the start of the Second World War in 1939 until the declaration of the State of Israel in 1948, Palestine was rocked by restive uncertainty, forcing the Vatikiotis family (and the wider Greek community) to make plans for their own security. They started by sending children overseas for education; ultimately, circumstances forced them to emigrate and disperse.

My father had glimpses of the troubled Mandate of Palestine during the long summer holidays he spent back home in between semesters:

> What was memorable about the outbreak of hostilities between the Arabs and the Jews, and the escalation of that violence the more the British distanced themselves from the conflict and prepared to depart from the scene, was the vociferous bravado of our Arab acquaintances, the talk of neighbours and the general assumption that the Jews did not stand a prayer against the more numerous Arabs, supported as they were by their fellow Arab neighbours. But one could not help noticing that it was mainly Arabs who were leaving Palestine; Jews, on the contrary, were coming in by every possible route and conveyance, and mainly illegally.

Most Greeks in Palestine, like my grandfather, were salaried employees of the British Mandate. They led a comfortable existence and had no stake in the struggle between Arab and Jew, yet their welfare was tied to the colonial administration that both Arabs and Jews were fighting to be rid of. Caught in the middle, they were understandably nervous. 'They did not involve themselves with either side of the conflict,' my father wrote. 'They remained cautiously aloof and circumspect.'

This sudden vulnerability underlines the fact that very few of the Greeks in Palestine had assimilated. By and large, they had migrated either to serve the Greek Church, as had my grandmother's family, the Meimarakis, or to make a living, like my great-grandfather Baba Yannis in Acre. My father was clear on this point: 'One commonly held myth about Greeks . . . held that Greeks, in contrast to all other foreign communities, assimilated easily and comfortably in the Arab environment. This was simply not so.'

If anything, he argued, the Greeks were very particular about creating their own exclusive cultural world, revolving around the Church and the school. Indeed, the Ottoman protection of the Greek Orthodox Church encouraged this. There were those Greeks, especially from Asia Minor, who had settled in an earlier period as Ottoman subjects and who embraced the notion of being common subjects of the more liberal new Ottomanism of the reform era. However, those who – like Baba Yannis – came trading on boats from the islands retained their Greek identity yet enjoyed Ottoman protection under the umbrella of the Greek Orthodox Church. There were always exceptions to the rule, with integration among Greeks who married into the Arab Orthodox community and became Arabised, eventually losing all trace of their identity, like George, the owner of the guest house where I stayed in Haifa.

The Second World War and the outbreak of hostilities between Arabs and Jews forced the Greek community to turn inwards. Just as with the Italians in Egypt, links to the mother country had strengthened during the inter-war period. Travel back to the home country to visit family relatives became easier. Many started to feel more Greek, not just in cultural or religious terms but also nationalistically. My father witnessed fierce arguments erupting at cafés in Haifa frequented by Greeks over Greek politics. Such feelings intensified with the Axis occupation of Greece in 1941, when a steady stream of refugees found their way to Palestine during this time, carrying news from 'home'.[1] The Greek army encouraged its citizens living in Palestine to sign up for service against the invading Germans. The Greek king, George II, even visited Palestine to drum up loyalty, and a handful of Greek army units were subsequently stationed there. A newsreel from 1942 shows the king standing beside the Greek patriarch, the pair of them inspecting Greek military units in front of a throng of local Greeks wearing traditional costume, waving their blue-and-white Greek national flags alongside the Union Jack. This stirring of patriotic spirit among the Palestinian Greek community – of belonging to a country many if not most had never seen – was perhaps just as well, given what was about to happen.

Yet for all this cultural pride and aloofness, young Palestine-born Greeks like my father Panayiotis actually felt closer to the Arab community than to the Jews. They had grown up speaking Arabic, they had Arab friends at the Christian schools they attended, and in church they rubbed shoulders with Arab Orthodox members of the congregation. Jews began to appear in larger numbers only in the 1930s, and tended to erect exclusive Jewish quarters, towns and settlements – the kibbutzim – throughout the country. And so, while caught in the middle, many Greeks tended to have more understanding of and therefore sympathy for the Arab cause.

'It may be safely and accurately asserted,' my father wrote in 1980, 'that the Greeks tended to observe the protest strikes called by the Arabs during the 1936–39 rebellion, and that their private sympathies, if they had any, were weighted on the Arab side.' I felt this palpably with members of my extended family in Greece, who all spoke Arabic to varying degrees of fluency and had relatives married into Arab families dispersed across the Middle East. I sensed it in my father, despite his calculated academic impartiality and deep affection for his Jewish friends. And as I found out later from his diary, his private sentiments, at least in the early years of the Palestinian struggle, were very much with the Liberation Movement because his earliest childhood friends were among its founding members.

To occupy his time back in Haifa during the long summer holidays during the war, my father found a traineeship with the Iraq Petroleum Company, whose offices were situated along Vine Street – a few steps away from Mosul Lane. He also became a singer in a local band that found itself much in demand entertaining Arabs who were forbidden from visiting Jewish-owned clubs or bars.

'As the Arab-Jewish contest was starting up again,' he wrote rather casually in his memoir, 'the Greeks, with a bit of unstructured research, discovered there was a market for their amateur musical and entertainment talents.' His band of musicians played the rooftop garden at the upmarket Grand Hotel Nassar, owned by a prominent Palestinian Christian clan, and patronised by the Arab elite who held weddings and dinner parties there. 'We became rather popular very quickly,' he wrote, 'and engagements for private functions proliferated.'

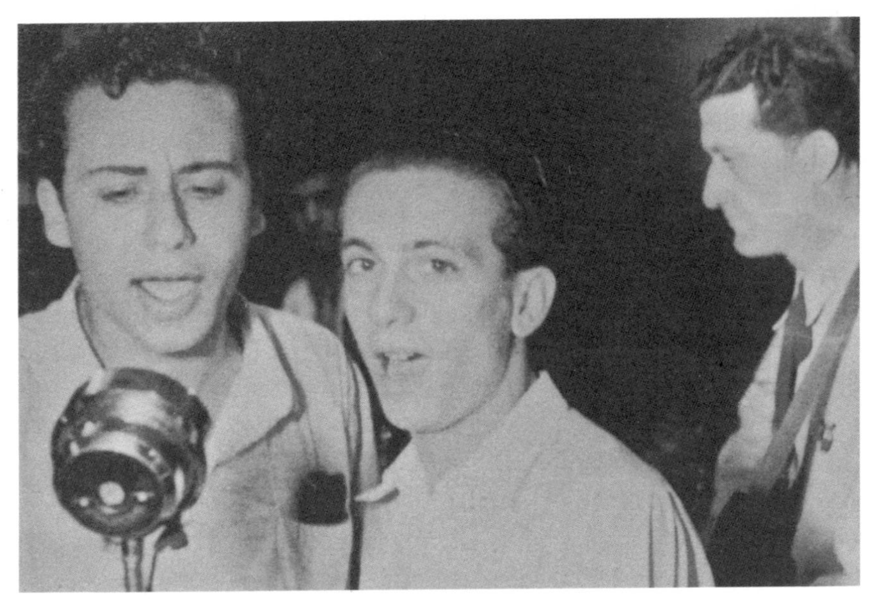

Panayiotis Vatikiotis (left) singing at the Grand Hotel Nassar in 1945

Contracts followed from other quarters, including Boutagy's beer garden in the German Colony, and by 1947, 'custom was bursting at the seams as the Arabs no longer ventured to Jewish places of entertainment.' Yet much as there was money to be made and fun to be had over the holidays, there were also perils. On the afternoon of 22 July 1946, as my father and a friend waited for a train back to Haifa at the old Ottoman station in central Jerusalem, an explosion rocked the city. The bomb had ripped through the southern wing of the King David Hotel, which collapsed like a concertina. The hotel, built by rich Italian Jews from Cairo, among them the Mosseri family, was only fifteen years old. The imposing stone-faced building perched on a hill had been the focal point of British social life, and the headquarters of the British Mandate's secretariat. Ninety-one people died in the blast, which was caused by 350 kilos of high explosive packed into milk canisters deposited by members of the Irgun in the hotel basement.[2] Of the dead, forty-one were Arabs, twenty-eight were British and seventeen were Jews. The one Greek casualty was eighteen-year-old Chrysanthe Antippa, who had just started working as a typist in the secretariat office located in the hotel's southern wing. Her father was a decorated civil servant, well liked and highly regarded, and she was a friend of my father's. Her death shocked the Greek community.

It is hard to imagine the reverberations this attack sent, not just through the Greek community but to all others in Palestine. As a point of comparison, it had approximately the same level of epoch-changing impact as al-Qaeda's attacks on the Twin Towers in New York. There is a vivid scene in *Exodus*, Otto Preminger's classic 1960 film of the struggle to establish the State of Israel, where the teenage Danish Jewish refugee, Karen Hansen, emerges from a hospital where she has just been reunited with her mentally ill father and witnesses the King David blown up before her eyes. She collapses in a hysteria of weeping and Paul Newman, who plays the male lead as Israeli military officer Ari Ben Canaan, carries her back inside. Many Arabs could not understand why the Jews were attacking the British with such ferocity, writes the Palestinian Ghada Karmi in her soulful memoir *In Search of Fatima*; after all, it was under the British Mandate that they had been encouraged to emigrate in large numbers. At the same time, it is clear from writing of the period – and since – that the Arabs did not anticipate the British leaving them to the mercies of the Jews, and all the hatred and recrimination that would follow for generations.

In 1985, I was working as a journalist for the BBC in Jerusalem. One day I wandered into the refurbished King David Hotel, and was passing through the revolving glass doors at the main entrance at the precise time that Yitzhak Rabin, former Israeli prime minister, then in opposition, was leaving. Our eyes met through the glass; I'll never forget the glimmer of apprehension in his pale-blue eyes.

Before the bombing, the British forces had exercised restraint dealing with the Irgun and Lehi (also referred to as the Stern Gang), the two fanatically anti-British Zionist outfits.[3] There was none of the brutality and indiscriminate sweeps through villages that were common during the Arab Revolt. Many Jews were imprisoned, but harsh sentences were avoided. The feeling in London was that with everything that had happened to the Jews under the Nazis, the government could not afford the spectre of comparison.

'One hundred thousand Englishmen are being kept away from their homes and work for a senseless squalid war with the Jews. We are getting ourselves hated and mocked by the world,' noted Winston Churchill, then an MP in the House of Commons. Yet despite the distinct and obvious differences in their treatment, the Jews suspected many British officials, including the High Commissioner, Malcolm MacDonald, and his military commander General Sir Evelyn 'Bubbles' Barker, of anti-Jewish sentiment. Orders like the one issued by General Barker after the King David Hotel bombing did little to dispel their fears. Barker, who was having an affair with the widow of the famed Arab nationalist George Antonius, ordered all his soldiers to avoid any social interaction with the Jewish community. Somewhat unfortunately, his order also argued for 'punishing the Jews in a way that race dislikes as much as any, by striking at their pockets and showing our contempt for them'.

Britain's ponderous prevarication over Palestine has long been debated. The root of the problem was of course Britain's original contradictory promises – a homeland for the Jews (as per Arthur Balfour's Declaration in 1917) and kingdoms for the Arabs (as per the McMahon commitments). Running in the background throughout the pro-Zionist period since had been British Foreign Office anxiety about the strategic consequences of abandoning the Arabs. As public opinion in Britain swung behind the Jewish cause in the wake of revelations about the Holocaust, the Whitehall mandarins still had their cold, impassionate gaze fixed on the oilfields of Iraq and, of course, the Suez Canal. And just as Jewish demands for statehood reached a crescendo in 1947, Britain was trying to shore up relations with Egypt and Iraq, both implacably opposed to the creation of a Jewish state. Unable to resolve this dilemma, British officials kicked the problem elsewhere, into the lap of another joint commission headed by the United States.

Aftermath of the bombing of the King David Hotel in Jerusalem

As the months of denouement ticked down, my father found it increasingly difficult to escape the violence; at one point he was caught in the crossfire when officers from British Special Branch pursued a Jewish suspect. On another occasion he was stopped by a squad of British troops and asked for his identification card. Not having one on him, he was detained at a police station until my grandfather Jerasimous arrived to vouch for him. Around the Vatikiotis family in Haifa, the Arab and Jewish communities diverged and started to prepare for confrontation: 'Several young Arabs whom I had known from various neighbourhoods boasted in those days that they were now armed; I only hoped they knew how to use these weapons. In fact, one of them, who carried a hand gun in his pocket, shot himself accidentally in the leg and groin.'

This was all so unsettling for my grandfather with his tidy, bureaucratic mind conditioned by the comforting certainty of railway timetables and the polite probity of his avuncular British supervisors. As his world started to fall apart, he naturally relied on the British for security. When my grandfather's mother Evmorphia died in 1947, an armoured car was called to take her coffin to the cemetery.

The Arab Revolt and the subsequent reign of terror led by Irgun and the Lehi had the effect of either eliminating the moderates on both sides or of marginalising their voices. Noises off, calls for peaceful coexistence fell on deaf ears. Arab and Jewish extremists also made it impossible for the British to maintain control, bearing in mind that events were unfolding against a backdrop of diminishing respect for and patience with colonial rule – anywhere. British rule in East Africa, in India and in Malaya was under pressure and facing mounting resistance. It was in this context that Britain essentially threw in the towel on Palestine and it became a problem instead for the whole world at the United Nations.

The European colonial powers were fond of using partition as a tool of imperial rule: the Sykes-Picot Agreement divided areas north and south of a line drawn from Acre to Kirkuk in Iraq in 1916; Allenby ordered the partition of Jerusalem into separate quarters after he rolled into the city in 1917; and the British Mandate of Palestine established in 1923 was the result of the partitioning of the Ottoman Empire. The Peel Commission, having failed to persuade the Arabs and Jews to rub along in a plural Palestinian state, in 1937 recommended partition as a post-colonial formula – which a decade later was presented to the United Nations as the only practical solution. The resulting UN resolution 181(II), which considered that the 'present situation in Palestine is one which is likely to impair the general welfare and friendly relations among nations', was passed in the General Assembly on 29 November 1947. The resolution called for termination of the British Mandate by August 1948 and the immediate establishment of two independent states, one Arab, the other Jewish, with a vaguely worded 'Special International Regime for the city of Jerusalem'. The resolution, far from acting as a salve, was in fact salt in festering wounds, prompting the outbreak of open hostilities. As partitions go, it was not as immediately deadly as that of India, which happened the same year – displacing an estimated 12 million people and resulting in the deaths of more than a million. Nevertheless, the resolution set the scene for three Arab-Israeli Wars, massive long-term displacement, international terrorism, the ongoing tragedy of Palestine and – sadly – the end of the Middle East as my parents and their parents knew it. My father put it in terms that I find remarkably detached, given the three generations of Vatikiotis family who had made Palestine home: 'Many of us realized then and there that we must leave that part of the world for good; there was no place for the outsider in such a cauldron of passionate and exclusive nationalist pursuits. We and our parents came to terms with the fact that the relative idyll of the inter-war period had come to an end.'

There was, in any case, little time for reflection or hesitation: the British pulled out early, on 15 May 1948. 'In 1917 the British entered Jerusalem to the sounds of trumpets,' wrote the Jerusalem-based Greek dentist John Tleel, 'they left unceremoniously and without fanfare, plunging Jerusalem and the entire region into an endless state of chaos.' It was evident from the beginning that the new State of Israel had no intention of honouring the implicit and explicit terms of partition – that Arabs could stay in Israel, or that Jerusalem would be established as an internationally governed city.

The Palestinian Arabs for their part refused to accept the formation of Israel and expected the armies from neighbouring Arab states promptly to march in and drive the Jews into the Mediterranean Sea. For the first weeks after the UN vote there were incidents of stonings, lynchings and other random acts of mob unrest including burning and looting of both Jewish and Arab properties. Jewish-settler militia blew up the Semiramis Hotel in the Katamon area of Jerusalem; Arab fighters answered by blowing up the Jewish Agency and Ben Yehuda Street in a mainly Jewish part of town. The Arab population went on strike. Jews and Arabs (mostly Jordanian troops who moved quickly to occupy the Old City after partition was announced)[4] took potshots at each other over city walls, and in between uncertain truces the periodic shelling killed hundreds, including civilians.

'The battles went on,' wrote the Palestinian chronicler Wasif Jawhariyyeh. 'At home we went through hell, sleeping to the sound of explosion, machine guns, rifles and fires around us day and night until we concluded that life . . . had become unbearable.'

Arabs began streaming out of Haifa as the Jewish armed forces (the *Haganah*) surrounded the city. Frightened Palestinian residents of West Jerusalem fled behind the walls of the Old City. The Arab exodus, my father concluded, was a result of 'intimidation, fear, panic, disorganization, lack of guidance and leadership and hopes for an early return to their homes soon after the Jews had been defeated by superior Arab military forces and power'. According to my father, the Greeks shared some of these same fears and concerns: 'there was an implied overtone of distaste that they might have to live under Jewish political masters.' Understandably: their memory was of languid

Ottoman tolerance and neglect followed by benign patronage under the British Mandate, which valued these Levantines precisely because they were neither Arab nor Jew.

The scars of partition and the three subsequent Arab-Israeli Wars have mostly been papered over in modern Israel. No one in Jerusalem today pays attention to the so-called Green Line, the seven-kilometre border cleaving the city into East and West, established after the First Arab-Israeli War of 1948. The whole of the Old City lies on the eastern, Jordanian-held side of the line. The Palestinians refer to partition in 1947 as *al-Nakbha*, the 'catastrophe'. Today, by UN estimates, almost 6 million Palestinians living outside Israel are descended from the original population of 1.4 million or so who lived in Palestine at the time of partition, half of whom fled. Almost 2 million of them are crammed into the Gaza Strip, a self-governing zone along the coast of less than 400 square kilometres. Close to 3 million Palestinians live in the West Bank, the landlocked area taken by Jordan after the 1948 Arab-Israeli War and later designated for Palestinians and governed by them after the 1993 Oslo Accords – although in reality Israel controls and administers a large swathe of the area and has threatened formal annexation. High-security walls and screens seal off Palestinian areas from Israel proper.

Strolling through the old Mamilla district of Jerusalem outside Jaffa Gate today is to experience a twenty-first-century-mall experience dressed in biblical stone. In 1948 this was no-man's-land between the Israeli and Arab-held sectors, an area repeatedly shelled. The Savvides photography salon where my grandmother, Paraskevi, worked before she married has been spirited into an upscale shopping street, the ghosts hiding behind plate-glass windows displaying Nike trainers and North Face sportswear. Against this baffling backdrop, I set out one chilly March evening to meet the last remnants of the Greek community in Palestine.

'Come, please come. We will all be together.'

Anastasi Damanios, leader of the Greek community, invited me to a screening of *The Last Note*, a disturbing film about the Nazi massacre of 200 Greek prisoners in May 1944. We were a group of about six: two chatty women from the Greek Consulate, an unhappy Greek policeman on loan to the European Union mission, and three living relics from families of the colony who still live there. The screening took place at a cinema club not far from Jaffa Gate.

After watching the harrowing story, which included gory execution scenes shot in slow motion, we left to visit the Greek Community Centre. Established in 1902 by a priest called Eftimios, the low-slung stone building set in a spacious garden and shaded by pine trees has served as a community hall and gathering place ever since. A small annex facing the street that was the first Greek grocery store in the neighbourhood now stands empty.

We huddled in a side room, sheltering from a chill wind outside and cupping our hands around hot mugs of sage tea. The pungent aroma of the herbal infusion transported me to the desiccated thorn-scrub hills of Hydra, and to my grandparent's tiny flat in Athens. I tried to imagine my grandparents' wedding banquet, which was held here in August 1923, the scent of pine and orange blossom blending with tobacco smoke and the more pungent aroma of roasting lamb.

Inside, the walls of the centre were crowded with framed group photographs of the community in its prime, church-led parades dominated by the bushy beards of corpulent priests and the proud moustaches and straw boaters of pillars of the community. Pride of place was given to the enterprising Father Eftimios, who in the late nineteenth century revived the community by harnessing revenue raised for the church and extending that to the building of the colony. In addition to weddings, the centre hosted other rites of passage including christenings and celebrations of religious feast days. Today there are fewer than 150 Greeks in Palestine; the dust gathering on the photo frames seems in places as thick as the icing on a wedding cake.

Anastasi's careworn features and slight stoop belie his great energy and keen sense of humour. Like my father, he is of Greek and Arab Orthodox heritage, from the town of Canaan in Galilee, where he was born in 1941. A residual Greek, he has lived in Israel all his life and long since retired from the civil service. Anastasi remembers the *Nakbha;* he was seven when his family – the only Greeks in what was then a predominantly Christian Arab town – were protected by the church. 'The priest took us in and sat us under the lemon tree,' said Anastasi. 'He told us whatever happens to us will happen to him. He saved us from becoming refugees.'

Later, Anastasi and I visited the church in Canaan together. The lemon tree under which he sheltered with his family during those initial days after partition still grows in a courtyard outside. We passed the site of his old home, now a four-storey apartment building close to the mosque. He pointed out a ruined stone house nearby that had once belonged to the family of Tariq Aziz, Saddam Hussein's ebullient foreign minister at the time of the modern Gulf Wars. Another ruined house, much larger, was the divan of Zahir al-Umar, the Palestinian warlord who managed to wrestle a high degree of autonomy from the Ottomans in the eighteenth century and helped rebuild Acre and Haifa.

Arab neighbours stopped and greeted Anastasi warmly, kissing him on both cheeks. Here he is called Abu George, after his father. He speaks flawless Arabic, Hebrew and Greek, as well as English. I stood beside him, envious and impotent, language-poor Levantine that I am. It was one of those moments on my journey that awakened in me a longing to recover the past, painful as it has clearly been for someone like Anastasi. His family was fortunate; they were allowed to stay.

Later, over delicious lamb kebabs served on long metal skewers and with a mouth-watering array of *mezze*, Anastasi recalled the filming of *Exodus*, which had used Canaan as a location. 'In fact, they took over our home. We all moved into one room. It was 1959, and I remember meeting Paul Newman, his wife, Joanne Woodward, and Otto Preminger.'

Back in Jerusalem and on my way to visit the patriarchate, I stopped at the ancient vaulted clinic belonging to Nicholas Ninos, the last Greek dentist in the Old City. Nicholas has a particular way of reminding his patients of his identity: he has painted a Greek flag on the ceiling, offsetting the striking contrast between the modern dental equipment and the medieval yellow-stone wall. 'It looks nice, but isn't all that hygienic,' admits Nicholas, with a twinkle in his large grey eyes.

Nicholas, who was born in the Old City, is the son of a dentist. The family home is opposite Saint Dimitri's, the Greek school attached to the patriarchate where my grandfather Jerasimous studied. Rich as the Church is, much of the money in those days was spent on supporting its adherents. Nicholas lives among spirits and ghosts and married into a Levantine family who claim ancestry from Portugal. He and his wife raised three boys; his wife, a clinical psychiatrist, opted to leave for the United States. 'I don't know whether to leave or stay,' sighs Nicholas, now in his sixties. Most Greeks have left, and those who remain are almost forgotten.

Nicholas Ninos: the last Greek dentist in Jerusalem

Archbishop Aristarchus is the octogenarian assistant to the Greek patriarch Theophilus III. Crouching behind a desk piled high with papers, he told me that Saint Dimitri's school closed in 1970. Built around an ancient church dedicated to a fourth-century saint, the school continued to function until the 1967 war, when Jaffa Gate was closed as the edge of Jordanian territory before being taken by the Israelis. The school moved up the hill to Mount Zion, close to the Orthodox cemetery, where on a Sunday morning a stooped nun in a dusty old black habit offers coffee and sweets to those visiting the tombs.

'We used to have a lot of Greek boys, but gradually the community depleted,' Aristarchus said as he hastily signed documents, barely reading them, breaking off only to wave a hand in languid emphasis and eye me impassively over his reading glasses.

Around the office I was told that he is regarded as a living saint.

'There are still young men who come from Greece interested in serving the Church – some of them stay on as monks, but not all,' he continued. 'As monks their responsibility is to protect the holy places. We also have pastoral duties towards our congregation in the Arab-speaking community . . . our Church helps maintain their religious identity. That's why we translated the testaments into Arabic in the eighteenth century.'

Seventy years after partition, the Greeks themselves may have almost all gone, but what remains of the Church, and the hallowed real estate it owns and governs? Listening to the old archbishop, I recalled the make-believe reclusive earldom of Gormenghast, which the British twentieth-century writer Mervyn Peake confected for boys like me growing up in England. Beleaguered and besieged, the earldom fell back on tiresome and tedious rituals to maintain a sense of order. The Greek Orthodox patriarchate in today's Israeli setting is just as isolated and threatened by its surroundings; its refuge in ritual and tradition just as pronounced a survival mechanism. It seems almost inconceivable that this ancient Church has survived centuries of war and invasion, yet still clings to the ancient stones, nourished by its archaic traditions and rituals. What has changed, however, is the extent to which it can claim to be Greek.

A couple of hundred metres from the entrance to the patriarchate, down a covered street lined with shops catering to tourists, is the non-descript door to the Arab Orthodox Welfare Society, run by Nora Quirt. Nora presides over a small museum housed in a 670-year-old Mamluk-era building that backs on to the old cistern – Hezekiah's pool – that was a major source of water for the Old City, fed by an aqueduct that ran under Jaffa Gate channeled from the larger Mamilla reservoir to the west. Today the empty cistern, a sizeable patch of land about the size of a football field, belongs to the Islamic *Waqf*, and like many other features in the Old City of Jerusalem, the ancient pool is threatened by Israeli developers who want to turn it into a shopping mall.

Nora's family, a landowning Arab clan with property outside the walls just adjacent to the site of the King David Hotel, built an Arab Orthodox church, Saint George's, which was taken over by Israelis and turned into a meeting hall after 1948. The land was lost, and Nora and her siblings were educated overseas. She would have left herself, she told me from behind an antique desk piled high with papers, but before he died her father told her: 'Nora, don't forget.' She abandoned plans to move to the USA and stayed in the region, initially working in Jordan and eventually retiring to Jerusalem to establish the museum and run a gift shop by New Gate to fund the society.

'I regret the Greeks have gone. The diversity they provided was very important,' Nora said as we sipped coffee and were cooled by a breeze blowing in from the empty cistern below. 'The Greeks were the educated, cultural face of the city,' she added. 'I felt that these people were adding a colourful mosaic. Jerusalem with all of its holy sites was truly internationalised – there was no real discrimination – everyone minded their own business really.'

And what of the Church?

'I don't deny I'm a residual Greek,' Nora replied without hesitation. 'I go to church and I pray in Greek and Arabic.'

But when she showed me a handwritten copy of the New Testament in Arabic in a dusty corner of the museum, her views turned bitter. She mentioned that patriarchate lawyers have tried to force her to pay rent for the museum – even though she claims to have bought the property. Most of the old shops along David Street, leading down from Jaffa Gate, where her museum is situated, sit on patriarchate land. The rents, she said, are 'old', so often nominal.

'In Ottoman times they would have been owned by Arab Orthodox families, now all gone. Today,' she said, 'the Hebronites have moved in.' The people she calls Hebronites are devout Muslim Palestinian Arabs who have in recent years taken over the shops and cafés once owned by the Arab Christians, or by Greeks and Armenians. 'As long as Israel is in charge here,' she said with a downcast look, 'there will be no more cosmopolitan existence.'

Partition, the *Nakbha* and the end of my father's family sojourn in Palestine was only the beginning of a much longer and ongoing contest over land and identity. Tracing my family's history, I kept stumbling into the conflict. Every day came the sharp pain, a bit like stubbing one's toe on the same corner of the bed each morning. The drivers of this conflict haven't changed appreciably in seventy years; the bitterness and rancour over who has a right to live in the land once called Palestine, now called Israel, never fades; only one side ever seems to be winning.

I have never directly been a victim of this conflict; I don't know the pain of loss in the same way that Palestinians who lost their land and homes, or the countless victims of war and insurgency on both sides of the Arab and Jewish divide. All the same, I identify with the conflict, which is part of my heritage. And so throughout my life, each outrage, each failure to reach a consensus on forging peace, has left me feeling a dull pain within – unlike any of the other appalling human tragedies I have encountered as a journalist and peacemaker.

*

For most of my time in Jerusalem I stayed at the crumbling but magnificent New Imperial Hotel, tucked just inside Jaffa Gate on the western edge of the Old City. The entrance to the hotel is halfway up an alley next door to a flower shop run by an elderly couple and a younger man selling freshly squeezed orange juice from a stall.

The New Imperial is managed by Walid Dajani, a Palestinian Muslim, whose family has run the 120-year-old property since the 1960s. Allenby, according to Walid, passed the hotel on his walk into the city that fateful day in December 1917, and was a friend of the famous tour operator Thomas Cook – the same Thomas Cook who had arranged the visit to Jerusalem of Kaiser Wilhelm at the start of the century, and for which occasion the New Imperial was built. And as Allenby walked through the gates on his way to the *Qishle*, the Ottoman police station, he stopped briefly at the Thomas Cook offices.

Allenby – again according to Walid – met an office boy inside and asked him to join him at the police station, where he apparently gave the boy some money and sent him on his way. 'This boy, a Christian Arab, was close to my father, Muhammad Dajani,' relates Walid in his untidy office, a conflagration of bills and papers, its walls plastered with pictures, most of them of Walid with city notables. 'So, when the boy showed the money to my father, my father asked him to go back and ask for permission to sell fuel in the city from the back of a donkey, which he did, and that's how we started our business.' Eventually the Dajani enterprise grew into an export and import business – they imported British bully beef.

This story is typical of the scrupulously maintained and detailed memory Palestinians have of the loss of so much of their land and property: they can pinpoint exactly who helped whom; who saved what and when, reciting at exhaustive length the whole unfolding tragedy of loss. Many of them keep the keys to the property they abandoned in the vain hope that one day they can return. Walid's father rescued friends from West Jerusalem after 1948, installing them in the New Imperial. The Dajanis, who had the means to leave, settled in Egypt for a while, returning to reopen their business in the relative peace of the era that followed the 1967 Six-Day War. 'My father remembered this hotel, so he went to the patriarchate and said he would be willing to take it over. He opened a cinema on the second floor to pay for renovations.'

*

After scouring Jerusalem for the relics of my own father's era, my last few discussions before leaving focused on the future. Inevitably these conversations gravitated towards the proximate threat to the city's unique status in the eyes of millions of Christians and Muslims, as well as Jews. Upwards of 3 million pilgrims travelled to Jerusalem in 2018. During my stay in Jerusalem in 2019 that figure was expected to reach 5 million, more than half of them Christians.

The worry is how much longer these pilgrims will come, in the face of concerted efforts by conservative activists to undermine the foothold non-Jewish religions have here. These more extreme elements wish to restore the primacy of Judaism as it was in King Solomon's era three millennia ago. Already, according to the patriarchate, the Christian population has fallen from 50,000 just after partition in 1947 to around 6,000 today. The Christian community, the Greek Orthodox Church argues, is squeezed between the Jewish majority of Israel and the Muslim majority of Palestine. Jaffa Gate, the entrance to the small Christian quarter, is in a sense the nut between the two arms of a giant cracker, one extending west that is predominantly Jewish, the other to the east, which for now is predominantly Muslim and Arab.

Conservative Jewish groups have mostly abandoned the violent pressure tactics of the partition era. Today they deploy stealthy entrepreneurial and legislative means: such as a bill in parliament to make it illegal for churches to own land, and a controversial buyout of long leases on properties dominating the entrance to the Christian quarter just inside Jaffa Gate. What is at stake, the Christians say, is the city's ecumenical status. The Greek Orthodox patriarchate, which owns much of the land in question, is pushing back, but the struggle unfolding in the courts and in Israel's parliament is up against determined, militant activists who use international lawyers and offshore investment vehicles to outmanoeuvre and outspend the Greek Church and its mainly Arab tenants.

At the heart of the case at Jaffa Gate is a contract signed a decade ago between the patriarchate and a Jewish organisation called Ateret Cohanim, which is dedicated to establishing Jewish occupancy and ownership across the whole of Jerusalem. The contract transferred the leases on three pieces of Church-owned land and the buildings on them at the edge of the Christian quarter by Jaffa Gate, including the New Imperial Hotel. The patriarchate appealed in an Israeli court that the lease transfer contract was drawn up with a former financial manager who had been bribed – allegedly – to sign away the lease (and who has since been arrested in Greece). Just recently, an Israeli district court upheld the contract. Ateret Cohanim has begun foreclosure proceedings on the two hotels. The Dajanis argue that the contract should be annulled; as long-term tenants they were never informed of the change of leaseholder before the signing.

The case, which drags on, has driven a wedge between the Greek Orthodox Church and its Arab Orthodox congregation, widening an already apparent divide. Many Palestinians suspect the Church was out to make money at the expense of their land and heritage. The patriarch who preceded Theophilus, and under whose watch the controversial lease was signed in 2004, was effectively imprisoned in the patriarchate until he left quietly for Greece in 2019. The case has highlighted the patriarchate's isolation; fiercely guarding his independence, Theophilus has refused to seek help from the Greek state to intervene. However, more recently, the patriarch launched a public-relations campaign in the United States, where Ateret Cohanim does most of its fundraising. Somewhat more successfully, he enlisted the help of Russia's President Vladimir Putin, who in 2019 put in a word with the Israeli government to bring a stay of legal action against the Jaffa Gate properties; nevertheless, the legal wrangling continued.

Walid told me he lives from day to day. Pointing to a stack of unpaid bills, he claims that legal action by the property's 'new owners' had shut down his bank accounts and threatened to cut utilities – electricity and water – to the hotel. 'What do I say to the people I employ?' he said with tears in his eyes.

I retreated to the roof terrace, where the sounds of Jerusalem at dusk have not changed in centuries, a descending cadence of church bells mingle with the ascending semi-tonal appeals of the Muslim call to prayer. As a child of this city, by blood – both Arab and Jewish – and by the quirks of its history, I was instinctively fearful of moves to suppress its ancient antagonistic diversity. My Levantine blood yearns for peaceful compromise, however unlikely it seems. I was reminded of a fable by the great thirteenth-century Anatolian storyteller and sage Nasr el-din Hodja, whose two wives were constantly asking him which one of them was his favourite. 'I love you both the same,' was always his answer, but they did not accept this, and asked him again: 'Which one of us do you love the most?' Finally, he secretly gave each of them a blue bead, privately instructing each woman that she should tell no one of the gift. After that, whenever either of the wives asked which was his favourite, he would say: 'I love best the one with the blue bead.' Hodja captures the wisdom of the ancients, who managed the contradictions and incompatibilities of mixed society in the Middle East. At the same time, like my father and his father before him, I was acutely conscious of our status as sojourners in a land we cannot claim, even with the strong whiff of ancestry and the power of the Greek Church. Perhaps, to paraphrase the late Israeli rabbi Menachem Froman: the land does not belong to anyone in particular; we all belong to the land.

CHAPTER ELEVEN

Dispersal and Desolation

'We're incomplete, unfinished. The most charmingly disappointed people I know of.'

Donatienne Sapriel, Egyptian Jewish painter (as told to Jacqueline Shohet Kahanoff), 1973

Back in Cairo, after partition and the waves of migration that ensued, my father Panayiotis was finishing his studies at the American University and mixing with people who were fleeing the outbreak of a bloody civil war between Jews and Arabs. Those with means were first to leave, such as the better-off Christian families and Greeks, from urban areas. For those avoiding the swelling refugee camps along the Gaza Strip, Egypt was one of the closest places to seek shelter, as was Lebanon. Both countries could be reached overland within a few hours. Despite the proximity, my father lost contact with his parents. Telephone lines were expensive and were then reserved mainly for military communication; the post, despatched by rail, was disrupted after partition. He knew his parents were in danger, their future precarious. By the early spring of 1948, with Israeli forces on the verge of capturing Haifa, the streets of the city were subject to ambushes and incessant, often indiscriminate sniper fire. Cut off, and with nowhere else to go, Panayiotis fortunately landed a job teaching at the university as soon as he graduated, giving him a front-row seat at the unfolding, anguishing drama we have come to know as the Middle East Conflict. 'It was a novel, bizarre phenomenon and experience,' he wrote, 'watching the uprooting of a people from a country they had inhabited for at least 800 years and the disintegration, through dispersal and exile, of a community.'

Cairo in 1947 was seething with militancy and unrest. The nationalists who had carried the torch of Egyptian independence from the start of the twentieth century (led initially by Saad Zaghloul and the Wafd Party), were splintered and discredited; tarred by years of privilege and corruption, preyed upon by devious British administrators who sought to co-opt and harness Egypt's nationalist politicians to their interests and pit them against the monarchy. King Farouk, not yet thirty, was scarred by the war and tainted by the company he kept – mostly pro-fascist Levantine advisors and grasping socialite procurers for the royal bedroom.

Egypt after the end of the Second World War was significantly wealthier than during the inter-war period, mainly because of the British army's massive spending spree and the war effort's boost to local industry. However, most of this wealth ended up in the pockets of the rich, and when the war was over local unemployment and poverty rose significantly. In 1945 Egypt's infant mortality rate was 153 per 1,000; there were fewer than 5,000 doctors in the entire country (its population was 19 million), and due to the unchecked prevalence of bilharzia and trachoma, Egypt had the highest ratio of blind people in the world. The overall situation was compounded in 1947 by a cholera outbreak that felled 35,000 in a matter of months.

Against this backdrop of elite abuse of power, appalling poverty and economic stress, the Wafd Party continued to govern Egypt, albeit without popular backing. The resulting vacuum was filled by new emerging forces on the Islamic right and communist left. Both were radical, found strong support among the poor, and were willing to use violence.

The post-war freedom to organise and protest turbo-charged popular anger over the continued British presence and spilled on to the streets throughout the year. Students and workers clashed with Egyptian police and British army personnel in February and March, and later in 1947 in other cities. Hundreds died. The protests were organised by the *Ikhwan* or Muslim Brotherhood, originally a moderate Islamic movement that eschewed violence when it was founded in Egypt in 1928. There was also mobilisation of popular anger by an array of left-wing intellectual groups and labour outfits infiltrated by communists, a recent import actively backed by Soviet Russia.[1] However, Islamic activism had a competitive edge in the struggle for Egyptian popular support, as Islamic sentiment had been employed by the Wafd and other nationalist groups in the inter-war period to bolster flagging support. It was this religious stream of militancy that ultimately gained ascendancy, slowly capturing the popular nationalist narrative and steering Egypt away from its European moorings, with enduring consequences.

My experience of life in Cairo in the mid-1970s, and then during subsequent, briefer, visits during, just before and after the Arab Spring uprising of 2011, has helped me gauge the distance modern Egypt has travelled from the cosmopolitan era that spanned the mid-nineteenth to the mid-twentieth century.

In 1976 I was fresh out of high school when I arrived in Cairo to enrol at the American University, signing up for Arabic-language classes. I had very little money and was forced to teach on the side to earn more. I was up for adventure. I found a room in a student hostel near the university campus on Shariah Falaki. By night I wandered through Bab el-Louk market, soaking in its sights and smells: the grocery store with mountains of dusty oranges and gigantic watermelons; the bakery selling hot unleavened bread with a floury crust for one piastre; the confectioner selling biscuits in tins embossed with a portrait of Egypt's most revered singer, Umm Kulthum. Buzzing, naked neon strip lights and yellowing bulbs hung over great brass pots of *foule*, the Egyptian staple. For those with more to spend, a shop window piled high with the pale, bloodless offal of sheep and cows declared its delicacy 'liver and brain'. Blackouts were common, and as candles and gas burners replaced the glare of neon, the whole neighbourhood suddenly felt very far away from the city around me.

I fell into a morning routine going to class, finding my way along the chaotic street, raising my hand to the man who mended shoes, shaded under his tattered canvas awning, past the stall selling old 78 records from America and – oddly – empty shampoo bottles, avoiding the same mangy dog curled up outside the fresh chicken shop and the trickles of blood that advertised the slaughter within. Turning another corner, I stepped into the dressed marble tidiness of the campus, grabbing a coffee, an egg sandwich and a copy of the *Egyptian Gazette*. It didn't seem all that very different from the world my father had known in the mid-1940s. Only it was.

One of my first meetings soon after my arrival was with an official at the Ministry of Information: Doctor Mursi Saad el-Din, who was a friend of my father's.[2] All smiles and affability, despite his rank as an under-secretary of state, he asked me to join him in a screening room to view newly made propaganda films. They were made using good-looking, middle-class Egyptian actors playing the parts of poor villagers. Egypt in the mid-1970s was a troubled place, plagued by rising prices for staples and falling wages. The government's propaganda was aimed at countering the Muslim Brotherhood's appeal to the poor and its calls for Islamic orthodoxy. The clean-shaven actor with his square jaw and well-clipped sideburns was not a convincing peasant. I could almost smell the expensive after-shave.

Wide-eyed and hungry for experience, I was taken during my first week to the Shooting Club, where rich Egyptian women in beehive hairdos and flouncy, loudly patterned dresses watched their husbands aim for pigeons released by *galabiya*-clad groundsmen. Yet, roaming the back streets of old Cairo, even then there was evidence that the government was losing the battle against advancing Islamic orthodoxy. The piety of the poor was evident – a taxi driver apologised profusely when he drove me the wrong way to my destination so he could head eastwards and pray while at the wheel. All the same, there was diversity. I went to parties in Ma'adi and out by the pyramids where young, high-class Egyptians drank copious amounts of alcohol, drove wildly around the city in open-top cars, and let their hair down. There was a pronounced duality to Egyptian society: the majority of people were pushed by poverty and hopelessness towards Islamic orthodoxy, while the rich elite clung to the fading remnants of the belle époque. As the Egyptian writer Waguih Ghali wrote in his semi-autobiographical novel *Beer in the Snooker Club*, published in 1964: 'Cairo and Alexandria were cosmopolitan not so much because they contained foreigners, but because the Egyptian born in them is himself a stranger in his own land.'

By the time I returned to Cairo thirty years later, in 2006, the stage was already set for the mass protests that were to topple the government of President Hosni Mubarak in 2011. The remnants of the cosmopolitan elite were mostly gone, replaced by a fawning nouveau riche who were just barely hanging on to the coat tails of government patronage. Young people, much of the educated middle class, were evidently pious and far more conservative than fellow students I had known thirty years before. Women mostly wore hijab, and many were fully veiled. This was a familiar story for me. In Indonesia I witnessed the transformation of a mostly secular Muslim majority from the mid-1980s to a more avowedly pious and observant Muslim community, less tolerant of minorities in their midst and slaves to narrow-minded dogma preached from mosques financed by the Kingdom of Saudi Arabia. Back in Cairo, men sported prayer marks on their foreheads, and the cold beers I had enjoyed in restaurants were harder to find. Cairo was for the first time since the early nineteenth century truly an Arab and Muslim city, its European veneer rotting away unattended in the heat. When I revealed the heritage of my family, there was only a dim understanding of what was meant by 'Italian from Egypt'; by contrast, mentioning a parent from Palestine prompted broad smiles and enthusiastic handshakes.

The initial trigger for Egypt's pivot away from the Mediterranean and towards the Arab and Muslim world was an almost forgotten decision taken by the struggling Egyptian government led by Prime Minister Mustafa el-Nahas in the leading cosmopolitan centre of the region. In October 1944 El-Nahas joined with delegations from Lebanon, Iraq, Jordan and Syria in establishing a League of Arab States in what became known as the Alexandria Protocol. Concluded three years before partition, the protocol included a special resolution on Palestine, affirming its Arab identity and declaring that the newly established Arab League 'is second to none in regretting the woes which have been inflicted upon the Jews of Europe by European dictatorial states. But the question of these Jews should not be confused with Zionism, for there can be no greater injustice and aggression than solving the problem of the Jews of Europe by another injustice, i.e., by inflicting injustice on the Arabs of Palestine of various religions and denominations.' My father, writing in his *History of Egypt*, saw the Alexandria Protocol's significance as 'the basis of a new Arab-Islamic dimension of nationalist agitation – a political orientation for the masses'. The foreign community took it as a sign that Egypt no longer looked to Europe, another indication of their waning era.

For a century, Muhammad Ali and his mainly French-educated successors had strived to marry Egypt's future to that of modern Europe. There was no affinity with the Arabs. Muhammad Ali, the Albanian tobacco trader's son, saw the Arab hinterland as a place to dominate and control rather than relate to in brotherhood. He considered an alliance with France to invade the Maghreb, and annexed Syria and

Palestine to establish more independence from the Ottoman sultan in Istanbul, to whom he was notionally at least a vassal. Egypt's new rulers in the nineteenth century looked down on Arabs. Muhammad Ali's descendant, King Farouk, even married off one of his sisters to the Shah of Iran! The feeling was mutual: King Abdullah of Jordan reputedly said of Muhammad Ali, 'You don't make a gentleman of a Balkan farmer's son by making him a king.'

The shift in orientation was stark. My mother's family's Tuscan-style villas by the pyramids and along the Nile were built using a dynamic diversity of European manpower and expertise cultivated in a modern urban setting. These backdrops to a privileged way of life, like the scenery for the first performance of *Aida* in 1871, were imported. Dressed and lit, the scenery obscured from view the ordinary Egyptian peasant toiling in the Nile Delta and the waterless desert of the Bedouin Arabs beyond. It was in hyper-cosmopolitan Alexandria in 1944 that the calculus changed and Egypt instead started to see itself as a dominant force in the Arab world, embracing the starving, half-blind *fellaheen* and even the Bedouin beyond. In the eyes of the foreign community, the Muslim Brotherhood was to blame for this new nativist nationalist agenda, and its later reinforcement by anti-Jewish sentiment. Little wonder, then, that my mother's family saw the Muslim Brotherhood as a grave threat. Many years later, my mother was so upset when I told her I had met with a group of Muslim Brotherhood intellectuals based in Europe that she sent a registered letter asking me to promise never to meet them again.

The turning point for Levantine society just as the war ended was at first hard to recognise; life went on as before at Groppi's and at the Gezira Club. King Farouk graced soirées attended by the beautiful debutantes of prominent Jewish families, and preyed on them for assignations. My mother, just seventeen, was starting to enjoy her own debutante life, dancing the tango in night clubs to live orchestras and enjoying partying until dawn. But all the while popular protests grew more fearsome, assuming anti-Jewish and anti-foreign overtones. 'Often angry demonstrations brought frenzied shouts and white-robed crowds swirling and wielding sticks and stones outside our gates,' wrote Jean Naggar, a member of the prominent Jewish Mosseri family. 'The relentless cadence of the muezzin from the many minarets around the city . . . had become a call to arms.'

Set against this combustible backdrop, Egypt's commitment to join other Arab forces to prevent the establishment of the State of Israel stoked a furnace of hatred aimed at Jews and their foreign supporters, as seen through the lens of the partition vote. Following the UN vote, the Muslim Brotherhood launched violent attacks against foreign and Jewish-owned establishments in Cairo – including the American-owned Metro Cinema, in which my father had been blown up.[3] In May 1948 Egyptian troops marched into Palestine to join the other Arab armies fighting to destroy the fledgling Israeli state.

For my father, quite apart from the hazards of living in a city plagued by bomb attacks and assassinations – usually carried out using hand grenades – there was the whole question of which side to take. His Arab classmates were fired up about the burning issues of the day: anti-imperialism, revolutionary nationalism and the question of Palestine, all three issues linked in their eyes. Unlike the Levantines, to paraphrase the Egyptian Jewish writer Jacqueline Shohet Kahanoff, the Arabs knew what world they belonged to without having to ask themselves. For Panayiotis and other Levantines caught between two rapidly changing contexts, occidental and oriental, they had to choose. As a Greek, therefore an outsider, this wasn't his fight. Yet as an Arab-speaking Greek from Palestine he felt himself to be 'a Greek and yet semi-detached from Greece', and at the same time a 'sympathetic outsider' belonging to Arab Palestine, the land where he was born and raised.

The phrase 'semi-detached' haunts me, bringing to mind my own sense of not quite belonging in situations of revolt and protest where, as an outsider, I have identified strongly and would very much like to have belonged. I suspect my father felt similarly drawn, like any young man with a lively intellect, to the struggle for liberty and dignity. Perhaps, as for Jacqueline Shohet Kahanoff, who came of age a decade earlier than my father, there was also something of trying 'to break out of the narrow minority framework into which we were born, to strive toward something universal'. Kahanoff's parents were, like those of both my mother and father, 'pro-British as a matter of business and security and we were nationalist as a matter of principle'. The succeeding generation, my father and mother's contemporaries, sympathised with the rising tide of revolutionary nationalism, as it 'seemed the only way to reach a future that would include both our European mentors and the Arab masses [. . .] The Arabs and other colonized peoples were cultural hybrids by chance, while we, the Levantine, were unavoidably so, as if by vocation and destiny.' Being a hybrid nonetheless confers a certain amount of choice. The novelist Eric Ambler describes the leading Levantine character in his 1972 novel *The Levanter* as having a composite character, as if a committee – with each member holding different views on a given situation and reacting accordingly. I feel this metaphor describes rather well how we Levantines are always consulting with members of the committee who make up our personalities to decide the best course of action.

At any rate, for more mundane reasons my father needed to belong somewhere, or to someone. His rather impecunious existence consisted of an allowance of around three Egyptian pounds a week and a modest stipend from his teaching job. He treated himself to café outings at weekends, but otherwise lived on a meagre diet of sweet tea, bitter coffee, bowls of lentils with macaroni and five local cigarettes a day bought loose from a street vendor. Unlike my mother Patricia, nestled in the comfortable bosom of the Sornaga family villas and worried about whether their Egyptian servants might murder them in their beds, my father had more in common with the poorer Egyptian students at his university and their steaming passions, frustrations and dreams:

> The medical and law schools were the scenes of yelling crowds, screaming for justice with the animal smell of blood clear in their nostrils. These otherwise quiet and most of them poor youth, who would rather reflect and dream on their own, trapping their emotions inside a dark skinny frame, would shake with frenzy, hypnotized by the delirious, even though perverted joy which they experienced in their violent flailings against their enemy – actually the reality of their existence.

Yet many of his classmate firebrands were also from good Arab families of means. By day they joined the workers and screamed slogans like 'Death to the British and their collaborators – burn them, brother!' By night they dined with their parents at the elite Mohamed Ali Club, sometimes inviting my underfed father along. Pictures of him from this period depict a wiry, widely smiling figure with curly dark hair, his clothes threadbare.

Panayiotis Vatikiotis c.1945

He looks game for anything interesting. He enjoyed their hospitality; some became his friends. His popularity increased when he ghost-wrote their essay assignments; in return, he was taken along to Cairo's many bars and speakeasies. Regarded as a 'sympathetic outsider' who spoke their language and understood their culture, he joined in their hashish-infused conspiring. They debated fiercely whether to focus on fighting imperialism or on attacking the corrupt royalist regime, although anti-imperialism was an easier pitch – they were less inclined to bite the hand that fed them. My father, however, saw through these bourgeois street warriors; it was an early lesson in the unreliability of Arab elites.

The arrival of exiled Palestinians over the course of 1947–48 complicated my father's interested observer/outsider status. 'I faced a difficult problem,' he wrote. 'Should I join with Arab friends in the pro-Palestinian demonstrations that were now becoming more frequent against not just the Jews and Israel, but the rest of the world too for having allowed the Jews to acquire an independent state?' Some of his close friends in Cairo were actively Zionist; he also counted as friends most of the Palestinians involved in these early demonstrations. 'Many of them reminded me that my family too would soon have to move away from its home – and possessions.'

*

The Arab armies invading the newly declared State of Israel in May 1948 expected to sweep the lightly armed and still-evolving Israeli forces into the sea in a matter of weeks, if not days. The Arab armies of Egypt, Syria, Iraq and Jordan were numerically superior and better equipped. They enjoyed tacit British support. But Israel quickly requisitioned weaponry from stockpiles left over from the Second World War and with a mobile, highly motivated force they gained the upper hand. In October 1948 the Egyptian navy's flagship, the *Emir Farouk*, was sunk after being rammed by a wooden motorboat packed with explosives. Five hundred sailors died.

The aim of invasion was to forge a peace under the terms of which a single Palestinian state, including a protected Jewish minority, would be established. But by the time a final armistice was signed in February 1949, Israel had managed to expand its territory by about a third more than had been agreed under the terms of partition.

For Egypt, the first Arab-Israeli War proved destabilising. Martial law was declared in mid-1948, heralding a crackdown on radical elements behind the anti-government protests. The Muslim Brotherhood resisted and continued its campaign of assassinations: included on their hit list were two prime ministers, Ahmed Maher in 1945 and Mahmoud Nokrashy in 1948. The situation worsened after the February 1949 assassination by the Egyptian security police of the Brotherhood's supreme guide, Hassan al-Banna.

The country seemed ripe for revolution; there was little doubt that any popular-backed uprising would invoke anti-foreigner sentiment. As my father put it: 'Many of us realized then and there that we must leave that part of the world for good: there was no place for the outsider in such a cauldron of passionate and exclusive national pursuits.'

My mother and father left Egypt before the very end; their departure was part of a dispersal of the descendants of those families who had made their home in the Middle East for almost a century. Reversing the migratory direction of their forebears, they headed west, to an economically uncertain but safer realm of the post-war world. They left behind their homes, their possessions, their way of life.

Patricia Mumford in Cairo, 1950

My mother decided to leave Egypt in 1951: 'I missed my father and knew he was living on his own in London in ill-health,' she wrote. Around her the comfortable, affluent world was crumbling. 'I packed my bags and set sail for Southampton, my only asset some clothes and my British passport.' She wasn't only escaping the dangers of Cairo in revolt. Her uncle Samuele's death the same year opened a complex and contested inheritance battle that ensued among his five sisters. My grandmother Lidia, the youngest and least-educated Sornaga sister (and above all, married to an *inglese*) decided to join her family in England, nursing her husband Richard till he died of emphysema and other complications in 1960. As for my father, without a teaching job he needed to leave Cairo by the summer of 1949. His sister Artemis visited Cairo that spring on her way to Greece, with news at last of the family in Haifa, so he knew they were safe, having survived the battle for Haifa, which Israeli forces captured in 1947. It was obvious where he would have to go.

'Those of us who followed the news, those of us who were literate enough,' he wrote, 'realised or rather foresaw that the academic bonanza was going to open up in one direction, and that was the United States.' Armed with a scholarship to continue his studies at Johns Hopkins University, my father boarded a converted wartime troopship, the SS *Steel Apprentice*, at Port Said. 'Bewildered and hopeful,' he recorded in his private diary, 'I landed in Baltimore, a hot sweltering port city in Chesapeake Bay.'

SS Steel Apprentice

In January 1952, following a violent crackdown by British forces along the Suez Canal against rebellious auxiliary Egyptian police units, unrest fatally erupted. On the morning of Saturday, 26 January mobs of protestors swept through the heart of Cairo, looting and burning foreign-owned shops and premises. Symbols of wealth and privilege, from the Turf Club to the iconic Shepheard's Hotel, were burned to the ground. Dozens of foreigners who were caught by the frenzied mob were lynched. The mob also targeted the city's richer districts, including the Cairo built by Ismail Pasha seventy years prior in the image of Europe. 'We will put paid to all the pashas,' the crowd chanted.

Underscoring their point, Prime Minister Mustafa el-Nahas was having a pedicure that morning; his wife was at the hairdresser's. He ordered an armoured car to take her home. An Egyptian police officer, standing outside the Rivoli Cinema, was asked by a passer-by why nothing was being done about the looting going on all around them. He replied: 'Let the boys have some fun.' The amusements, which lasted all day, saw the destruction of 750 establishments, mostly foreign-owned, and the death of thirty people. This terrible day of rage and burning became known as 'Black Saturday' and for many marked the end of an era. By July, a military-led revolutionary council seized power and forced the abdication of King Farouk, ending the Muhammad Ali dynasty's long rule over Egypt and with it all the remaining protection and patronage the Levantines had enjoyed.

King Farouk went into exile in Italy. The king's kitchen Cabinet was comprised of Italians and Greeks, and many of his mistresses had been Jews. His sympathy for the Italians even extended to offering deposed King Victor Emmanuel hospitality in exile at his palace in Alexandria, a favour the Italians had granted Farouk's great-grandfather Ismail Pasha when he was forced to abdicate in the 1870s. Now it was time to return that favour.

Meanwhile in Palestine, now newly established Israel, my grandfather Jerasimous realised that, as tensions mounted between Arabs and Jews, his livelihood and family's security were under threat. What immediately affected him was the struggle for domination of the railway's sizeable labour force – the largest in the Mandate, with over 7,500 employees. In 1946, railway workers went on strike as the Jewish Histadrut (the Jewish national trade union movement) clashed with Arab workers over jobs and positions.

Rising levels of violence between the two communities also saw increasing attacks and acts of sabotage against the railway system, disrupting my grandfather's orderly existence and alarming his family. In April 1947, the Kantara–Haifa train was blown up, killing eight people. This was the same train my father had used to commute to university. In 1948 the railway's head office, Khoury House, was bombed. My grandfather, who in 1942 had been promoted to chief clerk, never mentioned the incident, but did say that his journey to work had become so perilous that he was occasionally ferried to and from the office in an armoured car. His job wasn't just dangerous, it was also coming to an end. After the British left in May 1948, Palestine Railways operations all but ceased. Accordingly, on the fifteenth of that month (the day the British Mandate ended), my grandfather's employment was terminated. 'There was no further chance of continuing Government Service particularly for foreigners,' he wrote in a typed resumé prepared for prospective employers, 'the desire for employing personnel with knowledge of Hebrew and national feelings having become strong after the change of regime.'

In the years after 1948 the Vatikiotis family struggled to remain in Haifa; yet they had nowhere else to go. My aunt Zoe, who was training for the opera, had been working at the Iraq Petroleum Company, as had my father, just up the road from Mosul Lane. And as partition happened, she had begun broadcasting recitals on the radio and appeared a few times on stage. On 24 June 1947 the main Jewish daily, *Haaretz*, published a review of one of her performances: '[she had an] excellent voice . . . a very wide range and is very pleasant to the listening ear. The legato and staccato were very good.' She was noticed at one recital by the conductor of the Israel National Opera and Philharmonic Orchestra, and might have landed a role there had she stayed on. My uncle Yannis, who had also embarked on a musical career, was by partition in 1947 studying viola at the conservatory in Athens. My aunt Artemis, the baby of the family, graduated from high school in 1949, two years after partition. She started work with the United Nations Relief and Works Agency, established that same year to assist Palestinian refugees.

In 1950 Jerasimous found a role in the complicated bureaucratic unwinding of the British Mandate. He served first as chief clerk, initially with the United Kingdom Claims Mission to Israel, which was tasked with sorting post-Mandate compensation and the return of British property, and then with the British Services Claims Mission. How sad it must have been for a man who all his life had worked as a civil servant for the Mandate to oversee the dismembering of its carcass.

When the commission's work came to an end, Jerasimous agonised over the decision to leave. Both his parents were buried in Acre, where he was born and grew up. His wife Paraskevi's better-off family had lost their home in the Katamon quarter in 1948, when her sisters and brothers left for Greece.

Finally, on 12 January 1954, Jerasimous and Paraskevi bade farewell to their beloved home in Mosul Lane and boarded the steamer SS *Messaria* with as much furniture and household goods as they could take – including a wooden wardrobe, two iron bedsteads and six wooden chairs. They were bound for Athens, a city they did not know in a country they had never lived in, yet as Greeks they belonged to. In the heartbreaking resumé he prepared shortly afterwards in search of work, my grandfather described himself as 'a refugee'. Even so, one of his first acts in Greece was to register his name and that of his family in the town hall of Hydra, the tiny island where his father had been born before settling in Palestine almost a century earlier.

Moving to Greece with her parents, Artemis continued working with refugees for the World Council of Churches but then emigrated to Canada in 1956. Zoe went to Rome to continue her training, supporting herself – and her studies – by working as a typist at the Indonesian legation to the Vatican, where she told me many years later that she briefly met Indonesia's founding president, the charismatic Sukarno. The pattern here is that these were well-educated and – more importantly – multilingual people going out in a post-war world that increasingly needed language skills and the ability to comprehend the more complex environment in Europe of occupying forces and refugees, for which their cosmopolitanism was an asset. A letter of recommendation from the Indonesian legation in 1954 cites Zoe's knowledge of Italian, English, French – and Indonesian! Artemis filled out forms noting that she spoke Arabic, Greek, English, French and Italian. My mother's cousin Giorgio Eberle, who settled in Rome, told me that when the Italians returned to Italy from Egypt, they mostly found jobs in travel and shipping companies because they spoke English. Many, like Giorgio, landed jobs at the newly established United Nations offices in Rome.

Panayiotis Vatikiotis, the Palestinian-Greek son of a railway official, prospered in the United States. Everyone in America called him 'PJ' or 'Taki'. In 1953 he obtained his PhD from the Paul H. Nitze School of Advanced International Studies at Johns Hopkins University in Washington, DC, and secured a teaching position in the political science department of Indiana University. Like many other immigrants of his generation, he opted to enlist in the US army, and secured both the funding for his postgraduate education and US citizenship. Fortunately, he was posted as an infantryman in occupied Germany, narrowly avoiding being sent to the horrors of the war in Korea. Tucked away on his return from the army in the mid-1950s in a large, comfortable Midwestern campus with imposing limestone faculty buildings and tidy tree-lined streets, my father nonetheless wondered if he, a transplanted Greek from Palestine, would last in this exciting Western world: 'Did I have the stamina and physical and moral resources to survive and prosper? And what did it mean to prosper?' he asked himself in the 1970s, as he started to gain attention in the field of Middle East politics.

My father felt there were too many influences, not all contradictory, on his earlier life, which had shaped his character and destiny:

'I confess I took to the Western cultural heritage and tradition with alacrity and voracious interest . . . But I was in limbo otherwise, for I was from the East and yet not of it [with only a] seamless web of suggestions, faded colours and evaporating smells, whiffs of familiar sounds and familiar but long dead characters, [and] without any real answers.'

What were the questions he needed answering? Sadly, despite the comforts and promise of an American mid-century life, later, after moving to less comfortable but more venerable London, Panayiotis remained ambivalent about the occidental world he had escaped to and greatly missed the oriental world he was forced to leave. 'I became thoroughly fed up with all the nice chaps telling me now we were all the same, when everything else told me we were not, and I always was impressed by the different dynamic of individual, social and political behaviour in the East.' Not the Middle East, mind you: the East.

My father's embrace of Western traditions and culture, something he needed to make his way in the adopted world of his adulthood, clashed discordantly with the realities unfolding in his childhood home. Eventually, he fell victim to the academic polarisation of Middle East studies. He was viewed with suspicion by the older generation of orientalist scholars who regarded him as too much of a native; at the same time, the revolutionary idealists of the Arab world suspected him of being pro-Jewish because he had Jewish friends and admirers, including the late Bernard Lewis, a British Jewish scholar of Islam, who lured him away from the United States to the School of Oriental and African Studies (SOAS) in London. When my father asked the American Palestinian scholar, Edward Said, why he had so savagely attacked him in his famous 1978 book *Orientalism*, Said replied: 'because you are a friend of Bernard Lewis'.[4] Staring out through the great glass windows of his corner office at SOAS, he was torn, not just between Arab and Jew, but also between what was perceived to be morally right and wrong. I know, now, where his heart lay: in the close friendships kindled in a sunlit classroom back in Haifa.

My father said or wrote very little about the Palestinian Liberation Movement, though I have a childhood memory of something he said publicly about the Arab-Israeli conflict that was printed in a coffee-table book on the 1967 Six-Day War: 'No Arab expects to get what he wants without an argument.' The glib comment masked his real feelings. By contrast, his diary reveals that he closely followed the fortunes of the Palestinian Liberation Organization, and mostly, to his private chagrin, their misfortunes. In the summer of 1972, he wrote: 'Several letters from Beirut make interesting reading. One from [redacted] in response to my inquiries about Wadie Haddad, stated flatly: your predictions about Wadie and his lot [i.e. the Popular Front for the Liberation of Palestine, PFLP] have come true. The movement is politically at an end and the overall situation of the Arabs is hopeless.'

In his diary my father lamented the manner in which some of the PLO's leaders had made 'good money' out of the Palestinian question – and how they fell prey to subversion, or worse, assassination, at the hands of Arab intelligence agencies who were already fed up with their revolution – as it was clear to them that Israel could not be defeated. On a visit to Cairo towards the end of 1972, he met Palestinian cadres whom he described as being of such low calibre that 'they need no enemies.' He added: 'Also met some of the PLO executive boys at the Shepheard's Bar during the Palestinian National Council Meeting.'

My father's contempt for the manner in which the Palestinian struggle unfolded after 1948 wasn't popular with Palestinians or those Westerners who idealistically cast it as a sacred revolution. His bitterness stemmed from the fact that he was close to the movement's early leaders and followed its evolution. He had visited Beirut in the late 1950s and then in the 1960s as his school friend Wadie Haddad and Wadie's comrades formulated their strategy. In 'The Commando', an unpublished short story my father wrote some years later, the character, Munir, appears to closely resemble his childhood friend:

> When Munir became deeply involved in the Arab Liberation Movement, it was the proper thing to do, just as it was the proper for him to respect his father's wishes and train in medicine. Munir also remembered how on that day he had suddenly flung the notes, together with the Anatomy textbook, into the trash basket.
>
> 'Who wants to be a doctor when one has no country to practice in,' he hissed. 'The Arabs, the Arabs . . . you'll see, our great national heroes will make short shrift of these upstart, grasping, cowardly Jews when the time comes.'
>
> That's what my father always told us, while he licked the asses of the English to build a home and send us to university.

'I say shit on the Arabs: those reactionary, feudalist, capitalist blood-suckers,' Munir spat out as he went on to tear up his class notes and every other bit of paper connected with his medical school career.

Later in the story the narrator, presumably my father, again cast as the 'sympathetic outsider', asks Munir/Haddad, who as the head of the armed wing of the PFLP planned a string of hijackings in the late 1960s and early 1970s, why in 1968 he masterminded the hijacking of an El Al flight en route from London to Tel Aviv. The exchange comes across as rather too vivid to be a figment of his imagination:

'Why did you do it?' I suddenly asked him.

'Do what? I didn't do anything: I only planned the operation.'

'OK, why did you plan such an operation then? What do you think it will accomplish? Anyone can threaten and take over an aircraft inflight, up there in mid-air,' I challenged him.

'Sure, sure. I know that. What do you take me for? Hanna and Issa and the others, they think it's extraordinary and heroic. Ah, the bums with their big talk. You know what the Movement's bank balance is? Five thousand pounds. You can't fight a pack of rabbits with that, let alone anything or anyone . . . But I'll be damned if I will lick the asses of all those presidents and kings for a penny. They are as much my enemies as the Enemy himself.'

I could imagine my father enjoying moments of candour like this with his friend Wadie Haddad. A year later, in 1969, my father tried to advise the Palestinian Movement on how to raise funds:

My research student [redacted], a member of the Palestine National Council, recently presented a memorandum to that body emphasizing the dangers of the al-Fath movement submitting to purely military action without a political base in the West Bank. Fears the West Bankers will grow feeling separate from the movement. Now I know why he discussed the movement with me in my room a month or so ago [early January] before he left for Beirut on the pretext that his father was ill. I recall telling him that without a levy imposed on all Palestinians (as the Jews did in the Mandate of Palestine) the movement would remain financially dependent on outside (Arab

> and other) sources. Lo and behold a Beirut newspaper report about this memorandum included in his list of recommendations, the imposition of a levy.

Throughout the ensuing turbulent years, which saw the birth of international terrorism at the hands of his Palestinian activist friends, my father quietly advised a number of his other friends and students on what he considered more realistic approaches to successful armed struggle, relying less on the fickle and selfish Arab states and more on cultivating effective membership and loyalty on the ground. He was criticised for questioning the Palestinian revolutionary spirit. Instead, he positioned himself as a realist, a sympathetic outsider speaking truth to his idealistic friends. During this period, he recorded in his diary several approaches from Israeli Zionist organisations. Although he refused to engage them, he was frequently tempted and on occasions tried to act as an intermediary, bringing Palestinians and Israelis together in his office or at home. He saw this as part of the Levantine character – always the insider-outsider, doing things, as he put it, 'in the Nasr el-din Hodja way' (a reference to the Anatolian sage). The committee members that comprised his complex Levantine character were always arguing; they never quite reached a consensus.

By April 1971 Panayiotis concluded that his revolutionary friends from the PFLP were a spent force: they had failed to replace the more moderate, state-accommodating Fatah movement led by the charismatic Yasser Arafat (1929–2004), for whom he had little time. 'Are the rats abandoning the sinking Palestinian ship of revolution?' he asked himself on the pages of his diary. As I read these breathless passages I wondered: was he – in his way – fighting for the liberation of Palestine, or was he simply being loyal to old friends? Or was he recording for posterity a testament of loyalty in the face of the criticism that battered him in the course of his career? I didn't have the chance to ask. My father died in 1997, long before I read his diary, which reveals a passion and love for the people he was forced to abandon, and a yearning for the land of his father and his grandfather before him. Even towards the end of his career, already ill with heart disease, my father worked tirelessly to find a way to bring Arab and Jew together, even though he had no faith that Israel was interested in a political settlement, just as he had no doubt that Arab states had not the slightest intention of accepting the State of Israel. It was just that they could not defeat it militarily. If he were alive today, I doubt he would have enjoyed being proven correct.

While teaching at Indiana my father had fallen in love with Lois Cammack, an attractive, vivacious student from Burlington in North Carolina, whom he had met during a semester in Baton Rouge, Louisiana. They married, and a son – my half-brother Eric – was born soon after. The marriage was short-lived, and almost as soon as his divorce came through my father contacted my mother Patricia Mumford, who was then living in London, and whom he had known briefly in Cairo when she worked at the British Council. They met several times afterwards socially; my mother, together with her sister Josie, was part of the social circuit in Cairo. For all the uncertainty of those final three years, there was a lot of gaiety and fun. The resumed relationship and courtship, conducted by mail, was swift and my parents were married in 1955 in Heidelberg, where my father was posted with the army.

The Palestinian Greek married the British-Italian Jew from Cairo in Germany in a brief civil ceremony followed by a reception in a beer *Stube* attended by army friends. The familiarity of their lost worlds no doubt fastened their union: my mother was by then working for *The Times* of London as a typist. She may have had a British passport and a British father, but her mother tongue was Italian, her heritage Jewish. And in contrast to her expansive, indulgent childhood in Egypt, the move to England resulted in a considerable reduction in her circumstances. My memories of childhood visits to my grandmother Lidia in her shoe-box-sized bedsit in Belsize Park revolve mainly around her strong Italian accent, her efforts to cook us pasta on a Belling one-ring electric stove, and the weekly copies of the Italian tabloid *Oggi*, which my mother took home after Lidia had read them.

Serving in Germany, my father worked for the US army judge advocate's office – apparently on account of his typing skills – defending American GIs on charges of soliciting prostitutes. I was born in Indianapolis a little under two years later after my father returned with my mother to bucolic Bloomington, Indiana, and to his teaching job. My sisters Helen and Daphne were born there subsequently. My father's elder brother Yannis joined us to study at Indiana University's highly regarded music conservatory. My father tried to persuade his refugee parents to emigrate from Greece, where Jerasimous was struggling to find work, and settle in. They nearly did, until my grandfather baulked – even after completing all the formalities needed for immigration. Years later my grandfather would rail at me against the Americans, whom he blamed for the end of the peaceful idyll in Palestine under British rule. No matter how hard I tried to correct his slanted view of history, Jerasimous remained a loyal servant of the British Mandate. He would raise one bony finger at me and lift his chin in that typically Arab gesture of negation. My grandfather harboured this view until he died in 1992; though he held a British passport, he never once set foot in Britain.

In 1966 we all moved as a family to the United Kingdom after my father accepted a position as Professor of Middle East Politics at SOAS. Here, occasionally, he would receive telephone calls from Palestinian Arabs who introduced themselves as his cousins, or the children of his cousins. In fact, four of my father's first cousins married Arab spouses and subsequently settled in Syria, Lebanon, Kuwait and in the Gulf. 'It is ironic,' my father wrote, 'that for someone who has been frequently accused of being anti-Arab because of his critical academic writing on Arab affairs, I belong to an extended kinship group of nearly one hundred *awlad 'arab*.' As, I suppose, do I.

CHAPTER TWELVE

The Suez Syndrome

> 'Arab nationalism has become a reality and a source of action after it had been a mere slogan . . . It has become the ideology of a whole region. The whole world supports us. Free men everywhere support us.'
>
> President Gamal Abdel Nasser, speaking in Port Said, 23 December 1956

Towards the end of one of my recent visits to Cairo I saw by chance a notice for a performance of *Aida*. I managed to buy a ticket online. The New Opera House is situated at the southern end of Gezira island in Zamalek, just about walking distance from where I was staying. A gift from Japan, and designed by Japanese and Egyptian architects, this brutalist concrete structure hinting at the Islamic was completed in 1988. Instead of a Verdi opera, the inaugural performance was a traditional Japanese Kabuki. I confess it was my first ever visit to the opera, and I was unsure what to expect. The doorman stopped me on the way in, for although I had the good sense to wear a jacket, I was unaware that more formal attire was required.

'Ties over there,' said the uniformed doorman, pointing towards the ticket booth. A stained acrylic tie knotted in place, I took my seat in the stalls. There were lots of empty seats, and none of the glitter and style of the belle époque set who attended the opening of Cairo's first opera house in 1871, though I saw a few Egyptian families dressed for the occasion – formal suits, silk ties and girls in frilly lace dresses. Cairo's elite live more than two hours' drive away on the desert fringe in walled and gated communities with names like Utopia, Dreamland and Beverly Hills and rarely make the trek to the city centre. I did spot a few Russians, though, wearing 'smart casual', and some rather bohemian-looking Europeans wearing creased linen jackets. The production was Egyptian, with a couple of token Europeans in leading roles and an Italian conductor. During the intervals the stalls let out on to a small refreshment area. No champagne and canapés, only tea, soft drinks and packaged snacks. A surly woman wearing a hijab tended the till. Without even a hint of pretence or opulence, everyone seemed to blend in well together; Verdi, who was reportedly in favour of opera for the people, would have been happy.

As I sat through the long performance, I wondered what would have become of Italians and Greeks in Egypt if they had stayed on? Almost certainly they would have integrated and become citizens, perhaps like the Chinese and Indians in Southeast Asia, who after an initial period of ethnic strife at independence evolved as a productive and successful commercial middle class, despite the lingering hostility and prejudice towards them. Luckily, Southeast Asia has enjoyed half a century of peace and prosperity; the Middle East, on the other hand, has been plunged into a never-ending period of violent sectarian conflict leaving little space or security for unprotected minorities. Equally, the disappearance of Levantine diversity and its displacement by hard national identities deprived the region of a social interface for fluid and productive mingling without the fixed boundaries that generate such tension today.

Just as I began this journey at the Suez Canal, so it ends here, with an Egyptian leader every bit as transformative as Muhammad Ali, the Albanian tax-collector-turned-mercenary soldier. Gamal Abdel Nasser was a soldier too, but he was a native Egyptian of Bedouin Arab ancestry, a son of the soil with a nativist and pan-Arab vision that transformed not just Egypt but also the wider region. As much as Muhammad Ali opened Egypt to the outside world and encouraged Europeans like my mother's family to settle there, Nasser presided over a second opening – one to his own people, who had been largely excluded from the upper levels of society prior to 1952. Nasser, my father wrote in his 1978 biography of the charismatic Egyptian leader, 'assumed the role of enabler in his dream to make Egypt independent of foreign control'.

Reflecting on the region's history over the century that spanned my family's sojourn in the Middle East, I realised that partition and the coercion that turned arbitrary colonial dividing lines into fixed boundaries was the driving centrifugal force tearing at the fabric of cosmopolitanism. Arguably, the process evolved over the course of the nineteenth century, beginning with the loss of the Ottoman Empire's European territories – Greece, and the Balkan states of Bosnia, Serbia and Bulgaria – which comprised sizeable non-Muslim communities once considered part of a heterogenous whole. Pressure on the rest of the Ottoman Empire from encroaching European powers and from Russia in the east to improve the rights and privileges of the sultan's remaining Christian subjects encouraged them to demand equality and bred resentment among the Muslim majority. Subsequently a pronounced assertion of Muslim orthodoxy emanating from Istanbul, desperate to shore up waning Ottoman legitimacy, and with support from the Arabian Peninsula, drove a wedge between Christianity and Islam, reinforced by the onset of the conflict between Arab and Jew in Palestine in the 1920s and culminating in the formal partition in 1947.

There was, if you like, another partition of sorts – one that saw the progressive leaching of Christian populations from Muslim lands in response to advancing European and Russian challenges to Ottoman power. As many as a million Christian Armenians and a sizeable number of Greeks living mostly in Anatolia were massacred after 1895, the result of the Ottoman Sultan Abdul Hamid II's bid to purge the empire of infidels, using pan-Islamic sentiment. The same fate befell the remaining Greek population of Asia Minor after the First World War. Several hundred thousand perished. Those who survived went into exile after 1922, when Turks killed or expelled the region's historical Greek and Christian communities.

These developments did not directly affect the Egypt and Palestine my parents grew up in, by then under British rule, but they cast an ever-growing sectarian shadow that slowly chilled easy mingling, ecumenical practices and the preservation of social status. It upset what Jacqueline Shohet Kahanoff called 'the delicate balance which allowed people belonging to various communities and religions to live together in fairly good harmony as long as various accommodations with the facts of life were never openly acknowledged.' Quite possibly, if the European powers had not disposed of the Ottoman dispensation, blinded as they were by their own craven territorial ambitions, Levantine society might have graduated from the somewhat crude and contingent arrangements of khedival Egypt into something more rooted in modern democratic pluralism, in which minorities had rights and a place defined by constitutional arrangement.

Instead, stealthy partition and dismemberment of the Ottoman realm set the stage for the wave of modern Arab nationalism that swept across the Middle East and Asia after the Second World War, and which in turn made the facts of life harder to ignore, precipitating both a cultural and ideological expunging of the cumulative cosmopolitan diversity of the preceding century. This nationalist surge demanded narratives rooted in narrow nativism and the struggle against imperialism. To borrow from the British anthropologist Ernest Gellner's conception of nationalism, which fits the modern Middle East well: a homogenised Arab, mainly Muslim 'high culture' was imposed on societies, which, at least in Ottoman times, were composed of a broader range of coexisting 'low cultures' – Arab and non-Arab as well as Muslim and non-Muslim.

The British Empire, beset by delusions that it was spreading civilised enlightenment, found it impossible to balance paternalistic regard for the nascent nationalist sentiment among its subject peoples with the greater need to secure its strategic and commercial interests. The tendency to put a premium on the latter, often with the use of force, fuelled the rise of anti-imperial sentiment. As independent states were forged out of former colonies, the forces shaping the identities of these new states generally militated against the survival of pluralism that flourished in the colonial era. From Egypt to Burma to Malaya, the post-colonial reality was that immigrants either imported or cultivated to serve imperial ends were considered uninvited guests. The social history of the post-colonial era is littered with the rupture and dislocation of plural societies. My family's Levantine milieu were no exception.

Jerasimous Vatikiotis, for all his roots in Acre, remained a Greek; Richard Mumford, among a large tribe of Italian Jewish in-laws, a sole Briton. He and the Sornagas were protected by the British 'veiled protectorate' and the Italian state. Every member of my Italian and Greek family sought the protection of the Capitulations, thereafter finding themselves citizens of modern European states they had not been born in, and to which many of them had never been. Just as in the pre-war period they were buffeted by the powerful ideological currents powering the emerging Allied and Axis confrontation, so too were they caught up in the passionate and violent whirlwind of the post-imperial environment.

My mother, who had attended the British school in Cairo, was pulled in one direction: 'We attended the Empire Day reception at the British Embassy and sang "God Save the King". We read Shakespeare and learned about the British Empire. We were told what the pink stood for in our atlases.' My father, with his Arab and Greek roots, was somewhat detached from the colonial setting. His father Jerasimous was a Freemason, an affiliation many Levantines and educated Arabs would use to boost their standing in a context where, as orientals rather than privileged occidentals, there was the need for status-conferring affiliation.

These Levantine families initially benefited economically and socially from the post-First World War colonial construct, but by the 1930s they were exposed to hatred and prejudice generated by colonial policies. They were caught in a limbo of sorts, a liminal and precarious existence, in spite of their affluence, which helps explain why Levantine culture can be hard to define and pin down. Unlike the mestizo in Latin America, or the Peranakan society of the Malay Peninsula, where the mixing of races also generated distinct cultures, cuisines and languages, the Levantines stayed pretty much in their own ethnic and religious lanes – Greek, Italian, Jewish or Orthodox Christian. They did not combine as such to produce a definitive creole-like culture. Attempts to define Levantinism have focused on inchoate, fragmented descriptors such as 'multi-faceted', 'fluid' or 'prismatic'. The Egyptian actor Omar Sharif, who made his name playing the role of Sherif Ali beside Peter O'Toole in David Lean's 1962 film *Lawrence of Arabia*, was born to Lebanese Christian parents in Alexandria. He spoke French, Greek, Italian, Spanish and Arabic and noted that his accent enabled him 'to play the role of a foreigner without anyone knowing exactly where I came from'.

It is often hard to get past the inherent hybridism of the occidental and oriental in Levantine society, which sits awkwardly in the turbulent context of clashing tribes and religions that has come to define the Middle East. The Levantines served as cultural intermediaries, imparting European styles and affectations to local elites, yet never quite managing to integrate with them. This explains why their era is lost and their legacy is shrouded by the whiff of colonial complicity.

This identity angst comes through in the pronounced ambivalence of my father's diary. He craved the association of nationalist Arabs – Egyptians, Palestinians; yet some of them branded him anti-Arab because of his association with Western scholars and scholarship. He struggled to find a cultural anchorage; he maintained close friendships with Egyptian literary luminaries such as Louis Awad, Magdi Wahba, Yusuf Idris and Naguib Mahfouz.[1] He quietly offered support for the Palestinian cause, because some of its leaders were his childhood friends; therefore, very much part of his identity. Yet he managed to alienate many of the young Palestinian idealists who beat a path to his office at the School of Oriental and African Studies – including one or two who went on to serve in leadership positions on the Palestinian National Council. 'He rejected mostly the fact that they were dreamers, and did not have practical programs,' an Arab former student of his wrote to me. 'I had the impression, he felt they were hopeless.'

Meanwhile, the Western establishment on both sides of the Atlantic didn't quite know what to make of this nervous fellow with a Greek name who spoke flawless English with no recognisable accent and who teased Arab and Jew alike socially. On a visit to Cairo in early 1973, a diplomat at the British Embassy made excuses for not agreeing to see my father: 'Sorry old man,' he records the diplomat saying, 'we heard about the people you've been seeing and wish to avoid you becoming a Consular case.' But my father had no time for dreamy British diplomats with their 'Lawrencian and Philbyite' tendencies; they seemed, he wrote, to have limited access to Egyptian society other than 'rich Copts – the *ingleezi* veneer types'.

Many of the foreigners forced to flee the dissolving Levantine world turned their backs forever on the Middle East to make new lives in far-off places like Canada, Australia and South Africa, capitalising on their multilingual talents and their sophisticated, international sensibility.[2] My father's acute longing for the Levant was exacerbated by the fact that he had made a career of its study, and moved in circles that were obsessed with events in the region and afflicted, as he put it, 'by a form of hysteria about this intractable problem'. This highly charged context helped distil his feelings into a bitter brew of confused allegiance and resentment.

As the Arab-Israeli conflict unfolded across the wars of 1967 and 1973, my father's stature grew in the world of Middle East studies. At one point in early 1974, while on sabbatical at Princeton University, he mused in his diary: 'Often, I have reflected on my stupidity because were one to have accepted every speaking engagement and writing solicitation over the last seven or eight years, one could easily have become quite rich! But I somehow always considered that source of income as constituting "misery money": the misery of both Arabs and Jews.'

Earlier generations of the Vatikiotis and Sornaga families were less dramatically conflicted about their identity. Living under Ottoman rule and its immediate aftermath, they benefited from arcane mechanisms and devices that cloaked the divisive issue of identity in a pragmatic carapace of convenience: the *millets* that imposed the responsibility of self-government on different communities; the Capitulations that guaranteed extra-territoriality, which oiled the wheels of commerce; and the Mixed Courts in Egypt that protected foreign financiers, merchants and professionals from being preyed on by unscrupulous officials – and without doubt covered up the exploitation of native workers. These were the essential ingredients of cosmopolitanism in Egypt and elsewhere in the Middle East. As Europe embarked on the violent fusion of disparate societies into bounded nation states, which promptly then fell upon each other in deadly combat, the Ottomans were content to foster and manage a more fluid diversity because it made their empire easier to tax and control. Albert Camus, the Nobel Prize-winning French novelist and philosopher who was born in North Africa, understood the bonding effect of Ottoman cosmopolitanism. With an eye on the looming Second World War, he observed that defining nationalities generated disintegration and conflict. Civilisation, he argued, nodding in the direction of Diogenes and the Stoics, does not lie in a greater degree of refinement, but in an awareness shared by a whole people.

Ephemeral as it was, the Ottoman-derived system of pluralism was, in its purest form, effective. Communal divides were well managed, and commercial benefits flowed. The downsides were high levels of inequality and the absence of social integration, the same phenomenon observed by the British colonial economist John Furnivall in the Far East of the 1930s: a sense of pluralism, as people 'who mingled but did not mix'.[3]

My great-grandfather Baba Yannis in Acre was comfortable in his own skin; despite fears that drove him into exile on a number of occasions, he was not persecuted by the late Ottoman government for choosing to remain Greek. Giacomo Sornaga, the Cairo Post Office manager and my maternal great-grandfather, although a patriot who chose to die in Italy, was also very much a loyal functionary of the prevailing khedival system in Egypt. Paradoxically, this earlier generation, who came of age at the end of the nineteenth century before the collapse of the Ottoman Empire and all the accompanying misery, was more integrated than the generation that followed. They were liberal in their way of thinking, they treated their Egyptian or Palestinian colleagues as equals, spoke local languages, and did not allow religious affiliation to limit their social and professional interactions. Perhaps, as well, this was because they matured before the era of British imperial control and administration, with its obsessive insistence on *divide et impera*.

Their children were less fortunate. The onset of the Second World War brought with it the toxic hatred of fascism, which magnified allegiances and divided foreign communities. 'The black of National Socialism and the Brown of the (Italian) *fascio* created a fault line of suspicion in our cosmopolitan and convivial society,' wrote the Alexandrian French journalist Paul Balta. The war itself upended the stability and bourgeois prosperity of their lives. By the end of the 1940s, unless all these foreigners had joined the emerging nationalist struggle – either Arab or Jewish – they were no longer welcome, yet even those who did were suspect. Greeks and Italians in Egypt did join communist-inspired labour movements that helped whip up anti-British sentiment in the 1940s. But these foreign fellow-travellers did not survive what came next.

The nationalist awakening that animated those poor students in Cairo my father rubbed shoulders with at roadside food stalls, as well as the better-off students from the American University whose essays he ghost-wrote for favours and a bit of cash, included a strong element from the Egyptian army. One aspect of the confusing 'veiled protectorate' arrangement from 1882 until notional independence in 1922 was the imposition of Britain's administrative control over the Egyptian army. Even after 1922, Britain held the reins tightly, only really letting go after evacuating their troops to the canal in 1948. The Egyptian officer corps benefited from British training and support, but with smouldering resentment among young officers, many of whom came for the first time from less privileged backgrounds.

Gamal Abdel Nasser was among these activist officers. Tall and gangly and with a lantern jaw, he came from a modest, land-owning family in Upper Egypt, and his father had been a postal worker in Alexandria. Like other nationalist leaders who emerged at the end of the colonial era, young Nasser became politically conscious as a student in the 1930s and participated in anti-colonial protests. He and his comrades grew disenchanted with the hopelessly corrupt and ineffective royalist government. The Egyptian army's disastrous defeat at the hands of the Israelis in 1949 left them embittered and angry. Fraudulent arms deals brokered by King Farouk and his cronies exposed the army to better-trained and -equipped Israeli forces. The young officers became actively seditious, calling themselves the 'free officer movement', eventually assuming control of Egypt in a July 1952 coup. From here on, the position of foreigners in Egypt became untenable.

It had been several centuries since a native Egyptian ruled the country; despite this, foreign civil administration and military protection of the Suez Canal stood in the way of Nasser's grand vision of the pan-Arab world he aimed to lead and the destruction of the State of Israel he hoped to achieve. As much as the 1944 Alexandria Protocol and the establishment of the Arab League propelled Egypt towards the Arab world, Nasser's nationalisation of the canal in July 1956 precipitated the final end of Egypt's embrace of Europe and hastened, at least for Egypt, a reorientation towards the emerging communist East, and to newly independent states in Asia and Africa. 'We dug the canal with our lives, our skulls, our bones and our blood,' Nasser thundered to a roaring, adoring crowd in a speech that lasted almost three hours. The European world looked on and worried about the fate of global trade and the 15,000 ships that passed through the canal each year. In Alexandria, Paul Balta recalls a sense of panic in the Levantine community and a scramble to book passages to France and Italy. Jewellery was either hidden or entrusted to friends and neighbours.

As with the building of the canal a century earlier, so its return to Egyptian hands drew the international community together in what was briefly the world's most serious crisis since the end of the Second World War. Britain and France, the two powers with most at stake, teamed up to oppose nationalisation and ultimately remove Nasser. And though India was now independent, with less need to maintain clear lines of communication between Bombay and London, Britain still received half of its crude oil through the canal. Nationalisation, in British Prime Minister Anthony Eden's words, meant that 'Nasser had his thumbs on our windpipe'. Eden was obsessed with destroying Nasser, and, together with French Prime Minister Guy Mollet, signed a secret protocol with Israel in the French town of Sèvres on 24 October 1956. Under the deal, Israel would invade the Sinai, provoking an Anglo-French ultimatum to withdraw; Israel would comply, leaving the way open for British and French forces to invade Egypt. The British also united Jordan and Iraq against Egypt's pan-Arab ambitions in what was known as the Baghdad Pact. Meanwhile, Washington and Moscow opposed these Anglo-French plans to seize the canal. Washington was annoyed with its European allies for focusing on the decaying remnants of their empires, when the emerging threat to Europe was from behind the Iron Curtain in the newly acquired Soviet satellite states. As the Suez Crisis brewed, Hungary rose up against Soviet rule, and America's two most powerful Cold War allies, the English and the French, were planning an invasion of Egypt!

Anglo-French dealings had attended the birth of the Suez Canal, which reflected their imperial rivalries at the start of the nineteenth century. Their failed joint invasion of the canal zone in early November 1956, which was code-named Operation Musketeer and involved an air and seaborne assault, was the last gasp of their imperial order. And while the wars we see today in Syria and Iraq might have little to do with events in Suez almost seventy years ago, the foundations for Russian and American involvement in these conflicts were laid during the Suez Crisis of 1956.

The Suez Crisis terrified what remained of Egypt's foreign community. The Greek prime minister, Konstantinos Karamanlis, sought assurances from Nasser that the sizeable Greek community of pilots, merchants and professionals would not be expelled. Nasser said he 'would do everything possible to dispel the worries of our brother Greeks'. Alex Kitroeff notes that some left-wing Greeks actually supported Nasser's move to nationalise the canal. In Alexandria, hopes that a negotiated solution would be found to the Suez Crisis dissolved. More and more people started to leave. A production of Samuel Beckett's *Waiting for Godot* in the city was 'a greater success than expected', recalls Paul Balta. The play expressed the confusion felt by the Levantine community: 'Godot is not coming but misfortune is likely to turn up.'

These events unfolded against the backdrop of a world dividing between communist and non-communist, and with idealism and optimism spreading across Africa and Asia as newly independent nations sought to break the bonds of colonial rule and strive for the influence of what Indonesia's President Sukarno referred to as 'new emerging forces'. Nasser was a prominent participant in the Asia-Afrika Conference convened by Sukarno in the Indonesian city of Bandung in 1955

– just one year before the Suez Crisis. 'This is the first intercontinental conference of coloured peoples in the history of mankind!' thundered Sukarno, wearing a crisp white uniform jacket and his trademark black velvet cap at the podium. 'It is a new departure in the history of the world that leaders of Asian and African peoples can meet together in their own countries to discuss and deliberate upon matters of common concern.'

For members of my mother's family still living in Egypt, one of the most immediate changes was a sharp turn towards the Eastern bloc. Alongside the arms deal with Czechoslovakia came East European technicians and engineers, who replaced Italians and Greeks. My mother's cousin, Giorgio Eberle, who was seventeen in 1956, visited East European trade and product fairs. He bought a cheap Czech bicycle, which quickly fell apart. But if the Greeks and other non-Jewish minorities hoped this new vision of Asian and African independence and modernity would save their livelihoods, the 1957 Egyptianisation laws sealed their fate otherwise.

The history of the Aswan Dam built across the Nile in Upper Egypt neatly captures the sudden shift in direction. The original low dam had been designed and built under British supervision by Greek and Italian engineers and workers at the end of the nineteenth century. A plan to reinforce and strengthen the dam was drawn up in the early 1950s by an Egyptian-Greek engineer, Adrian Daninos. But when the USA and Britain withdrew financial support for the project after the Suez Crisis, Nasser angrily turned the project over to a Soviet firm.[4] In truth, by this time European capital, expertise and manpower by which Egypt had been built and modernised for over a century was inconvenient. The *New York Times* correspondent Osgood Carruthers described the 1957 Egyptianisation laws as 'the real beginning of Nasser's revolution, signalling an end to Egypt's dependence on foreign advice, foreign experts and foreign assistance'. To Egyptians, he wrote as Cairo bureau chief in 1957, 'these foreign influences have served only foreign interests and have failed to benefit the people of Egypt.' Even so, in 1954, an Egyptian Greek by the name of Antigone Costanda won the Miss Egypt beauty contest and went on to be crowned Miss World.

In one of his last major books my father, whose love for Egypt and Egyptians equalled his passion for Palestine, tried to get into Nasser's mind in a psychoanalytical biography, *Nasser and His Generation*, published in 1978. One of his conclusions was that Nasser genuinely believed he was working for the benefit of his people. Nasser did not use his fourteen years as president to accumulate great wealth and power for himself or his family, he argued.[5] Rather, he believed in his own rhetoric: that he was paternalistic, lifting his fellow Egyptians out of poverty and restoring Egypt's prestige as leader of the Arab world. In this sense, and much like his contemporary, Sukarno, Nasser saw himself as an extension of his own people. He had no time at all for the European arts and culture that had bloomed in Cairo and Alexandria under the preceding dynasty of Muhammad Ali. In this sense nativist and nationalist narratives co-mingled, just as they did across other former colonies in Asia and Africa.

With the exception of the Jews, who were harassed and poorly treated, Nasser did not formally expel what remained of the foreign community, but his policies and actions made it increasingly difficult for them to stay unless they naturalised; his rhetoric and thunder about Egyptian blood and bones fanned populist anger against them. Assets were seized or sequestered. The pretextual Israeli invasion of the Sinai in October 1956 lent this anti-foreign sentiment an acutely anti-Jewish tone, which was exploited by the Muslim Brotherhood. 'The events precipitated by the nationalization of the Suez Canal in 1956 spun the Egyptian Jews relentlessly out of their comfortable homes and influential positions and scattered them around the globe,' wrote Jean Naggar, of the Jewish Mosseri family. 'To that privileged community, the crisis had exploded with the force of an asteroid colliding with the earth, destroying the work of generations.'

If, after 1955, Egypt lurched towards the East and embarked on a new era of Afro-Asian solidarity, after 1961 the country adopted socialist garb and, as a result, all foreign-owned enterprises were turned over to the state, including the proud Sornaga ceramics enterprise, which, as mentioned, was renamed the El-Nasr Company for Refractories and Ceramics – *el-nasr* in Arabic means great victory. By the time I arrived in Cairo as a student in the mid-1970s the name Nasr was a ubiquitous branding of anything Egyptian-made, including the cars originally designed by the Italian Fiat company. My first paid job in Cairo was teaching English to engineers from the Nasr car company.

The withdrawal of Jews and other foreigners from the Middle East created commercial opportunities that other minorities took advantage of. 'The vacuum created by the departure of the Jews', an exodus from Iraq to Israel in the early 1950s, 'was filled by the Shi'a. Urban and wealthy Shi'a families shared with the Jews exclusion from many areas of official life and pursued their fortunes in trade and finance,' argues the Arab academic Sami Zubaida. These replacement minorities, displacing the more diverse Levantine cohort, stored up for another day a new set of sectarian problems for countries such as Iraq, Lebanon and Syria. In Egypt, where only a handful of Jews, Greeks and Italians now live, the sad reality is that even traditional relations between the country's ancient Christian Copts – who comprise up to 20 per cent of the population – and the majority Muslims have suffered so badly that it has led to violence, largely inspired, if not instigated, by the militant Muslim Brotherhood. Thus, the modern Middle East may not be uniformly Arab – or uniformly Jewish, in the case of Israel – but the pockets of diversity that once contributed to the region's modernisation and development have either been emptied or replaced by new groups of people, many of them snared in violent sectarian conflict.

The Arab nationalist narrative that replaced the Ottoman and succeeding colonial dispensation has been less inclusive and tolerant of diversity – perhaps not surprisingly, as there was a need to bind together fragile new nation states. This push for national identities has put pressure on non-Arab minorities like the more than 2 million Kurds in Syria, for example, but also Christian Yezidis and Assyrians. They and other non-Arab and non-Sunni Muslim minorities were progressively alienated by the pan-Arab Ba'athist ideology that developed in Syria and Iraq. The Ba'ath Party, ostensibly an Arab socialist movement founded in Syria, did not emasculate confessional communities and minorities by forcing them to assimilate – it simply co-opted and dominated them, notes the Lebanese academic Nadim Shehadi. These subjugated minorities comprise the principal victims of the Iraq and Syrian conflicts that have afflicted the Arab world in the twenty-first century. The rise of Islamic State in the Levant after 2013, a by-product of these debilitating wars, hastened the degradation of diversity in Arab lands. While, in theory – and some limited practice – Islamic State allowed non-Muslim minorities to live under their ultra-conservative rule (so long as they paid a tax), in practice they were mistreated and forced to convert to Islam.

In this sense, to borrow from the French-Lebanese philosopher Amin Maalouf, just as Europe shaped Christianity and Judaism, rendering these ancient faiths alien to the oriental lands of their origin in the Middle East, so the harsh desert culture of the Arabian Peninsula has perhaps rendered Islam alien to its broader, more pluralistic historical origins in trade and exchange between Semitic peoples across the wider region. The culturally sophisticated and inclusive Islam of the Abbasid period, ruling from Baghdad in the eighth century, translated the philosophy and science of the ancient Greeks. This valuable knowledge was conveyed to Europe in the Middle Ages through the agency of enlightened Muslim governors who ruled parts of the Iberian Peninsula until the fifteenth century, and which in turn influenced the emerging Ottoman rulers in Istanbul. Cosmopolitanism, stripped of the baggage of orientalist nostalgia, had a distinctive DNA that can in fact be traced to Muslim interpretations of the ancient Greek and Roman civilisations, long before Europe's enlightenment. The rather inclusive notion of *Rum* or *Rumi* was very much part of the region's heritage, not some alien intrusion.

Perhaps it is not surprising that the Middle East is preponderantly viewed through the lens of modern European post-Second World War thinking. China's contribution to human progress by its technological innovation – inventing paper, the compass and movable type – was for a long time obscured by the dominance of European power and particularism. In much the same way, the Ottoman Empire's contribution to managing tolerance and diversity in the name of civic order and collective human endeavour has been masked by the brutal theocracy of Islamic State and lost in the rubble of the devastated cities of Syria and Iraq. Grieving cosmopolitanism should be less about mourning the loss of European influence in the Middle East and more about the manner in which later European intrusions unleashed new and destructive forces that left in their wake the ruins of this earlier age.

The colliding forces of imperial power and commercial interests that have underpinned the modern Middle East since then have not played out in the same way they did for Muhammad Ali in Egypt at the start of the nineteenth century. It is difficult, in fact, to understand fully the Middle East today using analogies from the past. The post-war empire represented by the United States was interested in two things: protecting the State of Israel, and safeguarding the flow of oil from Saudi

Arabia and the Gulf. Neither of these imperatives offered opportunities for outsiders in the way that building the Suez Canal transformed the region in the 1860s. Rather, they have coddled an inward-looking conservative Wahhabi-influenced monarchy in the Hejaz as it progressively bleached Arab culture of its cosmopolitan elements, and allowed Israeli society to be held hostage by a hardline Jewish orthodoxy that sees peaceful coexistence with Palestinians as a threat. By the mid-1970s, what was left of cosmopolitan Cairo had been invaded by the new Saudi and Gulf Arab elite flush with petrodollars. During this period, my father records in his diary, 'it was the Libyans who littered the bistros of Cairo and Alex, and especially in winter it is the Saudis, Kuwaitis and Gulf types'.

Today the nearest you come to cosmopolitan settings in the Middle East are the soaring steel-and-glass spires that have sprouted in the Gulf states, making Dubai, Qatar and Abu Dhabi the new Klondikes. But the societies these brash new principalities have nurtured, with their tiny, privileged, indigenous elites serviced by armies of low-paid immigrant workers mostly from South and Southeast Asia, make for an awkward parallel. Wandering through the Dubai Mall, one of the largest in the world, I found it hard to sense a connection between the starched-dish-dashed Emiratis emerging from their super-charged Mercedes and BMW SUVs and the smiling Filipina store assistants who staff the brand outlets that service Emirati tastes for luxury. The role of these mostly temporary Asian guest workers is vital but transactional and fleeting. They come and go; their income wired home by Western Union to support families far away. They build nothing of their own in this futuristic desert film set. Is this the new cosmopolitanism? Ironically, the Gulf Arabs and other entitled Middle Eastern elites prefer to spend their summers in Greece or the Italian Riviera, where they buy property and moor their yachts.

In Doha there are at least signs of an effort to celebrate the region's diversity. The Islamic Art Museum, designed by the late Chinese-American architect I.M. Pei, blends the harsh desert Islam of the Arabian Peninsula with delicate figurative arts from Shiite Iran and ornate calligraphic designs from fifteenth-century Anatolia, from which my great-uncle Samuele Sornaga drew inspiration for the glazed ceramic vases he produced at his factory in El-Wedy.

*

I embarked on writing this book as tens of thousands of refugees from the wars that have plagued the Levant since my parents left the region streamed out of the dust-and-rubble remains of their once-proud cities on to leaking rubber dinghies in the Mediterranean Sea. Using smartphones, they started telling their stories and chronicled their desperate flight to safety in southern and eastern Europe, hoping to reach relatives in countries like Germany and Sweden. In the first nine months of 2020 more than 25,000 migrants arrived on the shores of Italy, almost half from North Africa – the same shores from which more than 80,000 Italians had left for Egypt by the 1920s.

As I made my own journey I was acutely aware of the tragic reversal of fortunes across an arc of almost two centuries. In the mid-nineteenth century my European forebears took deck-class passage on steamers alongside piles of luggage and found refuge in the Levant. By the mid-twentieth century they were refugees heading back to Europe on slightly bigger steamers with their own set of luggage and, if they were lucky, jewellery and gold coins stuffed in their bedsteads. Now, seventy years later, their former hosts and neighbours from the Levant are struggling to join them, albeit with little more than backpacks, cheap bed mats and mobile phones.

The waters of the eastern Mediterranean are beguilingly warm. For centuries this sea carried the hopes of people over its white-tipped, deep-blue waves and just as easily swallowed their lives. The ancient world whose shores it laps welcomed them, and then in a blink of an era pushed them off again. Throughout the writing of this book, I wrestled with the paradoxes of Levantine history as it affected my own sense of identity. As a white person of Semitic heritage – both Arab and Jew – bearing a Greek name, I was subject to casual racial abuse and discrimination at school in England. *Wog* and *dago* were common nicknames for me in the schoolyard. Yes, I grew up in the comfort of a well-heated suburban home surrounded by books and infused with the insulation of moderate middle-income Britain; to quote the British peer and journalist Daniel Finkelstein, whose parents were wartime Jewish refugees, compared to where my parents came from at the end of the war, 'Pinner is nicer' – indeed, that was the north London suburb I grew up in.

I did not quite belong in England, yet had little idea about where I came from. My complicated and dislocated extended family left me few clues; they were too busy fitting in. Summers in Greece or Italy left me feeling almost as detached because my relatives there all spoke English and had been born and grew up somewhere else. It was only when I visited the Middle East – first Egypt and later Israel – that I started to feel something stir within: an emotional attachment. Yet, unlike my father, I was afforded a less privileged position. He was more of an insider than he cared to admit. I was simply a tourist visiting the old country.

Over these past few years, through conversations, yellowing papers and sepia-tinted photographs, and then visits to some of the landmarks and remnants of my family's life in Egypt and Palestine, I never once felt out of place. The journey allowed me to build a house in my mind with each of its rooms dedicated to different components of my family and the periods they lived through. Like anyone exploring their past, I feel enriched and privileged to know something about my direct antecedents and to have explored their lost world. The history I have learned in the process will – I hope – serve as a guide to the future. I understand the complex dynamics that bound Europe to the Middle East long before Europeans imposed imperial rule; I have a better sense of an era when identity was a resource, not a struggle. Identity in the modern era is all about projecting and affirming, a defensive posture that often results in confrontation. In the Levantine era identity was a fluid sense of belonging used to adapt as well as to hide. What we see today is that defined identity has become a driver of conflict, whereas for Levantines ambiguous identity was a shape-shifting means of survival.

Having said this, the Levantine world was not real in a concrete or bounded sense; the Levant is more of an expression than a geographical region. It inhabited a context in flux – one empire falling at the hands of others. The popular narrative of splendid cultural diversity and commercial fecundity clashed with realities of privilege and profound inequality, underpinned by deep and enduring prejudices. The term 'Levantine', or Levanter, can refer to a person from the Levant, a strong easterly wind in the Mediterranean – but it can also be pejorative, referring to a person who runs away leaving unpaid debts.

Yet, as a polyglot and, more specifically, a genetic by-product of a lost age, I feel threatened by singular identities and bullied by racial difference. 'CAUCASIAN', my identity card in Singapore screams at me in bold capitals; on the outside, perhaps. Inside I am really a Canaanite, a hotchpotch of DNA flung around desert caravanserais mingled with that of weary Iberian Sephardic outcasts and wild Ottoman Janissaries scything their way through the Balkans. I grew up bereft of the oriental moorings that my Middle Eastern antecedents clung to – I am neither a proper Jew, nor an observant Eastern Christian. People I know well smell the whiff of the Levant about me: a chronically malleable stance on everything; the way I assess the context of any question before giving an answer – these are classic Levantine characteristics. For the Levantine, outcomes invariably depend on circumstances. We never bet on a single option; we act the insider when we are really outsiders. Out of character, we are a bit lost and adrift. Far from worrying me, these characteristics constitute a lifeline to my heritage. I might have been satisfied with a conventional hyphenated identity – Greek and Italian, with a dash of Welsh. But that doesn't tell the whole story. Neither of my parents knew Greece or Italy until they were adults; my Greek grandparents arrived in Greece as refugees from Palestine! The superstructure of my identity was not just about where I came from but also when, how and why.

During the course of my journey I have thought a lot about the value of multidimensional identity, and have become convinced that delving into the history and complexity of our origins is a useful antiseptic against polarisation and hatred. The Ottomans knew this, which is why they devised a system of communal self-government that eschewed larger narratives of statehood and blended rather than homogenised ethnicity and faith. They placed a premium on creating the conditions for unhindered trade and commerce, which required the subjugation of rigid dogma and an emphasis on easy tolerance. A grasp of the complex cultural underpinnings of the Middle East helps us understand why this was possible. Today we see a grim landscape of sectarian conflict, streams of refugees flowing out of cities that have been reduced to rubble. This is misleading, monochromatic. For centuries the Middle East served as a bridge between the Occident and Orient; it was the veranda for great empires – Egyptian, Greek, Roman and Persian – and after they collapsed it became a repository of all their knowledge.

The history of my family in the Middle East straddled the spread of European thinking that nation states and affixed national identities were the most natural expressions of the brotherhood of man; yet, laudable as some may consider these ideas (and as Camus noted), they generated much suffering and loss – not least in the two world wars that scarred the twentieth century. For a short while, my family benefited from the cosmopolitan ethos the Ottomans employed to govern their empire, enshrined in the notion that non-Muslims who submitted to Muslim rule were protected and allowed to govern their own affairs as *millets*. However, by the dawn of the twentieth century, nationalist thinking from Europe had prised the different ethnic and religious components of the empire apart and endowed them with nationalist pretensions, thereby reversing the logic of cosmopolitanism that had been passed down from Alexander the Great.

There were two principal reasons for the burial of this constructive cosmopolitan complexity: European imperialism with its uni-dimensional line-drawing and obsession with partitioning lands and their peoples, and the parallel emergence of puritanical strains of Judaism and Islam that, as a consequence, acquired a commanding political agency. These twin developments over the past 200 years recast polity and society in the Middle East using a rigid set of rules and obligations, and established deadly binary identities to displace the fluid lattice of overlapping transactions that characterised Ottoman society. Leaving aside the fate of my Levantine family (which was, after all, merely to be displaced), the impact on the region has been immeasurable suffering and incalculable loss. Thus, this journey has left me with contradictory feelings. The inner doubts I once had about who I am and where I belong have disappeared; the how, the where and the when of my family's history have made me feel whole and confident. Yet I have mixed emotions about the legacy of the Levantine era, seen from the perspective of my generation. The serial wars and chronic displacement of people have left indelible scars which never heal.

A few years ago I walked into a pharmacy in Amman looking for cold medicine. The young woman behind the counter was chatty and told me she was the great-granddaughter of a Palestinian refugee who had settled in Jordan soon after 1947. With tears in her eyes she told me that her parents still keep the keys to their house on the other side of the River Jordan.

One memory that haunts me from these travels in search of my family are the piles of stones and broken arches of old ruined homes in Wadi Salib, the deserted Arab trading quarter of Haifa. And Johnny Mansour, the local historian, his eyes welling up as he described the systematic erasure of Haifa's cosmopolitan Arab past. Another is the sadness in the eyes of the older former Sornaga employees in El-Wedy, as they brewed coffee on a fire using discarded timbers from the partly demolished ceramics factory around them, which once harnessed Egyptian creativity and nurtured their families. These memories are all but lost in the sands – although in the words of the poet Edmond Jabès, the silence of the desert speaks.

EPILOGUE

The pocket watch I inherited from my father symbolises, for me, the intrusion of time on an ancient tradition of fluid, borderless coexistence that predates even the Ottomans. I admire – maybe even envy – the way the Ottomans engaged others to keep time by gazing at the stars, allowed each community to live by its own calendars, to measure time according to the ripening of fruit in orchards near the capital. In this way, time is defined broadly as a state of being rather than a purely linear trajectory always pushing us forward; it becomes more than a stern judge of our endeavours.

Travelling through the ruins of the cosmopolitan world my family inhabited, and whence they fled, I found myself trying to bend or roll back time, sometimes by keeping an eye out for survivors. In Cairo I made my way to the suburb of Heliopolis, where my mother lived as a child, and to a Roman Catholic hospice for the elderly – a modest, modern, low-rise building benefiting from huge windows and a well-tended garden set behind a high brick wall. A nurse led me from the lobby to a third-floor room where a woman lay reclining on an unmade bed. She was in her eighties, her wispy white hair spilling loosely over her shoulders. Her eyes were focused not on the door but on the dust-coated window letting in a milky, early-afternoon sun. This was Vanna, my mother's cousin, the last Sornaga living in Egypt. When the nurse announced my arrival, Vanna turned her head slowly and looked at me blankly. I went over to sit next to her, and gently held her arthritic hands. I wondered how she felt about what was left of the world she had grown up in. Perhaps she dreamed of the tram bells clanging as they swished along heat-buckled tracks, or the honking of old Fords and Packards rumbling along dusty thoroughfares, avoiding horse-drawn *gharries* clip-clopping their way through the city, pulling up at apartment buildings manned by shuffling, watery-eyed *boabs* watching the world go by, much as they do today, measuring time by the length of shadows.

My father's Ottoman pocket watch

NOTES

CHAPTER ONE: PIERCING THE SANDS

1. Official Egyptian statistics recorded 46,000 Italian citizens in the country in 1937, although this was probably an underestimate of the actual population of Italians as cited by M. Volait (1987).
2. The Ottomans infamously used a system of child slavery known as *devsirme* to fill the ranks of the empire's armies. Christian boys from the Ottoman western provinces across Eastern Europe were taken, forced to convert to Islam and incorporated into the army, albeit paid. In addition, many young Muslim men from the Balkan provinces found a path to power and glory by serving in the ranks of the sultan's armies. Muhammad Ali, born into an Albanian Muslim family, was one such. After a spell as a tax-collector he joined a band of Albanian mercenaries serving the sultan which was sent to Egypt in 1801.
3. In fact, Muhammad Ali and his successors hired a few American military advisors, avoiding Europeans to ensure that the army was free of the influence of 'entangling alliances', as related by Col. William McEntyre Dye in his 1880 account of *Moslem Egypt and Christian Abyssinia: or, Military Service Under the Khedive . . .* (Atkin and Prout Printers, New York). https://dl.wdl.org/2534/service/2534.pdf [Accessed: 18 May 2021]
4. One of the initial engineers involved in the French bid to build the canal was the Italian Luigi Negrelli, also known as Alois Negrelli, a gifted hydraulic engineer from the Italian Tyrol who played an important role in conceiving and designing the Suez Canal, though this is often forgotten. Before de Lesseps launched his own plans, Negrelli was part of an earlier French-led effort by a group of idealistic social reformers known as Saint Simonians to pierce the isthmus in the 1830s. This was interrupted by the 1848 revolutions that swept across Europe. De Lesseps invited Negrelli to join his team in 1855 and it was Negrelli's proposal of a canal without locks that prevailed, though he died in 1858 just a year before construction got under way.
5. P.H. Morgan, justice of the supreme court of Louisiana writing in *Appletons' Journal*, volume 8, issue 4 1880. Morgan's damning article was subject to an equally scathing rebuttal from de Lesseps, who denied the abuse of labour, and other charges Morgan made.

On the racism and prejudice experienced by Italian immigrants in the United States see: https://www.nytimes.com/interactive/2019/10/12/opinion/columbus-day-italian-american-racism.html [Accessed: 18 May 2021]

On the system of Mixed Courts see: Gabriel M. Wilner (1975) 'The Mixed Courts of Egypt: A Study on the use of Natural Law and Equity' in *Georgia Journal of International and Comparative Law*. https://digitalcommons.law.uga.edu/cgi/viewcontent.cgi?article=2283&context=gjicl [Accessed: 18 May 2021]

Mercedes Volait (1987) 'La Communauté italiennes et ses édiles', *Revue des mondes musulmans et de la Méditerranée* (46), pp. 137–56.

Tarek Osman (2011) *Egypt on the Brink: From the Rise of Nasser to the Fall of Mubarak*, New Haven, CT and London: Yale University Press.

Nicolas Pelham (2016) *Holy Lands: Reviving Pluralism in the Middle East*, New York: Columbia Global Reports.

Sami Zubaida (2010) *Beyond Islam: A New Understanding of the Middle East*, London: Bloomsbury.

Anthony M. Galatoli (1950) *Egypt in Mid-Passage*, Cairo: Urwand and Sons.

Arnold Wilson (1939) *The Suez Canal: Its Past, Present and Future*, London: Oxford University Press.

Robert T. Ridley (1998) *Napoleon's Proconsul in Egypt: The Life and Times of Bernardino Drovetti*, London: Rubicon Press.

Henry Dodwell (1931) *The Founder of Modern Egypt: A Study of Muhammad 'Ali*, Cambridge: Cambridge University Press.

David Landes (1958) *Bankers and Pashas*, London: Heinemann.

Eustace Reynolds-Ball (1898) *City of the Caliphs – A Popular Study of Cairo and its Environ and the Nile and its Antiquities*, Boston: Estes and Lauriat, T. Fisher Unwin.

Philip Mansel (2012) 'The Rise and Fall of Royal Alexandria', *The Court Historian* 17(2), December 2012.

Philip Mansel (2010) *Levant: Splendour and Catastrophe in the Mediterranean*, London: John Murray.

D.C.M. Platt (1971) 'The Levant Service', in Platt, *The Cinderella Service: British Consuls Since 1825*, London: Longman, pp. 125–79.

Alexander Kitroeff (2019) *The Greeks and the Making of Modern Egypt*, Cairo: American University of Cairo Press.

CHAPTER TWO: GRAND HOTEL DE LA POSTE

1. Obituary of Professor P.J. Vatikiotis by Professor Charles Tripp, SOAS, 12 January 1998.
2. *Among Arabs and Jews* was published by Weidenfeld & Nicolson in 1991. The basic information about my Greek family and my father's personal recollections in this book provided a critical guide for me on this journey and I have drawn and quoted extensively from it throughout.

3. 'The Not So Magic East' is a compilation of four sketches set in Egypt and Palestine in the 1940s. There is an accompanying preface and encouraging letters from a couple of publishers rejecting them for publication. Manuscript in the author's possession.
4. Cairo hospital attack: https://www.theguardian.com/world/2019/aug/05/at-least-20-dead-and-47-injured-in-explosion-outside-cairo-hospital [Accessed: 18 May 2021]
5. On the disputes between companies operating along the Suez Canal see: https://www.wormsetcie.com/en/chronology [Accessed: 18 May 2021]

Lawrence Durrell quote: https://www.nytimes.com/1978/06/11/archives/with-durrell-in-egypt.html [Accessed: 18 May 2021]

Sylvia Modelski (2000) *Port Said Revisited*, New York: Faros.

Eustace Reynolds-Ball (1898) *City of the Caliphs – A Popular Study of Cairo and Its Environ and the Nile and Its Antiquities*, Boston: Estes and Lauriat, T. Fisher Unwin.

Sherif Boraie (ed.) (2013) *The Suez Canal: A History*, Cairo: Zeitouna.

Heather J. Sharkey (2011) 'The British and Foreign Bible Society in Port Said and the Suez Canal', *The Journal of Imperial and Commonwealth History*, 39(3), pp. 439–56.

Valérie Nicolas, Directrice de l'Alliance Française de Port-Saïd, in Marie-Laure Crosnier-Leconte et al. (2006), *Port-Saïd: Architectures XIXe-XXe siècles*, Institut français d'archéologie orientale du Caire (IFAO).

For more details on the shadowy modern war in the Sinai see: https://www.washingtonpost.com/opinions/global-opinions/war-has-ravaged-the-sinai-for-eight-years-why-dont-we-know-more-about-it/2019/06/01/58223886-8231-11e9-bce7-40b4105f7ca0_story.html [Accessed 18 May 2021]

Mostafa Mohielden Lofty (2018) 'Biographies of Port-Said: Everydayness of State, Dwellers, and Strangers.' Thesis Submitted to The Department of Sociology, Egyptology, and Anthropology, The American University of Cairo.

CHAPTER THREE: THE KHEDIVE'S GOLD

1. Family legend has it that their surname was originally Naga, to which was added the possibly Venetian honorific 'Sor'.
2. Gold sovereigns are still valued as a currency in Egypt.

Sources used to recreate the opening night of Verdi's *Aida* in Cairo:

http://english.ahram.org.eg/News/114382.aspx [Accessed: 18 May 2021]

https://musicwithvision.medici.tv/clef-notes/this-week-in-music-history/verdis-aida-premieres-1871/ [Accessed: 18 May 2021]

https://www.francemusique.fr/en/everything-you-always-wanted-know-about-aida-verdi-15685 [Accessed: 18 May 2021]

http://www.interlude.hk/front/verdi-aida-premiered-today-1871/ [Accessed: 18 May 2021]
http://www.egypttoday.com/Article/4/72262/Cairo-Opera-house-organizes-a-massive-concert-in-celebration-of [Accessed: 18 May 2021]
https://www.wqxr.org/story/verdis-emaidaem-and-its-role-egyptian-revolution/ [Accessed: 18 May 2021]

Denis Mack Smith (1997) *Modern Italy: A Political History*, New Haven, CT and London: Yale University Press.
Fausta Cialente, translated by Isabel Quigley (1963) *The Levantines: A Modern Novel of Distant World*, Boston: Houghton Mifflin.
Anouchka Lazarev (1997) 'Italians, Italianity and Fascism', in Robert Ilbert, Ilios Yannakis and Jacques Hassoun (eds) *Alexandria 1860–1960: The Brief Life of a Cosmopolitan Community*, Alexandria: Harpocrates Publishing.
Mohamed Ali Moh. Khalil (2009) 'The Italian Architecture in Alexandria, Egypt'. MSc thesis submitted to Kore University of Enna.
Trevor Mostyn (2006) *Egypt's Belle Epoque: Cairo and the Age of the Hedonists*, London: Tauris Parke.
L.A. Balboni (1906) *Italians in Egyptian Civil Life in the Nineteenth Century*, Alexandria: Tipo-litografico V. Penasson.
Mona Abaza (2013) *The Cotton Plantation Remembered: An Egyptian Family Story*, Cairo: American University of Cairo Press.
Alaa Al Aswany (2009) *Friendly Fire*, New York: Fourth Estate.

CHAPTER FOUR: BLUE BRICKS BY THE NILE

1. The Cattaui were Jews from Europe, almost certainly the Netherlands, who had settled in Egypt during the Fatimid period in the eighteenth century. They originally lived in Cairo's Jewish quarter, but then prospered as financiers in the nineteenth century and emerged and settled in palatial residences in the downtown area. Ennobled by both Ottomans and Europeans, the Cattaui were consummate players of both sides of the imperial fence – helping the Ottoman viceroys obtain the financing they needed and then also aiding the British as they gradually took over Egypt. The Suarez family were Sephardic Jews originally from Spain.
2. As a student of Southeast Asia, I read the works of William Skinner, an American sociologist who wrote about ethnic Chinese communities in Thailand and predicted their complete assimilation in the 1950s based on the melting-pot theory. Across Southeast Asia, Chinese communities thrive and have somewhat assimilated, but as China has risen, so there has been a revival of Chinese culture and language among these communities. My experiences in plural societies suggest that assimilation and integration is not a predictable one-way process; it is influenced by variable social and economic conditions. See G. William Skinner (1957) *Chinese Society in Thailand: An Analytical History*, Ithaca, NY: Cornell University Press.

3. Abdelhalim Ibrahim Abdelhalim was born in Al-Saff in 1941. He received his architectural training in Egypt and the United States, and is the designer of over 100 cultural, institutional and rehabilitation projects, including the Cultural Park for Children in Cairo and the American University in Cairo campus in New Cairo. I am grateful to his son Nour for information about the Sornaga factory.
4 For more on Egypt's new administrative capital, Al-Masa, see: https://placesjournal.org/article/the-anti-cairo/ [Accessed: 18 May 2021]

Alaa Al Aswany (2002) *The Yacoubian Building*, New York; Fourth Estate.
David S. Landes (1958) *Bankers and Pashas: International Finance and Economic Imperialism in Egypt*, London: Heinemann.
Dario Miccoli (2015) *Histories of the Jews of Egypt: An Imagined Bourgeoisie, 1880s–1950s*, London: Routledge.
Ronald Robinson and John Gallagher with Alice Denny (1961) *Africa and the Victorians: The Official Mind of Imperialism*, London: I.B. Tauris.
T.E. Lawrence (1927) *Seven Pillars of Wisdom*, London: Penguin.
P.J. Vatikiotis (1969) *The Modern History of Egypt*, London: Weidenfeld & Nicolson.
Alfred Milner (1904) *England in Egypt*, London: Edward Arnold (11th edn).
Alexander Kitroeff (2019) *The Greeks and the Making of Modern Egypt*, Cairo: American University of Cairo Press.

CHAPTER FIVE: BABA YANNIS SETTLES IN ACRE

1. Certain Greek thinkers of the classical era claimed heritage from the Levant and spent time teaching in the region. Their thinking and ideas left an indelible imprint on local customs and religion. The British former diplomat Gerard Russell has written a detailed exposition of this often-neglected nexus between ancient Greece and the Levant. He made a vivid journey into the world of the fringe religions of the Middle East, such as the Druze of Lebanon, whose beliefs are based on the ideas of Pythagoras, who, although born on the Ionian island of Samos, may have had a Lebanese father and was educated in Egypt. (Gerard Russell (2014) *Heirs to Forgotten Kingdoms: Journeys into the Disappearing Religions of the Middle East*, New York: Simon & Schuster.)
2. Russians came to Israel in sizeable numbers after the fall of the Berlin Wall and the collapse of the Soviet Union. Ostensibly, Israel welcomed Russian Jews, but many Russian Orthodox slipped under the net in search of a better life in the 'West'. Today there are thought to be approximately 70,000 to 100,000 Russian Orthodox believers in Israel, with many Jewish Russians turning to the Church after immigration.
3. As'ad Ghanem's latest book is *Palestinians in Israel: The Politics of Faith after Oslo*, published in 2018 by Cambridge University Press.

P.J. Vatikiotis (1991) *Among Arabs and Jews*, London; Weidenfeld & Nicolson.

Kostas Kostis (2018) *History's Spoiled Children: The Formation of the Modern Greek State*, Oxford: Oxford University Press.
P.J. Vatikiotis (1980) 'The Greek Community in Palestine: A Personal Memoir and Recollection'. Unpublished paper; Communication to the Conference on the History of Syria, Amman, Jordan 19–24 April 1980.
Simon Sebag Montefiore (2011) *Jerusalem: The Biography*, London: Weidenfeld & Nicolson.
Salim Tamari (2017) *The Great War and the Remaking of Palestine*, Oakland: University of California Press.
Salim Tamari (2009) *Mountain Against the Sea: Essays on Palestinian Society and Culture*, Berkeley: University of California Press.
Konstantinos Papastathis and Ruth Kark (2014) 'The Effect of the Young Turks Revolution on Religious Power Politics', *Jerusalem Quarterly* (Paris), 56–57, pp. 118–39.
Nicolas Pelham (2016) *Holy Lands: Reviving Pluralism in the Middle East*, New York: Columbia Global Reports.

CHAPTER SIX: BROTHER MAXIMOS IN A CAVE

1. In his autobiography, *Sometimes I Wonder* (New York: Farrar, Straus and Giroux, 1965) Hoagy Carmichael wrote: 'On Indiana Avenue stood the Book Nook, a randy temple smelling of socks, wet slickers, vanilla flavoring, face powder, and unread books. Its dim lights, its scarred walls, its marked up booths, and unsteady tables made campus history.'
2. For a good potted history of the colourful Cicurel family in Egypt see: http://www.hsje.org/SecondExodus/CICUREL.pdf [Accessed: 18 May 2021]

Walter B. Harris (1933) *East Again*, London: Keystone Library.
Jacob Norris (2013) 'Exporting the Holy Land: Artisans and Merchant Migrants in Ottoman-era Bethlehem.' https://lebanesestudies.ojs.chass.ncsu.edu/index.php/mashriq/article/view/13/14 [Accessed: 18 May 2021]
Raja Shehadeh (2017) *Where the Line is Drawn: Crossing Boundaries in Occupied Palestine*, London: Profile Books.
Alec Seath Kirkbride (1956) *A Crackle of Thorns: Experiences in the Middle East*, London: John Murray.
Simon Sebag Montefiore (2011) *Jerusalem: The Biography*, London: Weidenfeld & Nicolson.

Sources on Greek Orthodox monasteries:
https://www.npr.org/sections/parallels/2017/12/02/565464499/greek-orthodox-church-sells-land-in-israel-worrying-both-israelis-and-palestinia
https://www.youtube.com/watch?v=WvNaT46i4Dk [Accessed: 18 May 2021]
https://www.thejc.com/news/features/how-thomas-cook-helped-shape-the-israel-of-today-1.493690 [Accessed: 18 May 2021]

Saint Theodosius Monastery in Bethlehem:
https://en.jerusalem-patriarchate.info/holy-pilgrimage-sites/the-holy-monastery-of-saint-theodosius-the-cenobiarch/ [Accessed: 18 May 2021]
Saint John the Baptist's Monastery: http://orthochristian.com/110327.html [Accessed: 18 May 2021]
Saint Gerasimus Monastery, Jericho: https://www.seetheholyland.net/monastery-of-st-gerasimus/ [Accessed: 18 May 2021]
Mar Sabbas, Saint Sabbas Monastery: http://wysinfo.com/?page_id=4628 [Accessed: 18 May 2021]
https://www.ancient-origins.net/ancient-places-asia/living-remnants-early-christianity-mar-saba-monastery-007520 [Accessed: 18 May 2021]
https://stsabbas.org/jerusalem.html [Accessed: 18 May 2021]
On Greeks in Palestine: https://www.jpost.com/Local-Israel/In-Jerusalem/Its-all-Greek-to-me [Accessed: 18 May 2021]
To recreate Allenby's entry into in Jerusalem on 11 December 1917 I used the following sources:
https://www.haaretz.com/jewish/.premium-1917-general-allenby-shows-how-a-moral-man-conquers-jerusalem-1.5343853 [Accessed: 18 May 2021]
https://www.israel21c.org/a-general-and-a-gentleman-allenby-at-the-gates-of-jerusalem/ [Accessed: 18 May 2021]
https://www.timesofisrael.com/history-repeats-itself-as-lord-allenby-captures-jerusalems-old-city-again/ [Accessed: 18 May 2021]
https://www.criticalpast.com/video/65675050558_Sir-Edmund-Allenby_World-War-I_Jerusalem-proclamation_Jaffa-Gate [Accessed: 18 May 2021]
https://www.oneforisrael.org/bible-based-teaching-from-israel/israel/1917-end-muslim-rule-holy-land-foretold-bible/ [Accessed: 18 May 2021]
Warda Simha recalls the war years in Bethlehem:
https://sussex.figshare.com/articles/Warda_Simha_aged_93_from_Bethlehem_discussing_the_Ottoman_period_and_World_War_I/7271105/1 [Accessed: 18 May 2021]

CHAPTER SEVEN: PHILBY'S BATMAN

1. The Ottomans initially grew worried about British influence in the Middle East after the occupation of Egypt in 1882. This lent momentum to centralising reforms to protect the empire, which were particularly intrusive in the Hejaz, where the Ottomans feared that Muslim pilgrims from British India would become a pretext for occupation.
2. Alec Seath Kirkbride was posted to Kerak, where he was tasked with establishing a governing council. Coincidentally, his younger brother Alan was financial advisor to Philby and based in Amman, together with Dick Mumford.
3. Elizabeth was born sometime after the death of the 1st Baron Raglan, FitzRoy James Henry Somerset, the hapless general who commanded British forces in the Crimean War and was responsible for the disastrous Charge of the Light Brigade in 1854.

4. As chance would have it, Richard's widow, my grandmother Lidia, ended up in a room close to No. 4 Steeles Road in Belsize Park Gardens, her two unmarried Sornaga sisters living in a larger flat nearby after they were forced to leave Cairo in 1952.
5. Captain Frederick Gerard Peake was posted to Transjordan in 1920 to command a small mobile brigade to defend the territory. Its original composition was mostly locally recruited Chechens. The force later grew in size and eventually became the core of the Arab Legion, which although technically serving the Emir of Transjordan was staffed by British officers and paid for by Britain.
6. Henry Hugh Tudor, commander of the Auxiliaries in Ireland, had advised Churchill that up to 800 'absolutely reliable men' could be made available from those forces. The Auxiliaries had worked alongside the Black and Tans and the two policing divisions were often regarded as synonymous. The gendarmerie was founded at Churchill's initiative. https://www.irishtimes.com/culture/books/winston-churchill-sent-the-black-and-tans-to-palestine-1.3089140 [Accessed: 18 May 2021]

Scott Anderson (2013) *Lawrence in Arabia: War, Deceit, Imperial Folly and the Making of the Modern Middle East*, New York: Anchor Books.

James Barr (2011) *A Line in the Sand: Britain, France and the Struggle that Shaped the Middle East*, New York: Simon & Schuster.

Eugene L. Rogan (1996) *The Making of a Capital: Amman, 1918–1928* https://books.openedition.org/ifpo/8228?lang=en [Accessed: 18 May 2021]

Elizabeth Monroe (1973) *Philby of Arabia*, London: Faber & Faber.

Obituary of Lord Riddell, *Time Magazine*, 17 December 1934.

Saint Antony's College Middle East Archive: Mumford, Richard (1894–1960). GB165-0212. Photocopied TS reminiscences as confidential clerk to H. St J.B. Philby in Transjordan, twelve sheets.

Uriel Dann (1986) *Studies in the History of Transjordan 1920–1949: The Making of a State*, Boulder, CO: Westview.

Alec Seath Kirkbride (1956) *A Crackle of Thorns: Experiences in the Middle East*, London: John Murray.

Simon Sebag Montefiore (2011) *Jerusalem: The Biography*, London: Weidenfeld & Nicolson.

Mary Christina Wilson (1987) *King Abdullah, Britain and the Making of Jordan*, Cambridge: Cambridge University Press.

T.E. Lawrence (1935) *Seven Pillars of Wisdom*, London: Penguin.

Steven Morewood (2005) *The British Defence of Egypt, 1935–1940*, London: Frank Cass.

CHAPTER EIGHT: AMONG ARABS AND JEWS

1. Emile Touma was a prominent communist activist from the Palestinian community in Haifa before 1948. Today, his granddaughter Aida Touma-Sliman sits in

the Israeli Knesset as a member for the far-left Democratic Front for Peace and Equality (known in Hebrew as *Hadasha).*

2. Britain briefly considered settling the Jews in Uganda to avoid arguing with the Arabs. Had Moses been offered Uganda instead of Palestine, the Zionist leader Chaim Weizmann reportedly quipped, he would have broken the stone tablets.
3. Being Greek Orthodox, my father was raised to look down on the Roman Catholic Church. As a child he and his friends once spiked the holy water in a neighbourhood Catholic church with the red dye used to colour Greek Easter eggs, so that the Catholics emerged from church with red marks on their foreheads.
4. Wadie Haddad was born in 1927. After partition he fled to Lebanon with his family and attended the medical school at the American University in Beirut, where, together with another (unnamed) close friend of my father and a fellow Christian Palestinian, George Habbash, he established the Arab Nationalist Movement *Harakat al-Qawmiyyin al-Arab.* The pan-Arab and socialist ANM was the forerunner of the more militant Popular Front for the Liberation of Palestine established by Habbash in 1967. As a PFLP Executive member, Wadie Haddad was in favour of a campaign of violence to further the Palestinian cause. He planned and helped execute many of the hijackings and terrorist attacks that first occurred after 1968 and was the mastermind of the Entebbe hijacking of an Israeli airliner in 1976. He died in East Germany in 1978, allegedly after being poisoned by Israeli intelligence, although officially of cancer.

P.J. Vatikiotis (1991) *Among Arabs and Jews*, London: Weidenfeld & Nicolson.
Tom Segev (1999) *One Palestine, Complete: Jews and Arabs Under the British Mandate*, New York: Henry Holt.
John N. Tleel (2007) *I am Jerusalem*, Jerusalem: John N. Tleel.
Alec Kirkbride (1956) *A Crackle of Thorns: Experiences in the Middle East*, London: John Murray.
James Barr (2011) *A Line in the Sand: Britain, France and the Struggle that Shaped the Middle East*, New York: Simon & Schuster.
Salim Tamari and Issam Nassar (2014) *The Storyteller of Jerusalem: The Life and Times of Wasif Jawhariyyeh*, Northampton, MA: Institute of Palestine Studies and Olive Branch Press.
Ted Swedenburg (1995) *Memories of Revolt: The 1936–1939 Rebellion and the Palestinian National Past*, Fayetteville, AR: University of Arkansas Press.
Simon Sebag Montefiore (2011) *Jerusalem: The Biography*, London: Weidenfeld & Nicolson.

CHAPTER NINE: ROMMEL AT THE GATES

1. Egyptian anger at the Mixed Courts was inflamed after the murder of the prominent Jewish retail magnate Solomon Cicurel, who was stabbed in his luxury Giza townhouse in 1927. The case became a sensation after the chief suspects – two Italian domestic staff and a Greek driver – were tried in courts back in Italy and by a

Greek judge and jury sitting in Alexandria, which resulted in very light sentences. http://www.hsje.org/SecondExodus/CICUREL.pdf [Accessed: 18 May 2021]

2. Wavell noted in his very readable biography that after the 1922 Declaration Allenby was accused of having 'sold the pass' and given away Britain's position in Egypt. The delicate compromise that offered nominal independence in return for Britain retaining the 'liberty of actions' to protect a specific number of reserved interests – including the protection of foreigners – almost certainly ensured the survival of Britain's presence in Egypt until 1956.

John Rogers Shuman (1947) *Cairo Concerto*, New York: Harcourt Brace and Co.

Niall Barr (2004) *The Pendulum of War: The Three Battles of El Alamein*, New York: Overlook Press.

Jonathan Dimbleby (2012) *Destiny in the Desert: The Road to El Alamein – The Battle that Turned the Tide of World War II*, London: Pegasus Books.

Viscount Wavell (1943) *Allenby in Egypt: Being Volume II of Allenby: A Study in Greatness*, London: George G. Harrap.

Artemis Cooper (2006) *Cairo in the War 1939–45* London: John Murray.

Anthony Gorman (2015) 'The Italians of Egypt', in Anthony Gorman and Sossie Kasbarian (2015) *Diasporas of the Modern Middle East: Contextualising Community*, Edinburgh: Edinburgh University Press.

Anouchka Lazarev (1997) 'Italians, Italianity and Fascism', in Robert Ilbert, Ilios Yannakakis and Jacques Hassoun (eds) *Alexandria 1860–1960: The Brief Life of a Cosmopolitan Community*, Alexandria: Harpocrates Publishing.

Ilios Yannakakis (1997) 'Farewell Alexandria', ibid.

Rosetta Giuliani Caponetto (2015) *Fascist Hybridities: Representations of Racial Mixing and Diaspora Cultures under Mussolini*, London: Palgrave.

P.J. Vatikiotis (1985) *The Modern History of Egypt*, London: Weidenfeld & Nicolson.

William Stadiem (1991) *Too Rich: The High Life and Tragic Death of King Farouk*, London: Parkway Press.

Noël Coward (1994) *Middle East Diary*, New York: Doubleday Doran.

Max Rodenbeck (1998) *Cairo: The City Victorious*, Cairo: American University of Cairo Press.

Trevor Mostyn (2006) *Egypt's Belle Epoque: Cairo and the Age of the Hedonists*, London: Tauris Parke.

Lawrence Durrell (1957) *Justine*, London: Faber & Faber.

Olivia Manning (new edition 2014) *The Levant Trilogy*, London: Penguin Random House.

Sources on Italian internment in Egypt:

http://www.aaha.ch/cahiers/aaha-cahier-71-carbone.pdf [Accessed: 18 May 2021]

https://books.google.co.th/books?id=7fHnCwAAQBAJ&pg=PA222&lpg=PA222&dq=Italians+interned+in+Egypt&source=bl&ots=xjbA1el297&sig=AC-fU3U1UqG3puFDTeuCsb8w-lHvpWHQkUw&hl=en&sa=X&ved=2ahUKEwiptsWKjufnAhXHwjgGHfKNBgY4ChDoATABegQICRAB#v=onepage&q=Italians%20interned%20in%20Egypt&f=false [Accessed: 18 May 2021]

On Italian support for Arabs in Egypt and Palestine:
http://researchomnia.blogspot.com/2016/05/italian-propaganda-in-egypt-and.html [Accessed: 18 May 2021]

On the Metro Cinema in Cairo: http://cinematreasures.org/theaters/12765 [Accessed: 18 May 2021]

CHAPTER TEN: END OF DAYS IN PALESTINE

1. Sizeable numbers of Europeans fled to the Middle East during the Second World War and were housed in countries like Syria, which seventy years later was to be a major source of refugees into Europe. A British-led scheme known as the Middle East Relief and Refugee Administration, launched in 1942 and facilitated by officials based in Cairo, helped provide shelter for some 40,000 Poles, Greeks and Yugoslavs. https://www.washingtonpost.com/news/worldviews/wp/2016/06/02/the-forgotten-story-of-european-refugee-camps-in-the-middle-east/ [Accessed: 18 May 2021]
2. Controversially, the Irgun alleged they had telephoned a warning before setting off the blast and that the warning was not heeded.
3. The Lehi, or Stern Gang, was responsible for the daring assassination of the most senior British diplomat in the Middle East in Cairo in November 1944. https://www.jpost.com/opinion/op-ed-contributors/jewish-assassins-in-cairo-328913 [Accessed: 18 May 2021]
4. The Arab Legion was a British-officered Jordanian Arab force deployed at the end of the Mandate to protect the Arabs.

Tom Segev (1999) *One Palestine, Complete: Jews and Arabs Under the British Mandate*, New York: Holt.

Simon Sebag Montefiore (2011) *Jerusalem: The Biography*, London: Weidenfeld & Nicolson.

P.J. Vatikiotis (1991) *Among Arabs and Jews: A Personal Experience 1936–1990*, London: Weidenfeld & Nicolson.

Kati Marton (1994) *A Death in Jerusalem*, New York: Arcade Publishing.

King George II of Greece inspects Greek troops in Palestine: https://www.youtube.com/watch?v=NLGdHfXZeBw [Accessed: 18 May 2021]

UN Resolution 181 (11): https://unispal.un.org/DPA/DPR/unispal.nsf/0/7F0AF2BD897689B785256C330061D253 [Accessed: 18 May 2021]

Ghada Karmi (2002) *In Search of Fatima: A Palestinian Story*, London: Verso.

John N. Tleel (2007) *I Am Jerusalem*, John N. Tleel: Jerusalem.

Salim Tamari and Issam Nassar (2014) *The Storyteller of Jerusalem: The Life and Times of Wasif Jawhariyyeh, 1904–1948*, Northampton, MA: Olive Branch Press.

CHAPTER ELEVEN: DISPERSAL AND DESOLATION

1. There were many Egyptian Greeks and Italians who joined these socialist and communist movements in Egypt. The founder of the first communist movement in Egypt, Joseph Rosenthal, was a German Jew.
2. Dr Mursi Saad el-Din, a journalist and columnist, was head of the State Information Service and served as official spokesman for President Anwar el-Sadat. He died in 2013 at the age of ninety-two.
3. Years later, in August 1973, an Egyptian called Saad Zaghloul Fuad visited my father in London at his university office. He claimed to have known my father as a student at the American University in Cairo. My father could not recall meeting him. What he did remember is that the man was a well-known member of the militant group closely associated with Anwar Sadat, who later went on to become President of Egypt after Nasser's death in 1971. Fuad was arrested and tried for the Metro Cinema bombing in which my father almost died on 7 May 1947. He confessed to other attacks, but denied involvement in the Metro Cinema bombing. That day in my father's office, the former bomb-thrower alleged that neither he nor the Muslim Brotherhood were responsible: the bombing was carried out by a splinter group with whom he had personal grievances.
4. Edward Said was a Palestinian-American academic who taught literature at Columbia University in New York. His thesis in 'Orientalism', published in 1978, was that most Western-educated scholars were prejudiced against Arabs and the Arab cause based on long-held views of the East rooted in colonial narratives. My father once said that Edward Said 'introduced McCarthyism into Middle Eastern studies'. Five years after my father died I visited Bernard Lewis at his home in Princeton. I found the ageing scholar much embittered by his experience in the maelstrom of Middle East policymaking under the administration of George W. Bush. He had few nice things to say about anyone, including my father!

Waguih Ghali (1964) *Beer in the Snooker Club*, London: Penguin.
Jean Naggar (2008) *Sipping from the Nile: My Exodus from Egypt, A Memoir*, Stone Ridge, NY: Stony Creek Press.
Jacqueline Shohet Kahanoff, eds. Deborah A. Starr and Sasson Somekh (2011) *Mongrels or Marvels: The Levantine Writings of Jacqueline Shohet Kahanoff*, Stanford Studies in Jewish History and Culture, Stanford: Stanford University Press.
'Burning Down the House: Fifty years ago this week, Cairo went up in flames'; Fayza Hassan wonders who struck the first match, *Al-Ahram Weekly*, 24–30 January 2002, https://web.archive.org/web/20091108034353/http://weekly.ahram.org.eg/2002/570/sc3.htm# [Accessed: 18 May 2021]
P.J. Vatikiotis (1991) *Among Arabs and Jews*, London: Weidenfeld & Nicolson.
P.J. Vatikiotis, unpublished diaries (1968–76) in the author's possession.
P.J. Vatikiotis 'The Commando' from a collection of unpublished short stories titled 'The Not So Magic East'.

CHAPTER TWELVE: THE SUEZ SYNDROME

1. Louis Awad was a leading Arab intellectual who was literary editor of the Egyptian daily *Al-Ahram*; Magdi Wahba was Egypt's foremost literary critic and lexicographer – he translated many of the works of Naguib Mahfouz, who won the Nobel Prize in Literature in 1988. Yusuf Idris was a leading playwright and novelist.
2. Dimitri Tsafendas, a Greek of mixed African heritage who had family in Egypt earned notoriety in 1966 after he stabbed the then South African President, Hendrik Verwoerd. Much later George Bizos, a human rights lawyer in South Africa who campaigned against apartheid, represented Nelson Mandela in the famous Rivonia Trial in 1963.
3. Long before considering writing about Levantine society, my own graduate research in Southeast Asia drew me to the subject of pluralism. My doctoral thesis at Oxford University was on 'Ethnic Pluralism in the Northern Thai City of Chiangmai' (1984).
4. Earlier, in 1947, a stone plaque recording that the Aswan Low Dam, finished in 1902, had been 'excavated by Egyptians assisted by Greeks' and the 'stone dressed by skilled Italian workmen' was removed, allegedly because it did not 'shed a true light on things'.
5. My father's conviction about Nasser's probity was somewhat shaken by revelations of a USD 100 million 'Fund for the Protection of the Revolution' that Nasser had stashed in a Swiss bank account.

Ernest Gellner (1983) *Nations and Nationalism*, Ithaca NY: Cornell University Press.

Paul Balta (1997) '1956', in Robert Ilbert, Ilios Yannakakis and Jacques Hassoun (eds) *Alexandria 1860–1960: The Brief Life of a Cosmopolitan Community*, Alexandria: Harpocrates Publishing.

Alexander Kitroeff (2019) *The Greeks and the Making of Modern Egypt*, Cairo: American University of Cairo Press.

Jean Naggar (2008) *Sipping from the Nile: My Exodus from Egypt, A Memoir*. Stone Ridge, NY: Stony Creek Press.

Robert Vitalis (1995) *When Capitalists Collide: Business Conflict and the End of Empire in Egypt*, Berkeley: University of California Press.

Panayiotis Vatikiotis, unpublished diaries (1968–1976) in the author's possession.

Albert Camus (1963) *Carnets 1935–1942*, London: Hamish Hamilton.

Sami Zubaida (2010) *Beyond Islam: A New Understanding of the Middle East*, London: Bloomsbury.

Amin Maalouf, transl. Barbara Bray (2000) *On Identity*, London: Harvill Press.

Walter B. Laqueur (2018) 'The Generation That Shaped Our Understanding of the 20th Century Is Gone' in *Tablet*, July 26, 2018, https://www.tabletmag.com/sections/news/articles/walter-laqueur-generation-historians [Accessed: 18 May 2021]

Sami Zubaida (2010) 'Cosmopolitan citizenship in the Middle East' in Open Democracy, https://www.opendemocracy.net/en/cosmopolitan-citizenship-in-middle-east/ [Accessed: 18 May 2021]

ACKNOWLEDGEMENTS

Over the years that I planned, researched and finally made the journey that resulted in this book, many people have both encouraged and generously helped me. They included members of my immediate and extended family who not only provided documents, photographs and, very valuably, their memories, but also put up with my badgering questions. My late father Panayiotis was a wellspring of ideas; his delight in sharing family gossip and lore, the richness of his scholarship, and the vivid reflections and experiences he left in his private, unpublished papers lie at the core of this book and stimulated my interest in and exploration of the Levantine world.

My uncle John Mumford, who died in 2012, urged me to write this book and shared his own considerable knowledge and research on the family's history, especially the Mumfords. Once I embarked on the book, long discussions with my mother Patricia helped me experience what life was like growing up in the Levantine world. Her cousin Giorgio Eberle in Rome patiently guided me through the rich complexity of the Sornaga clan and provided a constant stream of detailed information about the Italians in Egypt. My cousin Michael Karzis in New York fed me a treasure trove of Vatikiotis family history and documentation and was a companion on this journey, in spirit at least.

Along the journey itself, there are many people to thank whom I cannot mention by name here because the Middle East today is a risky place for those who dwell on the past as well as contemplate the future. I am appreciative over many years to Professor Walid Kazziah, who first looked after me in Cairo when I showed up on his doorstep as a student in 1976 and later helped me think through my initial approach to the book. Also in Cairo, I am indebted to Sherin Darwish at the American University of Cairo for her limitless friendship, advice and support, and Mary Rogers for the use of her wonderful apartment in Zamalek.

Rami Nasrallah in Jerusalem has been a constant guide and friend, without whom my exploration of the Vatikiotis family history would never have advanced very far. I am grateful to Walid Salem for his deep knowledge and perspectives on Palestinian history and the contacts he generously shared: Johnny Mansour in Haifa, Nora Quirt and Walid Dajani in Jerusalem and Salim Tamari in Ramallah. Anastasi Damanios, the head of the Greek community in Jerusalem, offered me deep knowledge and warm companionship. Anna Koulouris gave me a warm welcome at the Greek Orthodox Patriarchate. Last but not least, I want to thank His Royal Highness Prince Hassan bin Talal of Jordan for his warm friendship, generous hospitality and intellectual inspiration for the conception of this book.

Shelley Kenigsberg kindly read and helped shape an initial draft of the book. Professor Charles Tripp, Dr Nadim Shehadi and Dr Anthony Gorman read versions and excerpts from final drafts, for which I am very grateful. As this is not a work of scholarship, their forbearance was both kind and indulgent.

My colleagues at the Centre for Humanitarian Dialogue working on the Middle East were especially helpful to me in the early stages of research, and I owe particular thanks to Lani Frerichs and Nir Rosen for their friendship and always very helpful advice. HD's Executive Director, David Harland, took a keen interest in the project and generously gave me the time to embark on the journey in search of my family.

Without the cajoling and editing skills of my resourceful and talented agent Kelly Falconer, I doubt this book would have proceeded very far. I am also grateful to Ian Pringle for his always valuable advice on what makes a good book. I am especially grateful to Alan Samson at Weidenfeld & Nicolson who kept faith with the idea of this book and, as always, gently nudged me in the right direction. The deft editing skills of Linden Lawson and Jo Whitford turned a very personal screed into a publishable manuscript.

Finally, the unwavering love, patience and support of my wife Janick, and two children, Chloe and Stefan, was a constant reminder that, regardless of the interesting history and context of the Levantine world I come from, family is above all what defines us.

ABOUT THE AUTHOR

Michael Vatikiotis is a graduate of the School of Oriental and African Studies in London and gained his doctorate from the University of Oxford. He is a member of the Asia Society's International Council and has more than a decade of experience working as a private diplomat and conflict mediator for the Geneva-based Centre for Humanitarian Dialogue. Prior to that he worked as a journalist in Asia for almost two decades, living in Indonesia, Malaysia, Thailand and Hong Kong. He is the author of two previous books on the politics of Southeast Asia and is based in Singapore.

INDEX